LITERARY CRITICISM AND CULTURAL THEORY

Edited by

William E. Cain
Professor of English
Wellesley College

A ROUTLEDGE SERIES

Literary Criticism and Cultural Theory

William E. Cain, *General Editor*

City/Stage/Globe

Performance and Space in Shakespeare's London

D.J. Hopkins

Routledge
New York & London

Routledge
Taylor & Francis Group
270 Madison Avenue
New York, NY 10016

Routledge
Taylor & Francis Group
2 Park Square
Milton Park, Abingdon
Oxon OX14 4RN

© 2008 by D.J. Hopkins
Routledge is an imprint of Taylor & Francis Group, an Informa business

Printed in the United States of America on acid-free paper
10 9 8 7 6 5 4 3 2 1

International Standard Book Number-13: 978-0-415-97694-7 (Hardcover)

Library of Congress Cataloging-in-Publication Data

Hopkins, D. J.
   City/stage/globe : performance and space in Shakespeare's London by D.J. Hopkins.
      p. cm. -- (Literary criticism and cultural theory)
   Includes bibliographical references and index.
   ISBN 0-415-97694-4
   1. Shakespeare, William, 1564-1616--Stage history--England--London.
2. Shakespeare, William, 1564-1616--Dramatic production.
3. Theater--England--London--History--16th century. 4.
Theater--England--London--History--17th century. 5. London
(England)--History--16th century. 6. London (England)--History--17th century. I.
Title.

PR3091.H65 2007
822.3'3--dc22   2007015935

Visit the Taylor & Francis Web site at
http://www.taylorandfrancis.com

and the Routledge Web site at
http://www.routledge.com

For Shelley

Contents

List of Figures

Acknowledgments

This project has been long in the making, and I owe thanks to many people. First among those to be addressed must be Robert Weimann, whose remarkable scholarship and acumen are matched only by his patience and hospitality. Robert's example as a theatre scholar, a colleague, and a friend is one that I will work to emulate (though falling short seems inevitable). Chapter Four is dedicated particularly to him.

Jim Carmody has been a fantastic source of advice and support for really quite a bit longer than anyone should have to be. It's Jim and Laurie's fault that I fell in love with Paris when I should have been thinking about London. Louis Montrose's involvement in this process was a welcome source of insight and support. Bryan Reynolds has been a valued collaborator and occasional adversary. Janet Smarr gave an early version of this text a close reading and valuable editorial advice. Support from San Diego State University's University Grants Program made it possible to assemble the images for this book. At SDSU, I have been particularly lucky in the support of my colleagues, especially Anne-Charlotte Harvey and Peter Larlham. Lastly, I owe thanks to my terrific research assistant, Amy May.

Portions of *City / Stage / Globe* have appeared in a number of forms and venues. Part of Chapter Three appeared in an issue of the *Symbolism Yearbook*. An earlier version of Chapter Four appeared in the collection of essays dedicated to Robert Weimann, *Rematerializing Shakespeare*. Parts of the book were "rehearsed" at numerous conferences. I would especially like to acknowledge the lively comments from participants at the Association for Theatre in Higher Education, the Group for Early Modern Cultural Studies, and Literary London conferences. More personally, I would like to thank Becky Steinberger for her friendship, generosity, and for making the Group for Early Modern Cultural Studies annual conference a collegial and productive venue for drafts of my work. Mark G. Aune, Joshua B. Fisher, Adam

Cohen, Sarah Werner, Marissa Greenberg, and Barbara Hodgdon have made my work more rewarding through their support and insight. The faculty, staff, and students of the Performing Arts Department at Washington University in St. Louis offered support along the way; Julie Jordan, Justin Blum, Deirdre O'Rourke, and Louise Edwards have been valued friends as well. San Diego State University's School of Theatre, Television, and Film has given this project a warm home for its completion.

Thanks to my Mom and Dad, whose love and support are, apparently, boundless. Danielle has been a great friend, colleague, and co-conspirator, especially during the early years of this project. And my debt to Shelley is enormous: the dedication of this book seems faint compensation.

Frontispiece: Satellite photo of Lower Manhattan, Sept. 12, 2001.
AP/Wide World Photos.

We look at the satellite photograph of New York City taken on Sept. 12 and our eyes go to the plume of smoke blowing off to the southwest from the tip of Manhattan. We barely notice the undisturbed grid of city streets reaching into the distance. They were, indeed, unnaturally quiet that day, but it was quietness, not extinction. There was a grace, an endurance, in the silence of those streets and of the country beyond them that we need to remember as carefully as we remember the burning debris of the World Trade Center.

The New York Times
September 11, 2002

Introduction

Cities and Spaces

To be lifted to the summit of the World Trade Center is to be lifted out of the city's grasp. [. . .] The exaltation of a scopic and gnostic drive: the fiction of knowledge is related to this lust to be a viewpoint and nothing more.

The 1370 foot high tower that serves as a prow for Manhattan continues to construct the fiction that creates readers, makes the complexity of the city readable, and immobilizes its opaque mobility in a transparent text.

Michel de Certeau[1]

Though the words "performance" and "space" figure prominently in its title, this book is as much about representation and history as performance and space. *City / Stage / Globe* takes as its subject the movement of history over a brief span of time and in one discrete location, though the referents that inform the discussion of that time and place range widely. My contention is that the culture of performance that had obtained in England throughout the medieval era began during the sixteenth century to be superceded by ideas and practices associated with Renaissance strategies of visual representation. London served as a gateway for and intensifier of these newly imported concepts of visuality, as it continued to serve as an organizing site for the repertory of ceremonies, practices, and performances that had formed the basis for social self-conception in previous centuries.

The intent of this project is to pursue a study of representation and space without recourse to increasingly moribund conceptions of the "image" or "text" of the city. The introduction of performance theory to studies of the early modern has transformed the discipline. I study performance to intercept my discontent with representation, and, following Henri Lefebvre, I study space to intercept my discontent with text.

1

> To underestimate, ignore, and diminish space amounts to the overes-
> timation of texts, written matter, and writing systems, along with the
> readable and the visible, to the point of assigning to these a monopoly
> on meaning. (Lefebvre 62)

Suspicious of ceding such a "monopoly on meaning" to textuality, I consider the origins and tensions surrounding the emergence of representational and spatial practices in the early modern era. Lefebvre observes
that in "Western Europe of the sixteenth century 'something' of decisive
importance took place" (268). While he is hesitant to define that "something" in historical or economic terms, Lefebvre is swift to locate that
"something" in space, particularly urban space.

The title of this project associates three categories of space-the urban,
the theatrical, and the cartographic-and considers the production and
operation of these spaces in the specific time and place defined broadly by
the life of Shakespeare. These spaces interacted and informed each other
at a time in which both the lived experience of the city and the ways in
which the city itself was represented in art and performance were undergoing considerable conceptual transformation. The work of this transformational reconception was accomplished in representation, and while the
physical terrain of Shakespeare's London was not radically different from
that of the medieval city, the spatial concepts innovated in this period
laid the theoretical groundwork for the radical transformations of London's topography to come. The coordinated operation of these cultural
forces produced the "hybrid spaces" characteristic of this distinct, liminal
moment in the history of London. In short, this book is the study of a
brief span of time in once city during which performing was supplanted
by looking.

At the outset of the early modern period, the representational media
of my title—theatre, cartography, and urbanism—each incurred a debt to
medieval practices of performance. Rather than considering early modern
space as static and distinct from medieval space, *City / Stage / Globe* exam-
ines the gradual introduction of the forms of visual representation that
would eventually supplant performance as an organizing feature of social
space. The development of artificial perspective in art, linear narrative in
drama, and global trade all played a role in the emergence of new spaces
throughout Europe.

As an example of performance history, *City / Stage / Globe* not only
organizes a selection of plays, pageants, maps, and masques in the historical and cultural contexts in which they emerged, but this project also uses

the tools of performance theory to locate the ways in which these (largely) ephemeral events contributed to lasting change in the spatial concepts and physical terrain of early modern London.

This book takes as its subject a particular city, at a particular time in its history—a time roughly bounded by the life of that city's most famous inhabitant. Though the texts and performances, objects and images considered in the following chapters are drawn primarily from "Shakespeare's London," the ideas that inform this study are not so strictly confined: while what follows focuses on a single city between the years 1564 and 1616, other cities in other times and places are implicated in this project, and indeed have informed it.

The epigrams that open this Preface are frequently quoted passages from Michel de Certeau's essay "Walking In the City"; these brief quotations introduce the principles that de Certeau argues have come to determine the spaces of contemporary cities like New York's Manhattan. In recent years these passages have come to be all the more meaningful for me: now, of course, the present tense of de Certeau's sentences serves as what I have called "an urban afterimage," memorializing in theoretical writing the view from the observation deck on the 110th floor of the World Trade Center (282 n15)·

I realize that it may seem anachronistic to use a satellite photo of Lower Manhattan as the frontispiece to a study of Shakespeare's London, and that it may seem equally out-of-place—or merely sentimental—to begin that same study with this quotation from de Certeau, an obsolete reference to a vanished example of postmodern architecture and twentieth-century western civic space. But the view from the top of the World Trade Center was not merely a grand achievement in public monumentality: for de Certeau, the image of cityspace achieved by that observation deck was the realization of an abstract concept in material form. From the 110th floor of the WTC, de Certeau saw the culmination in physical space of theories of urban visibility that had been developing for centuries. The WTC was a location that, de Certeau claimed, allowed one to be "a solar Eye, looking down like a god" on the readable text of the city, the consummation of western culture's longstanding "lust to be a viewpoint and nothing more" (92). However, de Certeau did not anticipate a view such as that of the frontispiece: not merely the approximation of a bird's-eye view provided by an observation deck, but the truly vertical view of a satellite miles above the earth, a view that effectively locates the viewer, however virtually, in the impossible perspective represented on many influential early modern maps.

However, while a city may be *viewed* from the cold comfort of low-earth orbit, it cannot be *lived* there, nor on an observation deck. A city is lived at ground level, at the level of human activity, and only there can a city be rebuilt. Architect Daniel Libeskind proposed a master plan for the World Trade Center site that proposed to redesign that location from the ground up, quite literally. Libeskind's plan preserved public access to the massive "bathtub" retaining wall that was the only surviving part of WTC buildings.[2] While this counter-monument, if in fact any part of it is built at all, would not provide the comfort of abstraction "from above," it would provide a view "from below," one perhaps occasionally disturbing and not readily available to legibility, but a view that would serve as a memorial to the pedestrian spatial stories of those who built and worked in the structures that rested on the bedrock of this foundation.[3]

Theories of space will be important in this study; theories of urban space and performance space will be predominant, and it should be noted that the two kinds of space are not mutually exclusive. As I have observed elsewhere, "the discourse surrounding concepts of space" has in the last decade or so developed into a defining feature of the fields of Theatre Studies and Performance Studies:

> Drawing inspiration and methodological resources from such disciplines as philosophy, human geography, and urban studies, scholars of theatre and performance have come to rely on theories of space to describe and define performances and theatrical events in the context of their cultural and physical surroundings. [. . .] Lefebvre's book *The Production of Space* (1974) and Michel Foucault's brief essay 'Of Other Spaces' (1967) have made essential contributions to this broad interdisciplinary field, particularly because of the ways these works think together the discourses of space and history. (2005, 319)

To this short list of important contributions to scholarly work at the intersection of space and performance should be added de Certeau's *The Practice of Everyday Life* (1984). The essays in this book have value for performance history because of the privileged status assigned to human physical activity in de Certeau's conceptions of space. The cities he describes are not the abstract, depopulated vacuums of other theorists' work; de Certeau's cities are composed the bodied pedestrians who walk the streets as much as they are composed of the pavement at ground level and the skyscrapers towering above.[4]

But not all city streets are paved nor defined by the built spaces characteristic of late-twentieth century Manhattan. The weak point in de

Certeau's conception of the modern is a failure to theorize the pre-modern. Though "Walking in the City" is detailed and specific in its descriptions of the present, this essay collapses distinctions between broad periods of the historical past, and further collapses the past into the present.

> Medieval or Renaissance painters represented the city as seen in a perspective that no eye had yet enjoyed. This fiction already made the medieval spectator into a celestial eye. [. . .] The totalizing eye imagined by the painters of earlier times lives on in our achievements. (92)

While the conclusion that de Certeau expresses here, that the forms of artificial representation of space associated with "views" and "perspective" have a lasting influence on the built spaces of 21st century cities, is one that will be reinforced by *City / Stage / Globe*, the passage nevertheless seems to suggest that such forms have existed in the same state for over a thousand years.

A vague phrase like "earlier times" might be forgiven if used in reference to a clearly defined term; here, however, those earlier times are either the "[m]edieval or Renaissance" periods—with an "or" to suggest that the choice is up to the reader and that the distinction between the two periods is neither substantial nor material. This indistinct discourse regarding pastness, which implies an inaccurate correspondence between past and present spatial conceptions, stems from a refusal to locate "the practice[s] of everyday life" in historical context with any specificity. However, it must be emphasized: the view from the top of the WTC, as de Certeau described it, does not participate in the same spatial practices as those prevalent in the medieval period; nor are the most prevalent spatial practices of medieval Europe identical to those of the "Renaissance." This book would be impossible without such distinct historical periodizing: the spaces discussed here are grouped around a time when contrasting ideas of space—some, longstanding traditional practices associated with the mediaeval era; others, newly emergent practices demonstrative of aesthetics and ideologies best described under the term "Renaissance"—coexisted in a single culture and in a single city. Many of the engagements of *City / Stage / Globe* can be traced back to a dissatisfaction with this passage from de Certeau, and a determination to explore and define the spatial concepts of those "earlier times."

The following chapters will focus on space, as performed and represented (the two functions are not mutually exclusive) in text and image, on stages, in streets, and on paper. The goal of *City / Stage / Globe* is to trace a performance genealogy of space in what I will describe as "postmedieval" London. In addition to space, "performance" serves not only as another object of study, but as the methodology of this study (Roach "Reconstructing," 8). The work of Joseph Roach, especially the study *Cities of the Dead: Circum-Atlantic Performance* (1996), has made valuable contributions to the methodology of theatre and performance. Roach describes his work as the production of "genealogies of performance": "genealogies of performance document—and suspect—the historical transmission and dissemination of cultural practices through collective representations" (Cities 25). Roach's influential work itself relies on the approach to history described by Foucault, whose description of the term "genealogy" is (perhaps appropriately) elliptical: "Genealogy does not pretend to go back in time to restore an unbroken continuity [. . .]; its duty is not to demonstrate that the past actively exists in the present," rather, a genealogy serves "to identify the accidents, the minute deviations—or conversely, the complete reversals—the errors, the false appraisals, and the faulty calculations that gave birth to those things that continue to exist and have value for us" ("Nietzsche" 146). Such an approach to history documents the fragmentary evidence of the past, describes reversals along with emergences,[5] while eschewing the forced—and often false—continuity of linear, Darwinian, historical narrative.

My use of the term "postmedieval" is an important element of the performance genealogy at work in this book. Not a word of my own coinage, "postmedieval" is a term used by historians to indicate a period in Western European history that follows the medieval, while emphasizing medieval influences on that succeeding period.[6] In my usage, this term designates a period of cultural change: "postmedieval" serves to periodize the overlap located at the end of the medieval and the beginning of the early modern periods in London, a period marked by uneven emergence of "Renaissance" cultural forms, and the continual recurrence of medieval spatial practices. When making broad historical generalizations, I will continue to use the conventional designations of "medieval" and "early modern," but "postmedieval" will describe a finite period of London's history during which performances, representations, and spaces were produced amid an admixture of cultural paradigms, not easily separated to either side of an arbitrary historical division.[7] The concept of the postmedieval is a tool that I deploy in the service of the performance genealogy pursued in these pages, and postmedieval London is the period studied in this volume.

The emphasis on performance in this project allows each chapter to pursue a wide range of cultural activities and to challenge the boundaries of the printed texts that so often mark the limits of conventional literary history. As Roach notes: "Texts may obscure what performance tends to reveal" (Roach, *Cities* 286).[8] The relationship between text and performance, as it manifests itself cultural forms, institutional policies, and theatrical practice, has become a topic of much critical discussion.[9] Rebecca Schneider and Diana Taylor have explored the value of performance as an alternative way of understanding the world and of communicating that understanding to others. Indeed Schneider and Taylor both challenge the seemingly self-evident definition of performance as an "ephemeral" form, and instead proposed performance as an epistemological alternative to literacy and literacy's more obviously lasting material forms-books, pamphlets, scholarly journals, and the full panoply of print media, contemporary and historical. Taylor differentiates between the cultural codes of print and performance through a distinction between "the archive" and the "repertoire" (2003):

> Even though the relationship between the archive and the repertoire
> is not by definition antagonistic or oppositional, written documents
> have repeatedly announced the disappearance of the performance
> practice [. . .]. Writing has served as a strategy for repudiating
> and foreclosing the very embodiedness it claims to describe. (36)

Though *City / Stage / Globe* was begun before the publication of Taylor's celebrated study *The Archive and the Repertoire* (2003), this project has been directed since its inception towards investigating the historical performances that are described in, implied by, intended for, and often erased by early modern English texts.

In a sustained, interdisciplinary exploration, Chapter One develops the idea of the "postmedieval" and the theoretical implications of this term. This chapter follows the gradual transition from medieval to early modern, focusing on the emergence of early modern cultural practices in 16th century London. The European middle ages, that epoch so casually glossed by de Certeau, was one dominated by a culture of performance. As a result, pre-modern visual and textual media relied on strategies of performance in ways that modern print media do not. Before print technology and its corollary, literacy, became near-ubiquitous features of western culture, the lived experience of Europe was permeated by discourses of performance. Recognition of this *performance culture* has been slow; scholarly studies have tended to rush to the relative security and putative stability of the study of printed matter from this period. Seeking to revise historical views that represent the movement of history as a switch that simply turns off the practices of a previous era and activates those of a new one, this chapter attempts to chart the uneven emergence of "Renaissance" concepts in conjunction with the persistent retention of traditional medieval ideas. Though individual performances may be temporal, performance as a culture-wide strategy for the organization of space proves to be surprisingly durable. This chapter concludes with a discussion of the textual ideologies of dramatic literature, a form in which issues of print and performance are necessarily intensely concentrated.

Proceeding from text to image, Chapter Two places renewed emphasis on the city, particularly maps, map images, and urban portraits of London. Providing a sense of historical trajectory, as did the previous chapter, this chapter surveys the evolving "canon" of urban representations of London. The work here is strongly interdisciplinary, and relies on studies in the history of cartography. I approach this material with a sense of respect, even a sense of debt: crossing borders, even disciplinary ones, is a dangerous business. My goal here is neither to replicate the work done by those whose disciplinary work is dedicated to cartographic history, nor to apply a "corrective" that that work. Rather, my purpose is expansive: I offer a theoretical supplement, introducing the theoretical apparatus of performance to a field where it is not conventionally applied. These analyses of a range of images not only chart the gradual increase in cartographic precision associated with the mapping practices of the early modern, but as well they chart the debt that early modern maps owe to the residual performance culture of the medieval era. The chapter is called "Pedestrian Mappings," a phrase drawn from work on urban space in a rather different cultural context.[10] Pedestrian mappings are cartographic activities that rely not only topographic organization but on physical activity of the mapper. In effect, pedestrian mappings are cartographic performances. The first maps considered in this chapter are quite evidently pedestrian mappings: they are essentially records of (or perhaps programs for) physical activity. But even in later examples, as early modern concepts of representation become the dominant organizing feature of these urban images, the city illustrated on these pages is visually determined by the physical activity of London's resident pedestrians. As Deleuze and Guattari have observed, "The map has to do with performance" (12).

The following "double chapter" deals with one specific urban, pedestrian performance: the royal entry of James I into London in 1604. Though one performance on one day, James's entry spawned a series of texts, each of which offers a distinct perspective not only on this event but on the city in which it occurred and on the uses of text in relation to a major civic performance. Ben Jonson and Thomas Dekker are the featured players in the drama that surrounds the entry, though the dramatic personae includes James, Shakespeare, and a number of other early modern pedestrians walking in the City of London. My consideration of this event is divided between a consideration of the textual politics that surround the printed volumes that left the presses following the entry, on the one hand, and on the other a study of the ways in which the performance itself might have served as a major force in the production of space in early modern London. The first part of the chapter pursues the relative security of textual study and literary history; the second part addresses the more tenuous, speculative consideration of the lasting consequences of a seemingly "ephemeral" performance.[11]

Each of Chapters Two, Three, and Four focuses on one of the representational media in this book's title. Two relates ideas of performance to the representational practices of mapping; Chapter Three discusses print and civic pageantry in the context of the streets of the city; and Chapter Four returns to the subject deferred since Chapter One: performance and the stage itself. This chapter continues an interest in historical relations between text and performance introduced in One and advanced in Three, an interest in what W.B. Worthen identifies as "a form of communication where writing bears in complex yet determinate ways on enactment: dramatic performance" (2003 5). This chapter insistently pursues the idea that while dramatic performance may be in "complex" ways determined by written words, live performance on a stage is not exclusively defined by written words-especially not live performance on a stage in Shakespeare's London, where relations between text and performance were undoubtedly flexible, and where embodied activity was still the chief form by which a dramatic text was "published" or made public.

Chapter Four also importantly considers the ways in which staged performance in Shakespeare's London was productive of space. The public theatre in the period served as a site that both demonstrated the lasting vitality of oral performance in early modern English culture and the laboratory for the development of new spatial practices, innovating urban space as well as social space. With innovations in urban space in mind, the chapter is devoted to two Roman plays, *Julius Caesar* and *Coriolanus*. These are not only the most urban of Shakespeare's texts, *Julius Caesar* and *Coriolanus* are themselves expressive of the historical movement of the postmedieval: straddling as they do the divides between the end of Elizabeth's reign and the beginning of James's, these plays help to chart the historical trajectory of performance in this cultural moment and the development of representation as a defining

feature of narrative drama. In considering the push-pull between the traditional pleasure of physical performance and the lure of emergent narrative representation, it is essential to bear in mind that the public theatre in which Shakespeare worked was not merely reflective of the developments in the physical space of London—the theatre was in fact a constitutive factor in those developments.

The conclusion is a long one, a chapter in itself, because it is less an ending than a beginning; as such its mode is more forward-looking than retrospective. Only in the conclusion do I begin to address one of the most notable spatial developments to emerge in London during the life of Shakespeare: the innovations associated with private court performance and the masques designed by Inigo Jones. These masques, written in collaboration (and often competition) with Jonson, offer an extraordinary range of opportunities to consider the interactions of space and performance, text and representation. However, the court masque also marks the beginning of the end of postmedieval London, and as a theatrical form outlives the era of the city that is the subject of this study. Accordingly, a glance at the spatial practices of the masque will serve to mark one endpoint of this study, and mark as well the beginning of my next book-length study. There are other endpoints: the conclusion is a catalog of endings, tracing as it does several of the trajectories followed in the course of this book to what must be only provisional conclusions. Included in this list of termini is the demise of the very city that has been both subject and object of study.

As offered in the subtitle of this book, *Performance and Space in Shakespeare's London*, the lifespan of Shakespeare provides the rough chronological parameters for this study. But the subject matter considered in *City / Stage / Globe* is by no means limited to events and texts between 1564 and 1616. I use the term "postmedieval" to interrupt any oversimplified estimation of the historical transition from medieval to early modern. The temptation to historical simplification is great in a project that covers a wide span of time. The remarkable range of reference in Julie Stone Peters's *Book* certainly beggars the range of my project: Peters regularly references in a single paragraph several writers working in different languages over a span of hundreds of years. As exciting as such referentiality can be, Peters's method often seems to admit an ahistorical and acultural tendency to conflate these reference points, to presume that with the emergence of print, the early modern culture established itself uniformly and without resistance or delay throughout Europe.

In order to avoid the temptation to collapse time and difference, I have adopted a two-fold approach to periodizing. First: I have suggested a period of overlapping cultural forces, a transitional period in which the performance culture of the medieval existed along with, and often in contest with, the emergent representational strategies of early modern culture. In London, this postmedieval period would have been startlingly dynamic, as social and representational practices changed amid urban spaces still determined by the topography of the medieval construction that dominated the city.

Second: To this awareness of historical situatedness and the movement of history over a limited span of time, I add the genealogy. The performance genealogy approach of Roach, predicated upon Foucault and Pierre Nora, facilitates the consideration of discontinuous events, practices, and representations. It allows me to indulge my sense that the course of true history never did run smooth. Though the majority of the material that I discuss is clustered around the accession of James and the death of Shakespeare, the full scope of the project ranges hundreds of years in either direction from those dates. Only by relying on the associative logic of the genealogy can a body of work range from the London-to-Rome itinerary drawn by Matthew Paris in 1252, to a *New York Times* article about Lower Manhattan from February of 2002.

An interdisciplinary project of such scope cannot hope to be exhaustive. In order to martial the range of material assembled here, I have resisted the urge to do as late medieval London did and spill beyond the boundaries of the city's walls in my discussion. The city serves as the primary category of space for this project, and it has framed and delimited the discourses of the project. Stanton Garner has called the city "a *lived* field of spatial meanings" (*Land/Scape/Theater* 102), and the goal of *City / Stage / Globe* is to understand how the city influences the production of meaning within its walls, and in turn, how the production of meaning influences the city.

Chapter One

Writing and Performing in "Postmedieval" London

> The Great Khan owns an atlas whose drawings depict the terrestrial globe all at once and continent by continent. [. . .]
> The atlas . . . reveals the form of cities that do not yet have a form or a name. [. . .] The catalogue of forms is endless: until every shape has found its city, new cities will continue to be born.
>
> Italo Calvino[1]

> Consider the case of a city-a space which is fashioned, shaped, and invested by social activities during a finite historical period.
>
> Henri Lefebvre[2]

One of the most famous images of Elizabeth I is a painting from late in her reign. The so-called "Ditchley portrait" by Marcus Gheeraerts (c.1592) was made to honor Elizabeth's progress to the estate of Sir Henry Lee in Ditchley (Harvey, *Maps* 4). In this image, Gheeraerts represents Elizabeth's relationship to the space of her nation and beyond. [Fig. 1] J.B. Harley observes that "Elizabeth stands with her feet planted on the map of England, the map symbolizing the association between crown and nation" ("Meaning" 33). And indeed, the surface on which Elizabeth is shown resembles the county maps of England produced by Christopher Saxton in the second half of the sixteenth century. With these county maps in mind, P.D.A. Harvey notes that Elizabeth stands on Lee's own county, Oxfordshire, and that Lee's home in Ditchley would be more or less nestled between the monarch's feet (*Maps* 4).[3]

Political interpretations prevail among discussions of this portrait, and one may conclude, as Louis Montrose observes in another context, that this image "provides compelling visual evidence for the consolidation of the powers of the dynastic state, and for the highly personalized nature of the political process, during the early modern period" ("Idols" 108). For Montrose, writing from the perspective of literary and cultural studies, the Ditchley portrait "asserts, in spectacular fashion [Elizabeth's] power over her land and over its inhabitants. The cartographic image transforms the land into a state" ("Gender" 14). Analysis of this image by cartographic historians, however, pursues other interpretations. Harley finds it "apt that Elizabeth I stands on a map of sixteenth-century England," because, given events to this point in the cultural history of early modern England, "Gheeraerts's picture shows how maps had already acquired abstract meanings" ("Maps" 295, "Tudor" 33). The use of maps as instruments of power thus might be seen to focus the attention of analysis to issues cartographic, an inversion of the critical attention that Montrose directs at the portrait and the government it implies.

My own view of this image incorporates elements of these general theories, that of the literary scholar as well as the cartographic historian; however, by way of a stepping-off point, I offer a correction to the observations of Harley and Harvey: in the Ditchley portrait, Elizabeth is *not* shown on a map. She is standing on a globe.

The curvature of the surface on which Elizabeth stands is clearly represented at the left side of the image, just off the right edge of the queen's gown. And even in the partial view of the southern portion of the British Isles, a viewer of the portrait can distinguish a distortion of the land mass that is typical of representation not on a flat surface, but on a spherical one. Roy Strong observed this feature of the portrait as early as 1977, in his famous study of Elizabethan portraiture and pageantry, in which he observes that Elizabeth "stands as an empress on the globe of the world" (154). More than merely providing a corrective to prevailing observations about the Ditchley portrait, Strong's observation inflects any understanding of the content of this image, forcing a re-evaluation of the portrait's cartographic and political meanings in response to this spatial precondition. A global perspective of this image would encourage interpretation in terms of international space and the complex network of representational relationships implied by this picture of the queen and, not just one county but, the world.

Of her own representational status, Elizabeth herself famously declared: "We princes, I tel you are set on stages, in the sight and viewe of all the world duely observed" (W. Scott 220). The Ditchley portrait provides a visual complement to Elizabeth's rhetorical "viewe" of her own position in relation to the world: one would not have to seek further than Shakespeare's countlessly repeated coinage "All the world's a stage" to find a pithy rendering of a popular commonplace of early modern European culture.[4] The Elizabethan world-as-stage maxim, however, is made spectacularly uncommon in the Ditchley portrait of Elizabeth herself. William Egginton argues, in his study of the

Figure 1: The "Ditchley Portrait" of Elizabeth I. Marcus Gheeraerts, c.1592. National Portrait Gallery, London

space of modernity, that the space of the "world" in Shakespeare's usage is a homely one consisting of "ordinary, everyday practices and conventions" (4). However, there is nothing "ordinary" about the space in and on which Elizabeth is represented. The "great globe itself" curves away beneath her feet, and thunder and lighting gather in the background of this potent theatrical disposition of the royal performer on a global stage.

Without wishing to overstate the significance of the Ditchley portrait in the cultural context of early modern England, I find that this image powerfully suggests the confluence of cultural forces that worked to determine the ways in which space was represented in England at the end of the sixteenth century. Without contradicting the politico-historical readings or the histories of cartography that I have previously cited, I choose to interrogate Gheeraerts's portrait for its representation of space. This image demonstrates a complex order of map-related concerns: the "concern with place" so critically important to representations in this period is displayed in the use of the globe (Helgerson 348), but is further made personal and even physical in the positioning of Ditchley at the very feet of the figure of Elizabeth. Though the full range of the space described in the Ditchley portrait is global, it is not to be forgotten that the occasion prompting the production of this image was local: the place of this location is represented, however minutely, in the space of the image itself, and even has come to serve as the name by which this image is known. "Ditchley," then, recurs not only as the appellation by which historians have come to know this portrait, but also as the geographical referent that locates this representation of Elizabeth in space and time. It is because of Ditchley that this image has the capacity to represent both spatial and chronological information: the Ditchley portrait can be seen not only to be like a map, it is also "a version of history" (Alpers 95).

But the portrait further discloses an awareness of the space-determining potential of performance. The disposition of body and setting in this image-as articulated in Elizabeth's own words: "We princes . . . are set on stages"-must be seen as a visual example of the rhetorical commonplace that Shakespeare so memorably captured. For one of Elizabeth's early modern subjects, this painting would have invoked a theatrical worldview, one not separate from political, cartographic, or representational issues. Among the many critical models for interpretation that one might use to unpack this portrait, I argue that performance theory must be added to the list, for in this period concepts of mapping and practices of performance were not so very different; indeed, it will be the argument of this book that these practices were inextricable.

The Ditchley portrait is a strong, finite example of the genealogical network suggested in my main title. Each of these terms, "city," "stage," and "globe," has meaning as an object, as a location, and as a term indicative of a representational form that was in the process of radical reinvention in England at the time that this portrait was made. And each of these representational forms contributes to and is informed by the performance-based perception of historical time that is the basis for this project. My approach is "geographic," in the sense that Edward Soja gives the term when he writes that: "geography is simultaneous, where language is 'sententious,' 'sequential'" (Soja, *Postmodern* 2).[5] Such a geographic attention to the joint history of performance and space informs a wide-ranging consideration of the multiple, simultaneous meanings that arise in performance from the interaction of different forms of spatial production, all of which draw on, however unevenly, both (physical) performance and (visual) representation.

My interrogation of the Ditchley portrait, as with the interrogations that follow, is inspired in no small part by the reinvention in contemporary cartographic thought initiated by J.B. Harley and David Woodward. In their massive, multivolume *History of Cartography*, Harley and Woodward introduce "an entirely new definition of 'map,' one that is neither too restrictive nor yet so general as to be meaningless" (xvi). Their definition:

> Maps are graphic representations that facilitate a spatial understanding of things, concepts, conditions, processes, or events in the human world. (xvi)

Given the ambitious span of their history, Harley and Woodward sought to define maps in such a way as to include the historical and cultural contexts essential to the full appreciation of maps as artifacts of human production, and to reappraise those images which had been excluded from cartographic history on the basis of "restrictive interpretations" that eliminated many examples—notably, medieval European and pre-modern non-European examples—from a place in previous histories of cartography.

Those who criticize this definition (Gillies, Gordon) do so at the risk of betraying their own narrow assumptions about the representations of space. Bernard Klein, under the influence of this new definition, recognizes that "geographical knowledge" in medieval and early modern Europe "embraced not merely topographical information in the narrow sense" but addressed itself as well to "multiple, overlapping and frequently contradictory forms of cultural and political identity" (11). In light of this redefinition, the Ditchley portrait itself and not merely the portion of a globe represented *in* the portrait, may be regarded as a species of map. Detached from the modern Western concept of an accurate representation of geography, Harley and Woodward admit into the definition of "map" a consideration of the culturally specific forces that inform mapping, which include not only spaces but events. Thus the portrait maps not only a location but the occasion of Elizabeth's arrival there. This relation of spatial and temporal forms in the Ditchley portrait displays the sublimated assumption that physical performance is the essential element that unifies subject and location. This portrait, then, is an early modern map that argues volubly that it is performance that puts bodies in place.

More than just a re-evaluation of Shakespeare's plays in relation to cartographic and theatrical history, this project deploys performance theory in an interrogation of the complex representations of space that propagated in Shakespeare's London. Montrose has suggested that Shakespeare's theatre is not merely an "inert product" of early modern British culture, but in fact "a source of cultural production" (*Purpose* 109, "Shaping" 31). In the context of my work, this means that Shakespeare's plays are not just redundantly reflecting popular ideas about space in general and the city in particular, but rather that Shakespeare's plays—along with the other cultural artifacts to be considered here-are in fact contributing to those ideas. Shakespeare's theatre had the capacity to generate material change: to produce space. The physical space of the city, the innovations in visual culture, and the representation of space in Shakespeare's plays all mutually informed each other. At a time of particularly acute social dynamism in London, the public theatre played a part in deciding what the city was, and what it could become. In other words, this is not just a study of the ways in which spatial change informed Shakespeare's plays, but of the ways that Shakespeare's plays were themselves productive of the spatial changes in which they participated. An understanding of the role of performance in early modern spatial practices is critical to a full appreciation made by the dramatic, theatrical performance to the spaces of early modern London.

In *Performance: A Critical Introduction*, Marvin Carlson explores at length the expanding field of study that is engaged with this unstable term. However, only at the very end of this exploration does Carlson offer any definitive statements, and only the penultimate sentence can be construed as a definition per se of performance:

> It is a specific event with its liminoid nature foregrounded, almost invariably clearly separated from the rest of life, presented by performers and attended by audiences both of whom regard the experience as made

> up of material to be interpreted, to be reflected upon, to be engaged in-emotionally, mentally, and perhaps even physically. (199)

Carlson's deferred definition offers an extension of the parameters of performance that are key to this study: he theorizes the effect of performance not only for the individual performer, but for those witnessing the performance. The famous coinage of Richard Schechner, "restored behavior" has become ubiquitous; while implying through its restoration that performance is linked to behaviors previously behaved by others, this phrase locates performance in the body of present-tense behavior. Similarly, a definition offered by Joseph Roach explicitly links the performer to a history of performance, but focuses on the individual: "the kinesthetic and vocal embodiment of social memory and self-invention" ("History" 23). The bodily occupation of shared space would seem to be a critically important element of performance, as Roach indicates, but no less important is the dialectical discourse that Carlson implies-placing notable emphasis on the role of the audience in performance. Though he makes a distinction between "performers" and "audiences," Carlson also makes it clear that the "material" of performance is equally available to members of each group, performers and audience alike, for interpretation, reflection, and engagement (199).

Just such an active, multivalent engagement with social space was evoked in traditional performances in the English medieval town: in the theatrical practices of seasonal performance, audiences and performers shared the social spaces of the town, shared the social knowledge restored and produced those public spaces, and shared even in the production of those spaces themselves.[6]

Robert Weimann observes of the field in general that "'Performance' has advanced to something like an ubiquitous concept which we use either to sound, or *intercept* our discontent with the epistemology of representation" (*Author's* 1, emphasis added). Weimann's work has, over several decades, interrogated the interaction between bodily performance and textual representation.[7] While the relation between performance and text will be a major engagement of this book, *City / Stage / Globe* includes among the representational forms considered visual discourses along with textual, in order to consider the full range of complex interactions between performance and representation along with the material consequences of those interactions. These material consequences include those that anticipate changes in urban social practices and even the physical spaces of the city.

The goal of this chapter is to develop a concept of the early modern imaginary as it obtained in London at the time of the birth of Shakespeare.

As the Ditchley portrait illustrates, emergent concepts of global space had, by the time of the portrait's painting circa 1592, begun to infiltrate the ideology of Elizabeth's court and her personal representational "sphere." Interrelated innovations in religion, literacy, print, and economy began to introduce to systems of social practice associated with the continental Renaissance to the British shores. My category of the "postmedieval" embraces a range of cultural transformations that marked this dynamic period in British history. The social "gallimaufry" that John Lyly describes in his preface to *Midas* responds to the decline of lineage society and the gradual disruption of an idea of community in which social action was predetermined and closely prescribed. Equally consequential was the breakup of locally organized economic units in favor of regional and, increasingly, global political and economic identities. Though my focus is on the interrelations of space, performance, and representation, the movement of these other social forces informed and drove the cultural shifts of the postmedieval period.

In conjunction with the emergence of print practices, the daily material conditions by which London was experienced by its inhabitants continued to be understood in terms of performance. Pre-modern urban practice was predicated upon a reliance on the experience of the city; the places of the city played an important role in the social performances of early modern London and as a result became sites of civic meaning and social memory (Roach, "History" 23). Over the course of a time period marked at the outset by Elizabeth's entry (1559) and closed with double finality by the death of Shakespeare and the publication of Jonson's *Works* (1616), the ceremonial performance of *representational space* is increasingly confronted by the culture-wide emergence of a visually dominated *representation of space*.

This is not to say that "the historical shift in question" was "one from sacramental civic *communitas* to disciplinary state hierarchy," a position that Louis Montrose rightly critiques (*Purpose* 23). This critique is echoed by Mullaney, who says of Elizabethan London: "things were not clearer in and of themselves as if possessed of some radiant phenomenological purity" (*Place* 10). Rather than ineffable qualities, Montrose describes this cultural movement "as one from a culture focused upon social dynamics within the local community to one that incorporates the local within a national framework" (Montrose, *Purpose* 23). While Montrose's cultural taxonomy is as compelling as his visual one, and equally politically engaged, this same cultural terrain can also be described in different terms.

In the history of cultural criticisms of London, this "historical shift" has often been conceived as one from a social system predicated upon "ceremony" and "ritual" to a more secular society.[8] And though important work has been done in the consideration of ritual and ceremony in society, this work subsequent has produced a more technically precise language: the language of performance studies.[9] The phrase "the ceremonial city" has become conventional in discussions of London (Smith, Strier, and Bevington; Gordon; Mullaney). This phrase relies on the path breaking work of Geertz and Turner, but it places conceptual limits on the ways in which urban practices can produce the city, limits that constrain investigation of the city to large scale, connotatively religious events, thereby occluding discussion of personal and secular microperformances; the word "ceremony" also excludes conventional theatre from a discussion of the forces that produced the city's spaces. In *City / Stage / Globe*, the "historical shift" in question will be framed as a transition from a performance culture to visual / textual one.

The understanding of medieval urban space in this project places an emphasis on bodily performance and the *eventmental* dimension of social space. The term "eventmental" was coined by Edward S. Casey in *The Fate of Place*, in which Casey argues that "place is not entitative [. . .] but eventmental, something in process, something unconfinable to [. . .] a simple location" (337). Casey's processual understanding of place is entirely compatible with my construction of a culture predicated upon the performance of location, the physical articulation of the space of the city. This kind of culture obtained in England's medieval period, and the continued influence of performance culture at the end of the 16th and into the 17th centuries was an essential precondition to the postmedieval.

Medieval performance practice—in both popular and ceremonial aspects—emphasized the relationship between the physical body and social space, two terms which "reacted on each other with a closeness which approaches identity" (James 21). By contrast, as Richard Rorty observes, the early modern era became obsessed with the Greeks' "ocular metaphors" (13) as well as by signifying practices which ceded dominance to representations of space, practices which eventually displaced the physical occupation of representational spaces—in the theatre as in the city—for the image of space in representation. Though etymologically the term "theatre" is derived from the Greek (meaning, "a place for seeing") late medieval theatre practice emphasized the first element in this definition, the importance of a communal "place" over individual opportunities for "seeing." Weimann makes use of a flexible understanding of performance "to establish a new nexus for doubleness and diversity in the purpose of playing and the function of (re)presentation" (*Author's* 11). With a similar goal of producing a "double" and diverse understanding of the relations of social practice and visual representation in this period, I choose to deploy performance to augment—and even intercept—the critical discourse surrounding cities, stages, and spaces that to this day remains for many scholars ossified around ideas of knowing based exclusively on texts. Jon McKenzie offers a valuable insight when he describes performance as "an onto-historical formation of power and knowledge" (18). While I remain unconvinced by aspects of McKenzie's study, *Perform or Else: From Discipline to Performance*, this basic insight has influenced this discussion. While McKenzie theorizes this formative property of performance as isolated to the postmodern period, I view performance as an onto-historical formation that exerted considerable force in the medieval and early modern periods, and indispensable to a full appreciation of the postmedieval transitional period considered in this study.

Studies by John Gillies and Stephen Mullaney loom large two of the discourses of space with which I am engaged: Shakespeare and cartography and Shakespeare and the city, respectively. Though there is much of merit in these scholars' works, each suffers from the same flaws: 1) a static view of the subject of study that attributes to all urbanisms / mappings the same qualities without regard for a diachronic understanding of culture and space that admits change and development over even a limited period of time; and 2) an unspoken assumption that literature and textuality are the appropriate ontologies for the investigation of the work of Shakespeare, an assumption that precipitates a neglect of performance as a representational force—including the performance of Shakespeare's theatre writing—that can contribute to urbanism and / or cartography as well as simply be influenced by those representational forms. Mullaney is at pains to observe that an event like Elizabeth I's coronation entry (see next section) can make meaning of the city, but he does not ever suggest that such performances can actually form and re-form urban space. And although Gillies discusses Shakespeare's "geographical imagination" from the outset of his study,[10] Gillies concludes that there is only a "metaphoric" relationship between theatre and cartography. The premise that fuels the present work is that the representational revolution that precipitated a "cartographic shift" in the early modern period not coincidentally is comparable to the innovations in space on the early modern stage-both the early modern map and the early modern theatre are products of the same representational revolution.

Bernard Klein, looking at this same period in European history, observes "a redefinition of contemporary spatiality: space defined in terms of the people using it [. . .] yields to its representation as a mathematical diagram as an abstract grid pattern inscribed on a blank sheet of paper" (19). My own view of this "redefinition" is consonant with Klein's, but neither so bleak nor so abrupt. Accordingly, the argument of *City / Stage / Globe* is that the structures by which space itself had been perceived, used, and understood for centuries were changing, and nowhere in England were these changes more acute than in London, where, in the decades bracketing 1600, a range of social pressures brought about a radical change in representational practices across the media of my title: the city / the stage / the globe-sites and practices associated by a "slash," rather than separated by comma.

This project is an investigation of what Lefebvre has called "the long history of space" (116). Lefebvre notes that since each historical period "has its own particular space, the shift from one mode to another must entail the production of a new space" (46). *City / Stage / Globe* is a consideration of just such a shift. No such historical shift, however, is ever abrupt and definitive, nor can the emergence of new spaces, or representational practices of space, be marked from a singular incident. Rather, the shift that I consider was a gradual, uneven, sporadic, and inconsistent transition that resulted in a period of spatial hybridity. The goal of this project is to examine the hybrid spaces of London, circa 1600.

In addition to his bleak view of early modern spatial representation, Klein additionally notes "the profound incongruity, the incommensurability, of the medieval and the Renaissance constructions of space" (18). With this point I must take issue. Space, in the period I consider, is marked by nothing if not the interaction and negotiation of medieval and early modern constructions of space. I use the phrase "spatial hybridity" to suggest the multivalent and flexible negotiations of the social and representational practices that activate, record, and perpetuate the dynamic spaces of this period, which were constructed—or, if you will, "spaced out"—by the very *commensurability* (contra Klein) of medieval and early modern spatial concepts.

It is in fact because of the interactions between these seemingly incongruous spatial practices that I find the term "early modern" an only provisionally helpful marker of periodicity. Although it would seem tautological that early modern London emerged during the early modern period, I suggest that this was not entirely the case. While concepts and practices associated with the early modern did indeed arrive in London during this period, the physical geography of the City of London remained decidedly that of a medieval town well into what is generally considered the early modern era.[11] More importantly, the spatial practices of medieval culture had not yet yielded in the face of supposedly incommensurable resistance from early modern thought. The negotiations between these practices would play out in maps and images, civic performance, on the public stage, and in other representational sites; the city proves to be both a physical location and the conceptual parameter par excellence for the reinventions of space that took place in this period. Lefebvre observes that: "Urban space was fated to become the theatre of a compromise between the declining feudal system" and the rising commercial and political powers which would come to define the early modern era (269). In other words, the space of the city became the stage (figuratively and literally) on which competing modes of material and spatial production were active, a space in turn defined by these same material and spatial activities at a critical historical juncture.

City / Stage / Globe locates in the early seventeenth century the emergence of ideas and practices of space that would govern the spaces of London for subsequent centuries and influence urban spatial thought and the physical space of the city even in the present; however, this project does not offer a simplistic discovery of the "origins" of the present in the past. Margreta de Grazia decries such presentist views of history, as I do: "There is a way in which seeing the Renaissance as the Early-Now commits itself to the very universalizing tendency that historicizing set out to avoid in the first place. As if *the* relevant history were a prior version of what we already are and live" (de Grazia 21). Despite de Grazia's incisive parody of "early modern" cultural studies, and in consonance with her resistance of a historiography that represents the past in terms of the present, my project insists that the ideas, performances, representations, and urbanizations of the past must be understood in historical context; and the recurring force of postmedieval spaces must be understood in the context of subsequent cultures and institutions.

In a critique of conventional narrativizing histories, especially in theatre studies, Michal Kobialka has called for "a postmodern archive," a practice of historiography that privileges the fragment, rather than succumbing to the false whole offered by teleologies of historical narrative. Following the model suggested by Kobialka, my project assembles a genealogy of texts, images, and performances: traces of postmedieval space that suggest the ways in which the city serves as the fragmentary repository of its own histories. While some poststructuralist ideologies might wish to deny the presence (and presentness) of the past in a two thousand year-old city like London, to do so would demonstrate a willful blindness to the terrain of spatial history and neglect the potent potential of the postmodern archive. My reading of the Ditchley portrait is situated within the compass of the postmodern archive and under the influence of the "complex genealogies" that Jody Enders assigns to theatre histories (xxix), and the chapters that follow similarly consider the interconnected cultural, material-and often immaterial-traces informing the production and performance of space in postmedieval London.

The operations that I discuss are historical. They are *events*. But the material consequences of the performances that comprised these events were not immediate; indeed, immediate consequences remain hard to locate in the physical space of London during the period of Shakespeare's life. The challenge of this work is to describe the gradual emergence of new forms of space and the ways in which the inhabitants of the city interacted with these spaces: the ways in which London's urban subjects described these spaces to each other and performed and practiced these spaces themselves. At the end-point of this book, I glance beyond the margins of the postmedieval to look at London after 1666. Only after the Great Fire destroyed the physical space of the postmedieval city could there begin a transformation of the topography of London that correlates with the representational developments of the turn of the seventeenth century.

At the time of this book's writing—a time that may still be called a millennial juncture—cities around the world are expanding in incompletely understood ways. The hybrid spaces of early modern London offer opportunities to investigate the "synekistic" moment circa 1600 that shaped and in many ways continues to inform our contemporary urban spaces, spaces which now seem to be undergoing another urban sea change.[12]

"THE WONDERFULL SPECTACLE"

> [. . .] if a man should say well, he could not better tearme the citie of London that time, than a stage wherein was shewed the wonderfull spectacle, of a noble hearted princesse toward her most loving people, and the people's exceding comfort in beholding so worthy a sovereign.
>
> Richard Mulcaster[13]

On January 14, 1559, Elizabeth Tudor made her way through the streets of London as part of the public theatrical performance which was the precedent to her coronation. The principal text describing this event, Richard Mulcaster's *The Quene's Majestie's Passage through the citie of London to westminster the daye before her coronacion*, not only sets out to record the series of theatrical displays and scenes that confronted Elizabeth but, notes Richard C. McCoy, this "unprecedented publication [. . .] made the event accessible to an even larger audience and preserved its glorious memory for all time" (245). As McCoy's hyperbolic tribute makes emphatically clear, Mulcaster's text sets out to articulate the "official" agenda for the progress. As in the epigram from Mulcaster above, Elizabeth is portrayed throughout *The Quene's Majestie's Passage* as a "noble hearted princesse," and the crowd that attended the event is portrayed as universal in its affection for Elizabeth and willingness to be her "most loving people" (Mulcaster 16). The suggestion of such uniformly positive reception justifiably elicits skepticism; as Sandra Logan notes: "such experiences were inescapably multivalent, different for differently positioned viewers" ("Making" 277). And indeed Elizabeth herself was one of the viewers whose position is the most complicated. Whatever interpretive bias may be expressed in Mulcaster's text, unless Mulcaster has engaged in the fabrication of several of the most intriguing events described in the *Passage*, Elizabeth herself must be seen as "one of the actors in the total pageant-part of the theatrical experience" (Bergeron, *English* 14). While she was, conventionally, the prime "viewer" of this event—the sovereign for whom this royal "entertainment" was prepared—Elizabeth also took on the role of a performer in this event, a particularly unconventional aspect of her royal entry, indeed, an aspect that broke with hundreds of years of tradition.

The description of Elizabeth I's accession day progress, published shortly after Elizabeth's coronation in 1559, attempts to limit the possible interpretations of this city-spanning urban performance. Mulcaster's text "reinforces the allegorical implications of the procession" in an effort to portray this occasion as one expressive of "cultural unity and interpretive stability" (Logan 253, 252). Recent considerations of this event, however, have undermined the security of any unity or stability that Mulcaster, and even some contemporary scholars, have assigned to this event, revealing the ways in which, in Susan Frye's words, "*The Queen's Majesty's Passage* demonstrates its own descriptive limitations in the gaps and omissions that can be found in its claim of unity" (Frye 33).[14] Much of what is to be learned of this public theatrical event from Mulcaster's text must be sought by reading against the intent of what Logan has called "the rhetorical occasion" of *The Quene's Majestie's Passage*: "events themselves differ for different viewers and participants, to such an extent that there can be no privileged viewpoint except one artificially produced through textual representation" (251). Thus, to consider the event represented by Mulcaster's text, the performance historian must read between the lines and beneath the surface of his pamphlet, peering through the "gaps" in its claims.

Among the insights that may be gleaned from a reading of Mulcaster's far-from-disinterested account of Elizabeth's passage is a sense of the space of the city. The theatricalized politics and politicized theatre of *The Quene's Majestie's Passage* serve as potent examples of the range of possible uses of urban space to construct and display social order and political authority in mid-sixteenth-century England. While this pre-coronation procession was part of a tradition of Tudor ceremonial entries into the City of London,[15] Elizabeth's procession was in many ways exceptional, particularly in the ways in which she herself chose to perform and interact with the event. For as

Mulcaster notes in the quote above, Elizabeth's *Passage* and similar civic ceremonies used London itself as a theatrical space. As Mullaney broadly claims, throughout the 16th century, the city itself was used as a venue for the "spectacular advertisement of social structure" (10). However, as the structures of English society changed in the course of sixteenth and early seventeenth centuries, so did the spectacles and that which they advertised.

The first stop along Elizabeth's progress was at Fenchurch Street, in the southeastern part of the City of London; there, Elizabeth was greeted by a child who concluded a speech of welcome with the words: "God thee preserve we praye, and wishe thee ever well."

> At which wordes of the last line the hole peple gave a great shout, wishing with one assent as the child had said. And the quene's majestie thanked most hartely both the citie for this her gentle receiving at the first, and also the peple for confirming the same. Here was noted in the Quene's majestie's countenance, during the time that the childe spake, besides a perpetual attentiveness in her face, a mervelous change in looke, as the childe's wordes touched either her person or the people's tonges and hertes. So that she with rejoysing visage did evidently declare that the woordes tooke no lesse place in her mynde, than they were most heartelye pronounced by the chylde [. . .].
>
> (Mulcaster 17)

Though Goldberg suggests that "the air of spontaneity that she maintained throughout her progress was manufactured at least in part," he nevertheless acknowledges that "Elizabeth plays the role in the spectacle of one taking part" (29), a role visible in the above quote, beneath Mulcaster's insistence on popular "rejoysing." Regardless of whether or not her performances were part of the original plan or repeated displays of inspired extemporaneous oratory, Elizabeth was an active participant in this event, responding to—and at times even *replying* to—the pageants staged for her.

The most significant, and frequently quoted, of Elizabeth's self-assertions came in her response to the pageant performed at Cheapside, at the time the major financial thoroughfare of the City of London. The fourth of eight stops along the route taken through the city, the pageant entitled "Truth, the Daughter of Time" was the critical nexus of the political, economic, religious, and gender issues with which the entire progress was engaged. The pageant itself featured two stage areas, "two hylles or mountaynes" of similar height; one of the hillsides was a blighted landscape, the other green and pleasant; the first bore the name "*Runiosa Respublica*, A decayed common weale," the other, "*Respublica bene instituta.* A florishyng commonweale" (Mulcaster 27, italics in original).[16] As well as being presented with lists of the various vices and virtues which could lead to either of these conditions in the common-wealth, Elizabeth was in the course of this pageant presented by a city official with an elaborately decorated bag of 1000 gold marks, and, at the end of the same pageant, an English-language Bible. Elizabeth's response to these atten-tions "renegotiates the terms of the gift as she gives her thanks for it" (Logan 257):

> I thanke my lord maior, his brethren, and you all. And wheras your request is that I should continue your good ladie and quene, be ye ensured, that I wil be as good unto you, as ever quene was to her people. No wille in me can lacke, neither doe I trust shall ther lacke any power. And perswade yourselves, that for the safetie and quietnes of you all, I will not spare, if nede be to spend my blood, god thanke you all.
>
> (Mulcaster 27)

At what might be described as the climax of the *Passage*, Elizabeth accepts a gift of gold offered by a city administrator and minutes later accepts an Eng-lish-language Bible—the latter acceptance forcing her to make a tacit, public acknowledgement that she would return England to the Protestant religion established by Henry VIII but interrupted by Mary I. Mulcaster's text gives the impression that Elizabeth's above oration was extemporaneous; the text also alludes to a few brief words, also presumably unstudied, that Elizabeth said later upon receiving the Bible. Regardless of whether or not Elizabeth knew in advance what would transpire in the course of her progress, whether or not her "spontaneous" orations were pre-planned, her role in the event was far from passive. Indeed, she must be seen as the most active of all the performers involved in the occasion.

As the result of Elizabeth's individual performing-verbal and physical-her progress must be seen as having two distinct audiences. The first of these audiences was Elizabeth herself, in the ruler's traditional role: observing as she moved through the city the various sites of a performance scripted and produced by her own subjects.[17] The second and ultimately more important audience was everyone else in attendance: the audience of London's popula-tion, present at Elizabeth's first performance of herself.

The ostensible premise of an English accession procession was the lavish welcome of the new monarch, who was given "access" to the city for the first time as ruler. However, the tone of Elizabeth's accession was often less than welcoming. Most of the individual pageants took the form of didactic allegories addressed to the young incoming monarch, dealing with such divisive issues as religion, heredity, political policy-all to the end of exhorting her to be a peaceful, stable, and even tractable ruler. But as the chief audience member and object of these theatrical exhortations, Elizabeth was not content to remain an idle auditor. Bergeron has noted that Elizabeth responded to each pageant along the progress route with the "theatrical flair" that would come to characterize her reign, and according to the text these performances were received with "great delectation" by her audience" of courtiers, attendants, City officials, as well as her more common subjects in the crowd (Bergeron 1985, 14).

In as much as these pageants were addressed to Elizabeth, she was their first and principal audience. However, Elizabeth was also very much an actor on this urban stage, performing in conjunction with the pageants for the secondary audience of this pageant: the people of London, be they "base and low personages" (Mulcaster 38) or the aldermen of the city who were the framers of the event. Frye notes that "the Court of Aldermen . . . organized the entry in order to represent its interests" (19), but even in the text paid for by the city, *The Quene's Majestie's Passage* suggests at least "two brief moments when Elizabeth steps outside the roles [the text] assigns her" (31). At times during the event, such as the acceptance of the gold or the Bible, when Elizabeth was forced to take physical action that had visible political meaning, her responses intercepted the seemingly monovocal intentions of these public transactions and provided Elizabeth with alternative ways of making meaning and of forming her political identity. In this, her first "public performance of herself as the ruler of England," Elizabeth was able to make the erstwhile "interpretive stability" of the *Passage* "unstable enough to be inverted, extended, and contested" (7). By making a place for herself in the performance of her own entry, Elizabeth was able to become more than a passive watcher addressed by this theatre event: she participated in the event, re-positioned its discourse, and interrupted the agenda of the pageant's framers.

Weimann's study of the practices of the late-sixteenth-century public theatre provides one way to describe the theatrical use of space that facilitated Elizabeth's interruptive performance. His discussion of the uses of *platea* space on the Elizabethan platform stage introduces portable theories of space that can be borrowed from a discussion of theatre and employed to reveal the tactics used by Elizabeth in the streets of London. In Weimann's development of the concept, the *platea* functions to break the frame, so to speak, of the theatrical apparatus. The *platea*, then, is: "an opening in *mise-en-scène* through which the place and time of the stage-as-stage and the cultural occasion itself are made either to assist or resist the socially and verbally elevated, spatially and temporally remote representation" (*Author's* 181).[18] In 1559, in an altogether different space, Elizabeth activated a similar use of *platea*: by asserting her right to participate in the "cultural occasion" of her own progress (181), Elizabeth could subvert the closure of the *Passage's* narrative by invoking the city-as-stage which underlies Mulcaster's description of the event in order to resist the insistent, patriarchal message of the city fathers. From her position in the urban *platea*, Elizabeth could offer a rebuttal to the message of the pageants—a kind of complex, political aside. While not able to assert her authority in exactly her own terms, she was able to engage with and qualify the terms set by the framers of the *Passage*.

In the face of the allegories of Time, Truth, and both Ruined and Flourishing nations, as well as more material displays of London's financial power and Protestant faith, Elizabeth side-stepped the terms of the implied performance contract by making an appeal that broke the boundaries of the allegorical representation. Elizabeth eluded the space of the representation with reference to the audience of the city and to herself, not as the figure of a queen, but as an individual, embodied performer (overtly drawing attention to her body, and even referencing her own "blood") and in so doing resisted the agenda set by the framers of this political theatre. Rather than the unconditional acceptance of the allegorical objects of the pageants (and the two real objects directly presented to her, the Bible and the gold) and the institutions they represented, Elizabeth's performance introduced the assumed precondition of her own "power," on which power, she implied by inversion, London's religious and financial institutions rely, as much as she will rely on those institutions.

While this extraordinary theatrical exchange between city and crown stands out in Mulcaster's account of Elizabeth's interactive *Passage*, the queen takes other opportunities to make other openings for self-performance in the conventionally "closed" structure of civic progress:

> How many nosegaies did her grace receive at poore women's handes? how ofttimes staied she her chariot, when she saw any simple body offer to speake to her grace? A branche of Rosemarie given to her grace with a supplication by a poore woman about fleetebridge, was sene in her chariot till her grace came to westminster [. . .].
>
> (Mulcaster 38)

Here, then, in her first public appearance as a monarch, Elizabeth can be seen to appropriate the space of the city, carving a space for herself from which to participate as agent in the cultural occasion of which she might otherwise have been a mere object.

The purpose of this brief, selective analysis of Elizabeth's royal entry is to demonstrate the value of performance in English culture an the culture of London in the middle of the 1500s. Indeed, Elizabeth's entry is demonstrative of what I refer to as a "performance culture": a community that relies on public performance-rather than, for example, visual representation or textual knowledge-to produce social meaning. A milestone in the historical genealogy that this book charts, *The Quenes Majestie's Passage* is richly demonstrative of both medieval practices of civic performance and of important, emergent traits of the early modern.

Crowding the narrow streets of the mid-sixteenth-century city, those Londoners attending Elizabeth's entry procession were not interested in merely gazing upon the individual pageant sites, however beautiful. Rather, their interest was also in being present as Elizabeth interacted with those pageants. Mullaney describes Elizabeth's "presence" as "the moving and vital force that brought the pageants to life and gave voice to the figures they contained" (*Place* 11). "Presence" has of course become a vexed issue in the study of theatre and performance,[19] and it is critically important for my project that performance be understood as more that just a question of presence. Simply "being there" is not an adequate conception of postmedieval performance and its potential as an animating force. It would be more accurate, though less poetic, to say that Elizabeth's accession provided the occasion for this event, and that her arrival at each station on the passage route gave the performers associated with each pageant a reason to voice their text, though it was not she herself who "gave voice to the figures." One might go so far as to suggest that the most notable figure animated by Elizabeth was Elizabeth herself, performing the role of the new queen, negotiating in an oblique way with her subjects, adding her voice to what would have been otherwise a univocal text.

The architect and urban theorist Bernard Tschumi states that the importance of architecture "resides in its ability to accelerate society's transformations through a careful agencing of spaces and events" (11). What Tschumi says of architecture can serve as an accurate description of the function of theatre as well: theatrical performance asserts both physical and narrative control over a given (representational) space or spaces, determines the conditions which apply to that space (representation), and introduces performers into those spaces whose embodied activities constitute the events (real or narrative) which occur in and are regulated by those spaces. Tschumi's description reveals the intensely theatrical faculties of architecture, but also provides language that can be used to describes theatre in terms of the regulation and "agencing" of space and the events or performances which occur in that space.

When applied to the conventional understanding of "theatre" as a public performance in which the space of the stage is determined by physical, conceptual, and narrative parameters that influence the activities of actors and the events which they perform, Tschumi's powerful formulation, "the careful agencing of space and events" can be seen to apply equally well to theatre as to architecture. But this same formulation empowers the term "theatrical" in a way that can describe the "careful agencing of spaces and events" beyond the conventional framework of theatre as public performance. A city-spanning event like Elizabeth's entry is "theatrical" in Tschumi's sense: it organizes the spaces of the city and innovates new spaces, spatial constructs appropriate to the events which will be performed in them. Notably, it is Elizabeth herself who is the principal agent in these spaces, endowed with the power to activate the events, to transform the spaces, and to rule the urban subjects themselves.

While this architecture-derived theory offers a way of thinking about the configuration of space in architecture and theatre, it presents a particular challenge for theatre historiography. As Sandra Logan has observed: "The problem of historiography is, above all else, a problem of the relationship between events and texts" (Logan 251). The texts which document past events "participate in the construction of perceptions about their historical context for future readers and writers" (Logan 252). Logan's observation is particularly acute for theatre studies, where the historical analysis of texts is often the only avenue by which to trace the histories of spaces and the events which took place in them. In Chapter Four, I will investigate these questions and challenges with examples drawn from Shakespeare.

Bergeron notes that those "spectators in the streets of London" attending a royal entry "are there to see the sovereign [. . .] as much as to see the planned dramatic activity"; that every audience member was aware of "participating in a theatrical experience can be of little doubt" (Bergeron, "Introduction" 14). But one must go further. For the secondary audience of *The Quene's Majestie's Passage*, the population of the city, the opportunity to stand as witness to the ceremonial performances for the new queen and her own theatrical participation in that ceremony was of prime importance. This was not a cult of celebrity but the way in which a citizen understood her or his relation to political power: through performance in the space of the city.

As Mulcaster states, "the citie of London" was "a stage wherein was shewed the wonderfull spectacle" of Elizabeth's first official entrance as monarch. In describing the relationship between the processional performance and the space of the city, Mulcaster's statement "exceeds the bounds of metaphor" in its accuracy (Mullaney 11), for although each individual pageant was the site of a stage, Elizabeth herself was also performing on the stage of the city itself, "in the sight and viewe" of London. Though Elizabeth's accession procession was not a performance explicitly *about* London, it was in a very real sense a performance *of* London: Elizabeth's accession day progress relied on the topology of London itself, relying on the performed and performable city for her "signifying power and political potential," to borrow a valuable phrase from Una Chaudhuri (5).

Mulcaster's text captures the heterogeneity of spatial production at this hybrid juncture in London's spatial history. Throughout *The Quene's Majestie's Passage*, the space of the "citie" is rhetorically equated to the space of a "stage" on which is displayed a civic "spectacle." In sixteenth century London, Elizabeth's entry was exceptional in the ways in which it produced social space: though in its course through the city, it's structure of serial allegorical dramatic performances, and it's general tone of fealty and welcome, *The Quene's Majestie's Passage* clearly demonstrates its participation in longstanding medieval traditions of royal pageantry. Yet, in the active performance of its central figure, a dialogic structure emerges at variance with medieval tradition. And the most important feature of this pageant is the one that facilitates all scholarly discussion of it: Mulcaster's printed document. Whether or not *The Quene's Majestie's Passage* does in fact faithfully "document" the events of Elizabeth's entry or provides instead a favorable fictionalization of those events is immaterial in the face of the material document itself: the unprecedented publication of an account of a royal entry. In a radical break with tradition, *The Quene's Majestie's Passage* is evidence of a need to record a performance and distribute it in print in a way that no previous entry had been treated before. The textualization of a royal performance was unprecedented, making this document and the event it (more or less) records landmarks in the emerging concept of the postmedieval.

Richard C. McCoy has noted that a "ceremonial" understanding of urban space marked the accession of Queen Elizabeth I, as performed in the course of her elaborate procession through the streets of London in 1559. However, as McCoy clarifies in his discussion of these two forms of social performance, "ceremony" is not the same as "ritual" (244). Elizabeth's progress was both a "secular and popular" event, precedent to the sacred rite of the coronation; but on this occasion the signifying power of the secular event "completely overshadowed the sacred ritual" (244). Several decades later, the coronation procession of James I in 1603 would demonstrate the increasing dissolution of the ritual significance already eroded under Elizabeth. Marked by visual spectacle and, in the words of Sidney Anglo, "stiff with classical allusions" (5), James's pageant entry was a departure from the mode of urban ceremony that had become traditional under the Tudor monarchs. As will be explored at length in Chapter Three, James's entry was an abstract, secular ceremony, celebrating the spectacle of power and emphasizing the perspective of a single ruling individual. Moreover, James's entry was not only documented by several competing accounts, the very event was in several ways self-documenting: the 1604 entry included aspects of the monumental and the archival in the course of its performance: that there was an entry at all in 1604 demonstrated a vestige of the traditional understanding of cityspace as the medium in which royal power was understood, made public, and connected to the historical past; yet, aspects of James's entry were more "spectacle" than "stage," serving simultaneously as a performance of social space and its negation. Though the static king of the 1604 entry seems to starkly contrast with the 1559 entry and the continually self-performing queen at its center, James's entry shares with Elizabeth's an important feature of postmedieval performance: staging in the space of the city an anxious competition between event and text. Hybridity of performance and textual cultures is one of the clearest markers of the postmedieval, as these entries demonstrate.[20]

THE CITY OF LONDON

Elizabeth's entry occurred at a time of extraordinary growth for London. By comparison to other major English cities, London was large in 1500, but by 1600 it dwarfed any city in the country and had firmly established itself as the equal in population of any city in Europe. The City's merchant communities had been important to royal finances for centuries, but London's financial strength had grown considerably throughout the sixteenth century. By 1604, London had become the overwhelmingly dominant hub of economic exchange in England.[21] In this same period, London's population grew by an astonishing degree. While the overall growth of the English population was in decline, London's population quadrupled from 50,000 (or fewer) inhabitants in 1500 to approximately 200,000 in 1600. In fact, this extraordinary growth had been accelerating. In 1550 London's population was approximately 60,000-75,000, a fifty percent increase over fifty years; yet by the end of the century the London's already dense population would more than double from its mid-century figures. London would continue to demonstrate such exponential population growth through 1650, by which time London's population had reached 400,000.[22] At the outset of the sixteenth century,

London was a modest medieval "town" compared to the standards set by continental European metropolises. However, by 1600 London had become one of the three most populous cities in Europe, exceeded in size only by Paris and Naples.

John Schofield describes late Elizabethan London as "a medieval city on the edge of spectacular expansion in the century to come" (*Topography* 319). Schofield participates in a tradition of urban historians who describe late sixteenth- and early seventeenth-century London as a city in transition. Lewis Mumford is one of the first to use the term "post-medieval" in relation to "the new urban complex" emerging in Europe at the outset of the seventeenth century (Mumford 345). The London through which Elizabeth passed in 1559 is described by social historian and urban geographer Christopher Friedrichs as a "post-medieval city," because even after a time at which most historians conventionally stop using the term "medieval," London had all the features of a medieval town. Friedrichs bases his assessment on the lack of topographical change in the city. The physical topography of this city was largely undifferentiated from that developed hundreds of years before. However, these urban historians' usages of the term "post-medieval" must be distinguished from mine: where they see a set of buildings measured against a conventional historical yardstick, I prefer to see a hybrid space of competing social and spatial practices, measured over cultural time. Over the course of the Elizabethan era, the introduction of early modern concepts and projections was bringing about a significant change in the urban imaginary, a change in the ways in which the city was conceived, practiced, and represented by its inhabitants. Though this change was gradual and did not immediately produce radical alteration in the city's topography, it is no less profound.

Cities concentrate not only numbers of people, but also the social forces which those people exert on a location. As Soja argues, the physical construction of a city cannot be taken as more significant than "the dynamic processes of innovations, development, and change associated with what can be broadly defined [. . .] as the social production of cityspace" ("Putting" 28). Thus it is not useful for this project to simply say that London "looked medieval" during the late 1500s; the idea of the early modern city was in development during this period, appearing in the city's spaces and in the behavior of its citizens, regardless of the appearance of the city itself.

The understanding of "space" in use should be clarified. I do not mean simply a catalog of the contents of a given location. Following the important work of twentieth-century spatial theorists like Lefebvre, de

Certeau, Casey, and others—part of "the explosion of writing on space that has characterized recent cultural studies" (Arnade et al 516)—the space I refer to is both the product of and the context for the social practices of a given people in given historical and cultural conditions. Space must be seen in terms of both the physical aspects of a naturally occurring geography and in terms of the social practices which have "fashioned, shaped and invested" the physical geography of a location "during a finite historical period" (Lefebvre 73). The city, as conceived here, is the assemblage of social spaces that Soja describes as "materially and conceptually constructed, simultaneously real-and-imagined" (Soja, *Thirdspace* 33). A fact-oriented reader may balk at the idea of a city that is even partially "imagined" as unproductive theorizing. But in fact the goal of *City / Stage / Globe* is to demonstrate that the *idea* of the city was a force with material consequences in Shakespeare's London. To understand how a "medieval-looking" city can be in complex ways both medieval and early modern, one must think together two conceptual forces: performance and representation.

The spatial dynamism of postmedieval London was expressed in a range of representational strategies that served to conceive the space of the early modern city long before that space was realized in the material geography of London. Elin Diamond defines representation as "the making visible (again) of what is lacking or what has disappeared" (85).[23] In her brief description of a complex function, Diamond suggests not only representation's filiation with visual discourses, but also its capacity to produce the new or to renew the absent. In London, during a period of study that extends from 1559-1616, representation served as the precedent to—and, indeed, the facilitator of—urbanization.

The forces of urbanization can be deployed in many ways. A wide range of work has considered the relationship between visual and textual representation in England "circa 1600"[24]. This relationship has dominated western representation since the sixteenth century (de Certeau), and the study of one or the other element in this relationship, or their operations together, was an important strain in late twentieth-century scholarship (W.J.T. Mitchell). However, my interest in representation in this period proceeds from an engagement with recent dissenting voices, particularly in the field of urban studies. Such self-described postmodern urbanism is engaged in a sweeping re-examination of the concepts and impulses that have conditioned the space of the contemporary city and the practices of the people who inhabit these cities.[25]

At the time of Elizabeth's entry into the city, the physical structure of early modern London was much as it had been for centuries. Though its population had been rising rapidly, construction was limited to individual, small scale efforts at providing and expanding living accommodations for the city's burgeoning lower classes whose numbers contributed to what Ian Munro calls London's "crowded spaces."[26] Friedrichs notes that, other than population growth, "in many of its most important aspects, the early modern city remained remarkably unchanged" over the sixteenth century (9). However, though continuity may have prevailed in the topography of the postmedieval city, the social practices of those urban spaces were in flux. Marvin Carlson observes that: "the theatre played a crucial role in the transition between medieval and baroque concepts of urban organization" (*Places* 23). Carlson quotes Pierre Lavedan, who notes that the principles governing the new urban space of the Renaissance

> were applied to the city only after having been, one might say, vulgarized by two intermediaries: the theatre and the art of the garden. The theatre ties geometry to urbanism.
>
> (*Places* 23) [27]

Following this assertion then, the urban development which must be charted in the early modern period is not so much one of a renovation of the physical geography of the city, but rather the emergence of a new theory of urbanism and a new set of spatial practices. This new ("imagined") urban space found expression in a number of different modes of representation before its form was in any way realized and stamped on the physical features of the city itself.

It is important to note that the space of this development extended beyond innovations in architecture. A single built structure might exemplify aspects of an emerging space, but only in a rather finite way. Though the interior spaces of a new structure might impose on a visitor structures which would be demonstrative of an emerging spatial practice, the pressure a single building could exert on external space—the space of the surrounding buildings and urban projections—would be necessarily more limited. Even a building such as Christopher Wren's rebuilt St. Paul's, still dominating the "skyline" of London, could not be said to govern the space of the city, despite its local significance.[28] Architecture alone is neither the source nor sole expression of the spatial practices emerging at this critical juncture in the history of the city. A study of built structures-a study that focused only on the "real" city to the exclusion of the "imagined"—studies only part of the city.

Without neglecting the physical structures and urban projections of early modern London, the range of spatial innovations to be considered must be broadened to include the modes of representation that designed and controlled space. These new representational practices—with correlative representations of space—did not merely interrupt existing spatial codes, as a new building might do, but served to utterly rewrite them. The era turned to some of the less permanent representational media for its most ambitious experiments on those spatial practices: gardens, cartography, and theatre served the rehearsal of spatial practices in ways that extended beyond the limitations of architecture. Richard Krautheimer notes the versatility of the impermanent experimentation that representation offered to urban development: "To remodel an entire town remained an ideal never to be achieved" in the early modern era; however, "the ideal city of the Renaissance [. . .] could be built [. . .] not in stone but only on the canvas of a stage backdrop" (355-6, 359). Krautheimer's observation about the limitations of urban development is based on constraints of time and money, and the inflexibility of the material substance of architecture. But this estimation presumes that architecture alone *could* reinvent the space of a city, were these constraints relieved, an estimation that overlooks the mutually constitutive relationship between architecture and the spatial practices that govern its use and development.

Mumford's comprehensive *The City in History* remains an important point of entry for the study of urban history. In his discussion of medieval town structure, Mumford makes clear that the essential aspect of a medieval town is not its visual appearance, but its use value as a place for social performance.

> Whatever the practical needs of the medieval town, it was above all things, in its busy turbulent life, a stage for the ceremonies of the Church. Therein lay its drama and its ideal consummation. [. . .] [N]o sedentary student, viewing this architecture in pictures, no superficial observer, taking up a position and attempting to plot out axes and formal relationships, is in a state to penetrate this urban setting even in its purely esthetic aspect. For the key to the visible city lies in the moving pageant or the procession: above all, in the great religious procession that winds about the streets and places before it finally debauches into the church or the cathedral for the great ceremony itself. Here is no static architecture. (277)

Mumford describes an understanding of urban space which is at considerable remove from our own cities. The medieval city was "a stage" for the urban rituals conducted by the city dwellers for the city dwellers themselves (277). The medieval city, Mumford argues, was not to be *looked at* but rather *performed in.* Such a spatial practice, in which the city itself was available as the representational space for self-referential public urban performances, facilitated the frequent events that constituted the European religious calendar. Through these performances in / of space, the medieval city was regularly "making sense of itself to itself," in Geertz's phrase, by means of community-spanning urban performance (167).

The whole of the city was a representational space, a heterogeneous site available to social performance. The social practices of the medieval city's population were bound up in what Charles Phythian-Adams has described as the "ceremonial or ritualized expression in action, in time" of "a coherent ceremonial pattern" (106), or what I might call a spatialized understanding of religion. Writing in particular of the ceremonies surrounding the feast of Corpus Christi, Mervyn James discusses the several events which comprised the celebration, but makes it clear that "[t]he feature to note however is the procession, in which the Corpus Christi becomes the point of reference in relation to which the structure of precedence and authority in the town is made visually present" (19). The consecrated host, "ceremonially carried through the principal thoroughfare" of the town, became the object that organized the social and religious relations of the community. Clergy, municipal officials, and guild leaders all followed in a procession that performed "the idea of the social order as body" in relation to the body of Christ.[29] Processions such as those associated with the feast of Corpus Christi took place in towns and cities throughout England: the medieval city was understood in terms of its *ritual topography*, the space for practices whereby "the community in its entirety was literally defining itself for all to see" (Phythian-Adams 107). Yet this was not a totalized or totalizing space: in her critique of univocal interpretations of medieval sacramental culture, Miri Rubin finds in the Corpus Christi processions "an exercise in self-portrayal which does not necessarily reflect consensus within a community, but rather juxtaposes symbols articulating one of many possible and competing visions of that community" (248). Similarly, despite frequent critical attempts to present its "cultural unity," Elizabeth's *passage* reveals a community in tension rather than "consensus."

The activities of medieval community were not based on "visions" or spectacles exclusively presented for others to "see"; the parades, processions, and public performances of cycle dramas and other plays may have been witnessed by others, but were in and of themselves means of producing the community by physically occupying the terrain of that community: its ritual topography. However, such a performance-based way of imagining urban space was on the wane even at the beginning of Elizabeth's reign. Treatises on and illustrations of the "ideal city" began to be disseminated from the print shops of Italy and the Netherlands, alongside influential cartographic innovations: maps and atlases that used new representational techniques to depict a new world. Forms of visual representation gradually began to supplant performance as the dominant medium of cultural expression. These images of ideal cities and idealized spaces had a powerful influence on the early modern imagination and, accordingly, on the way that space itself was imagined.

THE REPRESENTATIONAL TURN

In *The Birth and Rebirth of Pictorial Space*, art historian John White notes that the distribution of objects in any given medieval image was predicated upon "a hierarchic scale based on the importance of the person or object represented" (103) and not on any sense of "fidelity to nature" (Letts 30). However, one cannot accept fidelity to nature as a principle of "Renaissance" art, either. The "picture" that would come into being in the early modern period is not so much "natural" as representational, a conventionalized abstraction of nature.

The arts of the Renaissance have historically been described as distinct from those of the medieval era. The image system of the latter emphasized the subjective expression of a phenomenal, lived experience: a medieval painting of a location is not so much a landscape in a pictural sense as a topology, an image of location defined by the intersection of geographic space and ideology (Mullaney 10). The Renaissance picture came in to being along with the development of perspective, the impact of which on all aspects of spatial practice cannot be underestimated. White explains this development:

> Synthetic perspective may . . . be described as a thorough-going attempt to express an experience of visual reality which is only to be gained by a process of introspection, of asking what it is that is really seen. (275)

White's explanation suggests that, while the overt ideological content of medieval visual art is not a feature of Renaissance art, nevertheless, a "process of introspection" informs the kind of image-making that emerges at the outset of the early modern era such that Renaissance images must be seen as no more faithful to reality than the images of medieval art. Renaissance art merely substitutes a representation of space for representational spaces; such images remain ideological, but they work to conceal the ideologies that make such images possible.

Mitchell refers to what he calls a "Pictorial Turn" in order to describe "the way modern thought has re-oriented itself around visual paradigms" (9). Mitchell sums up the workings of this re-orientation with the phrase "picture theory," a phrase used in a dual sense; it refers both to "a theory of pictures" and a to pictorial way of thinking about theory, as one might say in colloquial parlance, "picture this." Mitchell's punning about picturing is a useful correlative to White's analysis of the rise of pictorial representation: "picture theory" condenses both the sense that picturing is an abstract process of representation and the sense that pictures and picturing have become the dominant metaphors for modern era. As another art historian, Christopher Braider, observes: "Far from being confined to the domain of visual and literary art, the pictorial serves as a central cultural model spanning the entire spectrum of modes of representation" (3). And Richard Rorty argues that picturing has become the central model of philosophy and even of thought itself.

As useful as many of Mitchell's observations about picture theory may be, I must assert a significant point of disagreement about the occurrence of the pictorial turn. While I do not contest that such a turn has taken place, when Mitchell writes that "*modern* thought has re-oriented itself around visual paradigms," the period he refers to as "modern" is the twentieth century (9, emphasis added). Though the pictorial indeed is intimately associated with the twentieth century, I rather locate the western cultural turn toward the pictorial at the rise of the historical modern, as indeed does Rorty (an author Mitchell quotes at some length), who locates in the work of Descartes the beginning of the modern obsession with the picture and metaphors of picturing. But perhaps no one better captures the conceptual workings of this turn than Heidegger, who goes so far as to define the divide between medieval and early modern eras in terms of picturing.

> The expressions "world picture of the modern age" and "modern world picture" both mean the same thing and both assume something that never could have been before, namely, a medieval and an ancient world picture. The world picture does not change from an earlier medieval one into a modern one, but rather the fact that the world becomes picture at all is what distinguishes the essence of the modern age.
>
> (Heidegger 130)

Here, in a passage from "The Age of the World Picture," Heidegger distills the key difference between these two eras, a difference struggling to resolve itself in the social and spatial fluctuations experienced in Shakespeare's life-time. Heidegger identifies a historical turning point, though a different "modern" moment from the one identified by Mitchell. For Heidegger, the start of the (early) modern era is marked its own "pictorial turn," one that relates subjectivity and power to practices of representation. And for Heidegger, picturing is a much more complex practice than Mitchell makes it out to be. Though Mitchell discusses the wide-ranging significance of pictures in twentieth-century western culture, and does not rule out the role of power in this significance, Heidegger sees the world-picturing practices that inaugurated the early modern era as constitutive of the system of power that prevails even in late modernity: "Hence world picture, when understood essentially, does not mean a picture of the world but the world conceived and grasped as picture" (Heidegger 129). Thus in the early modern era, the power to picture becomes the power to *appropriate*; writing on the politics of Heidegger's claim, Weimann comes to a conclusion that explains the cultural consequences of this representational shift: "'appropriation' as an act in literary history will have to be defined as both a text-appropriating as well as a world-appropriating activity" ("'Appropriation'" 465).

The representation of space, therefore, can be seen as inextricably linked with what Lefebvre calls "the abstract space" of early modern power. For Lefebvre, "the use value of a space of this kind is political—exclusively so" (287). Lefebvre sees in the abstract space of the early modern a kind of collapse, a "reduction of the 'real,' on the one hand, to a 'plan' existing in a void and endowed with no other qualities, and , on the other hand, to the flatness of a mirror, of an image, of pure spectacle [. . .]" (287).[30] Foucault, too, sees the transition from medieval space in terms of an explicit spatial collapse. In his brief, celebrated lecture "Of Other Spaces," Foucault provides sketches of the two sides of this historical divide, separated by what might be called a "spatial turn" rather than a pictorial one.

> One could say, by way of retracing this history of space very roughly, that in the Middle Ages there was a hierarchic ensemble of places: sacred places and profane places; protected places and open, exposed places; urban places and rural places [. . .]. It was this complete hierarchy, this opposition, this intersection of places that constituted what could very roughly be called medieval space: the space of emplacement. (22-23)

The many "places" that Foucault argues are constitutive of the medieval spatial system portray a society whose spatial practices function to particularize: in the medieval system, space was the product of lived experience. This is the space that Lefebvre calls "absolute space," where the means of production directly reflects social practice: "This space is 'lived' rather than conceived, and it is a representational space rather than a representation of space" (Lefebvre 236). The theories of both Foucault and Lefebvre correspond with the performance culture that I have described as dominant in medieval Europe. Medieval space, theorized in these terms, relies on what Casey calls the "eventmental" aspect of place: an environment determined by the events that "take place" there.[31]

After his brief, abstract description of medieval space, Foucault goes on to describe the space of the early modern.

> This [medieval] space of emplacement was opened up by Galileo. For the real scandal of Galileo's work lay not so much in his discovery, or rediscovery, that the earth revolved around the sun, but in his constitution of an infinite, and infinitely open space. In such a space the place of the Middle Ages turned out to be dissolved [. . .] a thing's place was no longer anything but a point in its movement, just as the stability of a thing was only its movement indefinitely slowed down. In other words, starting with Galileo and the seventeenth century, extension was substituted for localization. (23)

Foucault offers a somewhat idiosyncratic view of Western history, one that extends the middle ages into the seventeenth century, when the publication of Galileo's *Dialogue on the Great World Systems* brought him acclaim and infamy in 1632. But regardless of his chronology, Foucault's discussion of these two modes of production of space is a useful corollary to Lefebvre and Heidegger: the transition from medieval space into the space of the early modern is a movement from eventmental localization to visual, representational extension.

Whereas medieval space may be seen as a vertical accretion of performed events, the space of the modern was (and perhaps still is) a horizontal space, one conceived in representation, a space where practices of picturing were (and perhaps still are) used to establish a fixity in support of the "world-appropriating" activities that marked (and perhaps still mark) this era. The representations of space that came to dominate social practice "inverted the real space of Society" substituting instead pictures of place, representations which must be seen as "fundamentally unreal spaces" (Foucault, "Of Other Spaces" 24). The space that Foucault calls "fundamentally unreal" is the space that Heidegger and Lefebvre refer to as "abstract": space defined by subvert ideological systems: representational space. This is the meaning of "abstract" that will be deployed throughout this book, an abstraction produced by representations of space that might under other circumstances be called "realistic." Such "realistic" representations objectify that which is in representation, setting it apart from the viewer. Thus understood, abstract representation will be juxtaposed throughout this project with the concrete engagement of performance in various forms, and, in Chapter Two, with non-abstract representational strategies referred to by the term "collection."

Abstraction in this sense is an effect of representation. For Heidegger, "[t]he fundamental event of the modern age is the conquest of the world as picture" (134). This "conquest" is "accomplished in a setting-before, a representing, that aims at bringing each particular being before it in such a way that [one] can be sure, and that means be certain, of that being" (127). The force of representation to determine and fix the identity of an individual or a territory proceeds from the abstract: the separation of the representation from that-which-is-represented, or "the objectifying of whatever is" produces "an iconicity that in itself is self-contained" (Heidegger 127; Weimann, *Author's* 182). Thus Lefebvre views abstract space as the product of representation deployed in social conditions (primarily urban) for political uses (287). Such uses of representation in the space of the city emerged along with the early modern era.

> This was the point at which the town was conceptualized, when representations of space derived from the experience of river and sea voyages were applied to urban reality. The town was given written form-described graphically. Bird's-eye views and plans proliferated. And a language arose for speaking at once of the town and of the country [. . .]. This language was a *code of space*. (269, italics in original)

What Lefebvre calls a "code of space" is the abstract, Cartesian, picturing system that fuses representation and appropriation. The coding of space was an attempt to render the city legible via abstract representations, as if viewed "from above." Visual coding was an attempt at objectification and social control, an urban strategy as explicit and synthetic in its own way as the development of linear perspective.

Though Heidegger and Lefebvre view the early modern as prone to totalizing spaces, the subject of this study is rather given to what Braider has described as "the promiscuous intermingling of painting and theater" that prefigured "the space-time of modern geography and history" (3). A time of cultural promiscuity that also preceded, I might add, the period of modern urban space.

In the sections that follow, I will attempt to provide an introduction to specific social practices of space in the transitional period examined by this project. The consideration of such a transition is a calculated response to unhistorical "literary histories" or broadly theoretical studies that deal in a "before" and "after" that portray the histories of space, representation, and the city as altogether more tidy than I view them. The London that I examine participated in a promiscuous intermingling of spatial practices at the historic juncture of medieval and early modern cultures, a period when performance coexisted with representational picturing, and where for a brief time vertical and horizontal productions of space intersected.

THE NEW WORLD PICTURE

> Right Honourable, I do remember that being a youth, and one of Her Majesty's scholars at Westminster, that fruitful nursery, it was my hap to visit the chamber of Mr. Richard Hakluyt, my cousin, a gentleman of the Middle Temple, well known unto you, at a time when I found lying open upon his board certain books of cosmography, with a universal map. He, seeing me somewhat curious in view thereof, began to instruct my ignorance by showing me the division of the earth into three parts after the old account, and then, according to the latter and better distribution, into more. He pointed with his wand to all the known seas, gulfs, bays, straits, capes, rivers, empires, kingdoms, dukedoms and territories of each part, with declaration also of their special commodities and particular wants which, by the benefit of traffic and intercourse of merchants, are plentifully supplied. (Hakluyt 22)[32]

I began this section with an excerpt from Richard Hakluyt, whose fateful visit to his cousin's office introduced him to the two competing representations of space at work in his world, and to the cartographic practices to which he would dedicate the rest of his life. Though I will begin by discussing the maps of the medieval world (as did Hakluyt's cousin), maps whose residual cartographic potency informed the hybrid spaces of Hakluyt's world. Then, I will return to Hakluyt, his contemporaries, and their postmedieval world-picturing practices.

In "The Age of the World Picture," Heidegger articulates the historical shift to the early modern Era, a shift which he understands as a question of representation. For Heidegger, the representational practice subsumed under the term "world picture," is not merely one by which an individual responds

to the world by making a picture of it, rather, the world picture is a "norma-
tive" understanding of the world perceived "in its entirety" as visual representation: "Hence world picture, when understood essentially, does not mean a
picture of the world but the world conceived and grasped as picture" (129).
Heidegger goes on to discuss the uses of such a world-picturing project in
the service of appropriation. By setting the world before oneself as picture,
one creates a subject-object relationship which not only separates oneself
from the rest of the world (as object / picture), but makes the world available to the subject for instrumental use. For Heidegger, "[t]he fundamental
event of the modern age is the conquest of the world as picture" (134). The
world-picturing project that Heidegger sets out to describe is quite literally a
representational project in the service of world conquest.

A study of the emergence of world-picturing as a practice in the early
modern era would have to account not only for "the story of the domination
of the mind of the West by [primarily Greek] ocular metaphors" (Rorty 13),
but also the uses of world-picturing for the ends of "conquest," or representation understood as a "world-appropriating activity" (Weimann, "'Appropriation'" 465). In the latter case, the world-picturing uses of representation are
quite literally pictures of the world: maps and the cartographic practices that
bring them into being. Early modern cartography "helped advance and con-
summate the primacy of boundaries," a goal that links the emerging spatial
practices and colonial activities of the postmedieval period (Kirby 55).

However, in the medieval period cartography did not serve world-picturing appropriations. In fact, the map as it is understood today simply did
not exist in the Middle Ages. The map did not have the "autonomous" existence which de Certeau attributes to contemporary maps (121). J.B. Harley observes that maps "were confined to particular areas and to particular
occasions for which their use had become established by custom" (283). A
map did not preexist its use, nor was such a thing available for purchase as
a piece of domestic goods. P.D.A. Harvey makes the claim that "[a]ny one
map was drawn with one particular purpose, even one particular occasion,
in mind" (284). Harvey concludes: "If we are to evaluate a medieval map, or
even understand it at all, we must first know just why it was made" (284).
Thus, for the most part, during the medieval period, a map was the companion to the active practice of space, an effect of the eventmental. Given such
circumstances, Deleuze and Guattari's maxim "[t]he map has to do with performance" becomes particularly viable for medieval cartography (Deleuze
and Guattari 12).

The intimate relation of medieval maps and performance is based upon
Harvey's premise: the existence of a medieval map did not precede but rather

proceeded from the need for a particular use. Maps in this sense, were not even necessarily pictorial, as de Certeau notes:

> The first medieval maps included only the rectilinear marking out of itineraries (performative indications chiefly concerning pilgrimages), along with the stops one was to make (cities which one was to pass through, spend the night in, pray at, etc.) and distances calculated in hours or in days, that is, in terms of the time it would take to cover them on foot. Each of these maps is a memorandum prescribing actions. (120)

Such a map would be unintelligible to a casual user (of any time period) unfamiliar with its intended use. The ways in which such itineraries *prescribe* actions is discussed at length in Chapter Two. As intriguing as these itineraries are for this study, they were likely marginal artifacts in medieval spatial culture. The dominant artifacts of medieval mapping seem rather to have been calculated to *proscribe* action.

Of the very few varieties and extant examples of medieval maps, the *mappaemundi* present a particularly difficult case regarding use. Early twentieth-century map historian Charles Raymond Beazeley epitomizes the critical estimation of the *mappaemundi* prior to recent conceptual innovations in cartographic history. In his three volume study of *The Dawn of Modern Geography*, Beazeley displays a casual disregard for the forms of medieval map making; he dismisses two of the most exemplary *mappaemundi* simply because they do not correspond to his own understanding of the function of a map: "the non-scientific maps of the later Middle Ages [. . .] are of such complete futility [. . .] that a bare allusion to the monstrosities of *Hereford* and *Ebstorf* should suffice" (qtd. in Woodward 288). Beazeley's presumption that the Hereford Map *should be* scientific inevitably precludes an understanding of the *mappaemundi* on their own cultural terms. While the exact uses of the *mappaemundi* are not understood with certainty, when viewed in the context of medieval culture it is clear in general that the uses of the *mappaemundi* were not so much topographical as ideological.

I would like to return to the new definition of the term "map" that Harley and Woodward introduced in their *History of Cartography*:

> Maps are graphic representations that facilitate a spatial understanding of things, concepts, conditions, processes, or events in the human world. (xvi)

Edson draws on Harley and Woodward's influential re-definition to reap-praise the *mappaemundi*: "Such a broadened definition makes room for those medieval maps whose function was to organize physical space according to philosophical or religious principles" (15). She notes that "the great Hereford Cathedral map describes itself as an *estorie*, whose modern descendant is the word 'history'" (18). In his massive study of the Hereford map, Scott Wes-trem concludes that this map "was originally intended to play a role in the education or exhortation of a variety of people-readers, auditors [. . .] and viewers," some of whom would have been illiterate (xxii). Visitors to the Hereford map would have received "live human assistance in [their] efforts to comprehend the work" (Edson ix). The Hereford *mappamundi*, like the Ebstorf, must be understood as showing not just space, but a spatial version of history.

The edges of the Hereford image are marked by letters at the points where one might expect to find the cardinal directions, but rather than marking North, South, East, and West, the letters are M, O, R, and S, which spell out the Latin word for "death." This substitution is not evidence that the cardinal points were unimportant to the makers of the *mappaemundi*; in fact, all the maps in this category are quite specific about their directional "orientation"—east is always positioned at the top of these maps, associated with the geographical home of Christ. Rather, the "M-O-R-S" arrangement around the boundary lines of the *oikumene*, or the known world, is critical to the conceptual organization of this particular *mappamundi*, and prompts a generalization about this genre of mapping.

Mappaemundi represented not only space but time, and did so in a way that consistently demonstrated the influence of the Judeo-Christian world view. According to this world view, the only direction that needed to be explicitly spelled out on the *mappaemundi* was the only direction toward which all life moves: death. The boundaries marked on the Hereford *map-pamundi* not only show "the limits of the material world" (Harvey, *Medieval* 32), but they mark as well the limits of life itself. Beyond this space, the earthly sphere must give way to the space of divinity.

Similarly the Ebstorf *mappamundi* uses religious symbolism as a bound-ary for both time and space.[33] On the Ebstorf image, the head, hands, and feet of Christ are illustrated at the cardinal points; they mark the boundaries of *oikumene*, with the head in the East, and the feet opposite, immediately adjacent to Gibraltar and the Pillars of Hercules. As Edgerton concludes, no devout user of this *mappaemundi* could "think seriously of sailing away" beyond the limits set here "because that [. . .] would mean abandoning the Body of Christ" (29). The makers of the Ebstorf *mappamundi* used this dismembered representation of the Body of Christ to mark the limits of the known world.

The primary purpose of the *mappamundi* was "philosophical and didactic," with primary emphasis on the relationship between mortals and their God (Harvey 284). The *mappaemundi* served "to instruct the faithful about significant events in Christian history," and only secondarily did they serve as "a repository of contemporary geographical information," and this geographical information was valuable, Woodward argues, only in so far as it was "of use for planning pilgrimages and stimulating the intended traveler" (286, 288). Any resemblance between a feature on a *mappamundi* and "some part of the earth's surface [. . .] was quite incidental" (284).

The *mappaemundi* would at first seem not to resemble the "itineraries" for travel that de Certeau describes. Despite Woodward's suggestion that these circular maps were used in relation to travel, a *mappamundi* is not the kind of map that de Certeau had in mind when he generalized the medieval map as "a memorandum prescribing actions" (120). A subjective, Christianized history of locations and events is inscribed in each of the *mappaemundi*. The medieval "user" of one of these maps did not need to be planning a pilgrimage in order to receive "guidance" from such a map. The *mappaemundi* were descriptions of faith and faithful conduct, a wonderful example of topology: geography and ideology reflected equally in an image of location. Thus, the *mappaemundi* were designed not so much to help the faithful get from one place to another, rather the *mappaemundi* were designed to keep the faithful in place. By presenting the world as an unnavigable elsewhere, the *mappae-mundi* work perhaps less to inspire pilgrimage, as Woodward contends, than to constrain those who view such map images. *Mappaemundi* encourage the faithful to "keep their place" in the context of the divine "plan" that they display.

I have referred to "the faithful" in this discussion of the *mappaemundi* because the *mappaemundi* are not "autonomous" (again, per de Certeau's usage) as are contemporary maps. Medieval maps—the *mappaemundi* and others—do not exist outside the field of their predetermined use; moreover their use is limited to a predetermined community of potential users, a community determined by a shared ideology. Without the shared understanding of the ideological component of these topologies, the geographical component will remain unavailable. D.J. Gordon points out that in a "ceremonial" community such as that of medieval England, an image or "device":

> does not exist by itself; it has to be read; moreover, it has to be difficult to read. To read it is a kind of play, and its function is to define the

> group that can play-to establish the group's sense of coherence, identity,
> and security." (qtd. in Mullaney, *Place* 13)

So it is not as a result of incompetent construction, as Beazeley would suggest, that a contemporary observer of the *mappaemundi* (or another kind of medieval map) cannot easily recognize how to "use" these maps; they are in fact constructed to define and maintain a particular community by including as a precept of their construction an interpretive paradigm which would only be available to those within the community of origin, perhaps only a select few trained interpreters. This kind of spatial practice is entirely contrary to the world-picturing practices of "scientific" cartography.

Kathleen Kirby describes the "earlier spatial practices" of medieval Europe as forms of mapping "based on narrative" and promoting "a subject-in-process" (41). However, Kirby subsequently qualifies this statement, saying: "I maintain that narrative and pictorial maps share a common preconception of what knowledge is and how the subject is to obtain it" (47). Kirby's latter conflation of "narrative" and "pictorial" maps neglects a full understanding of what it means to be, in her phrase, "a subject-in-process." If one takes Kirby to mean by "narrative" the itineraries and world histories that constituted the two major map forms of the medieval period, then one must find "pictorial," or representational, maps of the early modern to be radically different from the maps-in-process exemplified by the itineraries discussed in Chapter Two. The former maps produce the subject as a fixed object, not as a subject-in-process, or, as I will argue later, a subject in performance.[34] Though Mitchell may note, following Foucault, that "the relation of language to painting is an infinite relation" (5), the narrative of the medieval itineraries does not articulate the kind of language-based narrative representation that appropriates space with the authority of Modern world-picturing. What Kirby calls "narrative" and "pictorial" maps are neither narratives nor pictures in the Modern (Heideggerian) senses of the words. Itineraries are representative of "earlier spatial practices," and as such the route they describe is not the document of a previous journey, rather itineraries are scripts for future travel. Such maps prompt a "subject-in-process" along the route of a journey intended to be taken in the present tense; such maps cannot be considered separately from the spatial practices that they entail.

By contrast with medieval itineraries, the *mappaemundi* cannot be mistaken for examples of a Heideggerian "world picture," despite a certain etymological homology. The abstract appropriation of space which marks world-picturing practices emerged along with the early modern era. As de Certeau notes: "Between the fifteenth and the seventeenth centuries, the map became more autonomous" (121). This autonomy takes the form of a new kind of spatial practice, one which simultaneously sees "the erasure of the itineraries" characteristic of the performance-oriented medieval maps and the rise of spatial practices that pictured the "land [as] stabilized by representation" (de Certeau 121, Kirby 46). During the sixteenth century, representation came to serve explicitly as part of a world-appropriating activity. Chandra Mukerji has argued that the cartographic technologies appearing in this period must be considered "capital goods," because they were "innovations in material culture that were *specifically designed to act as economic tools*":

> The geographical documents published and distributed in the late sixteenth century were a type of "capital good" whose proliferation in print and wide distribution affected the international balance of power by changing patterns of control over world trade. (81, italics in original)

As the Portuguese and Spanish began exploring what was for the Europeans a "new world," a reliable means had to be developed to direct sailors successfully and repeatedly to and from newly acquired holdings in the Americas. "Maps and geographical writings, as information fixed in a permanent form, replaced both memory and advice in accumulating and transmitting [. . .] information" (Mukerji 81). Prior to—and even at the outset of—Europe's Age of Exploration, methods of navigation relied on memory, verbally relayed advice, and, when close to shore, visual cues: the itinerant spatial practices which dominated the medieval era. To our twenty-first-century apprehensions, obsessed as we are in the west with communications technologies, such maritime procedures seem inadequate even for navigating the Mediterranean, and in the face of the vast expanses of the Atlantic and Pacific Oceans they were indeed of limited value. But these procedures reflect the hybrid understanding of space as well as the relationship of the individual to the world that adhered in postmedieval Europe—a relationship that, as Heidegger notes, was only just conceiving world-picturing practice.

Pre-modern map making and cartography did not rely on representational strategies to present the world as picture. Instead, premodern navigators used tools such as *portolan* charts, criss-crossed by their distinctive rhumb lines, to travel in coastal waters and the Mediterranean. These coastline charts were used in conjunction with oral directions and personal experience as supplementary tools of medieval European maritime travel.

The centuries of tradition and belief that tied European cartography to medieval spatial practices were overturned in a relatively short period of time in the 16th century. Ptolemy's *Geographica*, "a classic text brought out in the late fifteenth century [1482] along with hundreds of other works of interest to the humanists," re-introduced Europeans to "the scientific approach to geography" (Mukerji, *Graven* 99). Within one hundred years of this publishing milestone, European mapmaking was revolutionized first by Italian and then by Dutch atlases. And as the "publication of geographical information undermined Portuguese and Spanish control of the world's oceans, making it easier for other countries to participate in world trade" (Mukerji, *Graven* 85), sixteenth-century proponents of geography and navigation began to influence affairs of state.

The principal geographer of the sixteenth century was Abraham Ortelius, influential in "the intellectual circle that surrounded the emperor" and at the center of European cartographic representation. Ortelius is responsible for publishing in 1570 "the first wholly modern atlas" (Mukerji, *Graven* 104), and the first widely disseminated realization of the Modern world picture by which one "could master the world at a single glance" (Cosgrove, *Apollo's* 130). Ortelius subsequently precipitated one of the first great publishing sensations with his *Theatrum Orbis Terrarum*, or *The Theatre of the Whole World*. The word "theatre" in this period was not exclusively applied to purpose-built structures used for public performance; the word was used in a general way to describe any "container" for things one might want to look at. Such a container could be a building, a single room, or a book; in this case, the book was one that Ortelius himself described as "the eye of history" (qtd. in Gillies 71).[35]

The new cartography, like Ortelius's *Theatrum*, did not seek to accomplish the same goals as the medieval *mappaemundi*, did not enter spatial culture for the same reasons. Medieval mapping offered a vertical idea of culture, "a hierarchic ensemble of places," and sought to connect human experience to an ordered Christian cosmos (Foucault, "Of Other Spaces" 22). Though the *mappaemundi* included the individual in their conceptual territory, the individual did not have access to that territory through the *mappaemundi* themselves: these maps were understood as having a given meaning which could only be explicated by the clergy, a meaning that did not make space available to the individual, but rather made the individual available to Christian space. The goal of the new cartography was just the reverse. Though the individual was dissociated from the content of the new maps (for example, Ortelius's *Theatrum*), interpretation of those maps was open to the individual map user, as by association was the territory represented on the maps. No intermediary, clerical or otherwise, was necessary. This was a horizontal space, one that made the world available for travel and appropriation. Though ongoing explorations and continual map revisions conveyed a sense that the global mapping project was itself in-process, global cartography relied on paradigms of accuracy that translated the physical and visible to the geometric and pictural. As Heidegger observes: "truth has been transformed into the certainty of representation" (127). The representational strategies of the new mapping technology assured the user that however incomplete the picture, its accuracy was always total—regardless of the picture's actual accuracy.[36]

The explorations that constituted the English contribution to global knowledge had their own historian and patron. Hakluyt's accounts of the "Principal Navigations, Voyages, Traffics and Discoveries of the English Nation" were published in 1589, roughly contemporary with the work of Ortelius. "Hakluyt's own collections—*Divers Voyages* and *Principall Navigations*-bracketed the decade of the 1580s, appearing in 1582 and 1589 respectively" (Fuller 146–7). These volumes, usually referred to simply as "Hakluyt," helped to imprint the Americas and the new world picture in the popular imagination of Europeans, as well as helping to demonstrate to Elizabeth and her political advisors that investing in such ventures was worthwhile.

Hakluyt wanted to convey in his text a sense that the world was something "out there" available to the English for exploration and consumption-and as well, representation and appropriation. But this was not the whole picture conveyed by Hakluyt's narrative. His accounts emphasized the "payneful and personal" labor of those who sailed for months at a time in the squalid confines of a sixteenth-century ship. By contrast, Ortelius's map is an abstract, objectified space-quite literally a "world picture" to be used for "conquest"; Hakluyt, though presenting in many respects a similar world view—an abstract, objectified space available for instrumental use—also presents an embodied placeworld of pain and sweat and sea salt. His descriptions of his cousin's Middle Temple law office (littered with books and maps, old and new) and his own admission that the sprawling *Voyages* was a "burden" that he himself could see as remarkable only for its "huge toil and small profit" (24) reveal a sense of Hakluyt himself and his own personal efforts. The space of lived experience, immediate and concrete, was associated with the objective and objectifying cartographic pursuits that the book recounts.

This trace of the personal in Hakluyt's writing is in contrast with the depopulated abstraction of global representation that Hakluyt promotes. In this trace, Hakluyt's publications, for all their global ambition, retain the need to define themselves in relation to the individual performances of travel and writing that led to the production of these books. De Certeau locates a similar trace of personal effort at the margins of early modern maps:

> No doubt the proliferation of the "narrative" figures that have long
> been [the map's] stock-in-trade (ships, animals, and characters of all
> kinds) still had the function of indicating the operations-traveling,
> military, architectural, political or commercial-that make possible
> the fabrication of a geographical plan. Far from being "illustrations,"
> iconic glosses on the text, these figurations, like fragments of stories,
> mark on the map the historical operations from which it [the map]
> resulted [. . .]. (121)

In these figures we can see the intersection of spatial practices: on the one
hand, the iconic residue of itinerant, medieval mapping and the lived experience of travelers and map makers; on the other, the picture of a world,
made available to navigator and emperor alike because that world is made
other, is defined as separate from the self-identity of the map-using subject. Kirby notes that this othering is integral to early modern spatial practice: "Mapping separates the subject conceptually from his actual location.
While any representation could be said to do the same, this separation is
mapping's *purpose*, and it is judged successful only to the degree that it
does so" (50, italics in original). Though Ortelius made a significant break-
through, it would be some time before the apparatus of mapping made this
separation complete, before the spatial practices of the early modern era
perfected the picturing practices of represented space. Until then, "payneful and personal" projects like Hakluyt's and the fanciful figures at the
margins of maps give evidence of the hybrid cartographic spaces produced
in this period.

   One cultural coincidence of note: Hakluyt died in 1616, within
months of Shakespeare's death.

INVENTING THE IMAGE OF THE CITY

Hakluyt provides one example of the tensions surrounding the early modern representational and spatial practices emerging in England at the end
of the 16th century. Another traveler offers a significant contribution to the
history of space in this period, too, even though this latter traveler is the
author of a more modest, local record, in contrast with the global ambition
of Hakluyt's nautical navigations. In his famous *A Survey of London*, John
Stow tried to isolate and anchor London in a moment in time, a moment
just before his own, a moment in which Stow found London expanding
beyond the traditional limits (physical and conceptual) of the medieval
town that he admired.

Stow's *Survey* provides a sense of the anxieties that some Londoners felt at the end of the sixteenth century.

Stow writes disapprovingly about the expanding slums at the margins of the city, and registers his dissatisfaction with the Reformation through vague references and notable omissions. He also frequently recalls the "pastimes" of a bygone London, and laments the changes that have taken place around him.

> The youths of this city also have used on holy days after evening prayer, at their masters' doors, to exercise their wasters and bucklers; and the maidens, one of them playing on a timbrel, in sight of their masters and dames, to dance for garlands hung athwart the streets; which open pastimes in my youth being now suppressed, worse practices within doors are to be feared. (120)

In this passage, as in general, the *Survey* can be seen to be a kind of *textual memorial* in which Stow records a lost London and where he notes with concern "changes which offended against his social ideals" (Archer, "Nostalgia" 19). Ian Archer writes about the nostalgic tone of Stow's project and attempts to situate the *Survey* in the context of a changing metropolis. Archer resists any suggestion that Stow's project is "a new development," invoking William FitzStephen's twelfth-century "Description of the Most Noble City of London" as a case in point. However, Stow's nostalgic *Survey* is significantly different from FitzStephen's "Description": the latter is a brief encomium to his native city, written, it must be noted, almost entirely in the present tense. Stow's project is a sprawling neighborhood-by-neighborhood history that, as Archer himself notes at some length, glorifies London's past in comparison to the London in which Stow found himself at the end of the sixteenth century, a city newly composed of social elements which Stow finds "are to be feared" (120). Stow's fears of and for London relate not to changes in the topography of the city but changes in the social practices of London's inhabitants. Not London's physical state but its social fabric was changing, and it was in response to these changes that Stow composed his *Survey*. The title itself suggests the visual metaphors at work in this text: a picturing project through which Stow sought to "fix" the historical city in place and arrest its social evolution.

In this cartographic sense, Stow's writing must be seen as part of the "range of media and the sheer density of representations," which Archer notes appeared during this period. A text like the *Survey* must be considered alongside the "printed maps and panoramas" that "helped Londoners to

conceptualize their city as an integral body 'whole and entire of itself'"
("Nostalgia" 17). Stow's *Survey* is a text that demonstrates in its form a change
in the social and spatial practices of the city, a change in itself as radical as
any described in the *Survey* itself. Stow's *Survey* participates in the picturing
practices of the early modern representation of space, and as such his writing
project is in itself a significant example of the kinds of social change that
Stow himself resisted.

But Stow's picture of the city was not complete. Though Stow tried to
stabilize the city in text, medieval and early modern cities were not equally
available to being "read" as "text." Despite suggestions by numerous writers in
urban studies and the humanities, the postmedieval city was not "legible"—no
city is, in its entirety, though portions of many cities are built with such legibility in mind.[37] The transitional period that I have been discussing cites the
very beginning of the imposition of the idea of a legible city, and even that
beginning must be understood in terms of its mutually contaminating coexistence with non-legible performance practices of medieval space. Like the maps
of the middle ages, postmedieval city spaces were recondite territories meant
to be performed, lived, and experienced by an explicitly delimited community.
However much he may have wished to be representing a fixed image of the
city, Stow's *Survey*—and Stow himself—participates in the hybridity of postmedieval space.

The very practice of a survey is a kind of mapping. Harvey notes that
medieval Europeans "produced written descriptions where we would be more
likely to draw a map":

> [T]here survive many medieval written surveys which, without the aid
> of a map, set out in intricate detail the arable strips or other pieces of
> land belonging to a particular village or manor. (*Medieval* 8)

Stow's *Survey* seems self-consciously to "locate" itself in relation to this tradition. And although there is little doubt that the *Survey*'s goal is to "fix" London
as a static point of reference, there is certainly nothing static about the author
of the *Survey*: a reader of Stow's text experiences London, not from the "god's
eye view" of de Certeau's concept city, but from that of the pedestrian who is
navigating the streets and buildings and narrating these places with great personal knowledge. As a result, the *Survey* conveys not so much an image of London as a topography-in-process, a medieval notion of space that combines the
physical exploration of an urban space with the recollection of its events-what
Pierre Nora would call "*un milieu de memoire*" (7), a space in which memory is
actively performed. Stow's pedestrian performances inform his *Survey*, a textual

map in which the city's past is inextricable from its present. In its dual, even competing, representational agendas—a "Renaissance" picturing project coupled with a medieval sense of processual pedestrianism—Stow's *Survey* of 1598 is the epitome of a postmedieval mapping of London's eventmental spaces.

Though many twentieth-century urbanists, like Kevin Lynch, speak of "the image of the city" when referring to medieval urban spaces, such an image does not capture the urban practices that would have been available to the pedestrians of medieval and postmedieval spaces. The "apparent clarity or 'legibility' of the cityscape" that Lynch posits is a modern imposition, a practice of picturing imposed on a space never intended to be "seen" and "read." Ian Munro, writing of "the figure of the crowd in early modern drama and culture," argues that "efforts to contain or control the crowd, whether in political, literary, or theatrical manifestations, can be understood as attempts to control and make legible the symbolic space of the city" (ii, iii). But this understanding is one-sided, emphasizing the space of control and legibility that will come to shape the city, while failing to recognize the multiple understandings of space in this transitional period, many of which were not based on the legibility of images. The very idea of a "crowd" posits the inhabitants of the city as the definitional opposite of an authority that would seek "to control or contain" that crowd rather than a community that, while hierarchically distinct, is nevertheless a continuous social body in a productive relationship with its cityspace.

A self-described postmodern urbanist like Dear critiques the "voyeuristic, top-down perspective" uncritically adopted by numerous scholars, from Lynch to Munro. Dear urges urban and critical theorists alike "to relinquish the modernism inherent in these 'objective' representations of the urban text" in favor of a "postmodernism from below" (12). Relinquishing the need to view the legible image of the city is essential to an understanding of the hybrid space of postmedieval London: one must be able to negotiate the pedestrian itineraries of the ceremonial city as well as to "read" the emerging "imagetext" (Mitchell's term) of the early modern city-as-picture (9). A contemporary study of urban space may choose to "view" or "read" Elizabeth's spatially hybrid London according to this emergent abstract and abstracting practice, but it would be anachronistic to impose this view on postmedieval London's inhabitants, whose own "views" of their city were significantly more diverse.

A THEATRE OF COMPROMISE: POSTMEDIEVAL PERFORMANCE

Postmedieval (urban) space was given to a spatial heterogeneity, and the space of the stage was no exception. In the Prologue to his play *Midas*

(1592), John Lyly addresses in his own terms the shift in social practices taking place in his lifetime:

> At our exercises, Souldiers call for Tragedies, their object is bloud: Courtiers for Comedies, their subject is love: Countrymen for Pastoralles: Shepherds are their Saints. Trafficke and travell hath woven the nature of all Nations into ours, and made this land like Arras, full of devise, which was Broade-cloth, full of workemanshippe. Time hath confounded our mindes, our mindes the matter; but all commeth to this passe, that what heretofore hath been served in several dishes for a feaste, is now minced in a charger for a Gallimaufrey. (3: 115)

Here, as elsewhere in his Prologue, Lyly describes the confusion of social identities and practices that obtained during the cultural moment captured in this play. Lyly's comparison between "Arras" and "Broade-cloth" clearly describes the historical shift rapidly changing the social fabric of urban London. In Lyly's estimation, a uniformity of type marked medieval society: cultural mores were distinct, as were social strata. But the singular "Broade-cloth" of the medieval cosmology's hierarchical social and geographical distinctions has been replaced: "Arras," "woven" of many individual threads has become the prevailing metaphor of Lyly's relatively mobile late-sixteenth-century society. And like the world-picturing practices emerging in Elizabethan discourse, "Arras" is "full of devise": a tapestry, like a map, is an abstract representation. The concrete register on which "Broade-cloth," a non-representational fabric, exists has been superceded by "Arras," a network of threads interwoven in the service of the abstract: a picture, or many pictures.

Lyly also notes the impact that international trade and global travel have had on the refiguring of Elizabethan England. He attributes this cultural shift-from "Broade-cloth" to "Arras"—to the forces of "Trafficke and travell." Lyly concisely summarizes the impact of global exploration on early modern Europe. The expanding understanding of the space(s) of the globe, the efforts to expand the space and power of individual nations, and the intercourse among nations precipitated by expanding commerce all worked to bring about a cultural sea-change. The sense of place as a pre-understood cultural given is, in Lyly's Prologue, no longer sustainable: space has become both *here* and *elsewhere*-a new development for every Londoner, to be sure, but a particularly powerful development for the early modern stage.

Mullaney sees in Lyly's Prologue the "dismay expressed by Shakespeare's contemporaries over their increasingly unfamiliar and unruly city," a dismay expressive of "a community helplessly watching the symbols of [the city's] coherence [. . .] taken over and turned against it" (Mullaney 19). But the cultural shifts that Lyly identifies are not necessarily written in dismay. By contrast, Weimann sees in Lyly's Prologue not dismay nor even anxiety, but rather an awareness of a new potential:

> "a sense of the interdependence of variegated forms of cultural and social change emerged and [. . .] the impact on the theater of unheard-of-mobility and distant trade could first be articulated as a moment in and for poetics."
>
> ("Hodge-Podge" 38)

Lyly is not only noting the changes taking place in his newly dynamic world, but he is articulating the ways in which theatre practice will adapt and respond. Notably, Lyly's Prologue occurs introduces a play in which the social "Gallimaufrey" brought about by "Trafficke and travell" will prove to be a virtue.

The sophisticated cultural responses proposed in the Prologue to *Midas* and in the drama of other contemporaries of Shakespeare had their precedents. There were other responses to the first perceived movements of the shift from medieval to early modern world views, responses more firmly rooted in the medieval popular tradition. The late medieval play *Hickscorner*, probably written some time between the years 1497-1512, is one of these. The presentation of morality figures in this anonymous text accords with the conventional personifications of morality drama. However, the title character, who makes only a brief appearance in the play, is a somewhat different figure. Hickscorner[38] seems to be a kind of pirate who joins the personified vice figures of Freewill and Imagination and tells them of the places to which he has traveled.

> HICKSCORNER: Sirs, I have been in many a country;
> As in France, Ireland, and in Spain,
> Portingal, Sevile, also in Almaine;
> Friesland, Flanders, and in Burgoine,
> Calabria, Pugle, and Erragon,
> Britain, Biske, and also in Gascoine,
> Naples, Greece, and in middes of Scotland;
> At Cape Saint Vincent, and in the new found island,
> I have been in Gene and in Cowe,
> Also in the land of Rumbelow,
> Three mile out of hell;

At Rhodes, Constantine, and in Babylon,
In Cornwall, and in Northumberland,
Where men seethe rushes in gruel;
Yea, sir, in Chaldaea, Tartary, and India,
And in the Land of Women, that few men doth find:
In all these countries have I be. (69)

Hickscorner is a text that is clearly attempting to respond, however ambiguously, to the innovations in popular conception of the space of the world and the space of human activity at the outset of the 16th century. This ocean-going rogue cannot give a simple answer to the simple question, "Out of what country come ye?"; instead, he must recount all the countries that he has visited. However, the understanding of world travel that emerges from Hickscorner's account is a decidedly disordered one. Though the space presented in his monologue demonstrates the expanding geographical range of reference available under the medieval English cartographic imagination, yet Hickscorner's description does not take the form of a map-like "world picture"; rather it is an idiosyncratic performance of an understanding of location—an understanding exclusive to the subject-in-process, Hickscorner himself.

Though the list begins with familiar locations and nations neighboring on England, it gradually moves towards the exotic and unfamiliar. The fact that the "middes of Scotland" is located, sequentially, between Greece and North America ("the new found island," refers to Newfoundland, Canada) gives ample indication that this is not an itinerary for any plausible journey. Moreover, actual places are presented as adjacent to fantastic and legendary locations: "Rumbelow"-which is, according to Hickscorner, a suburb of hell—and "the Land of Women" rub shoulders with India, and Cornwall—places which are themselves far from proximate to each other. Indeed, he has been to both Constantinople and Babylon, different names for the same city in different historical periods.

Hickscorner's geography is not a world picture, but rather a playful litany of place names meant for performance. This litany presents a sense of "elsewhere," but one that, by absurd contrast, only serves to reinforce the immediacy of "here." However much the character Hickscorner may value travel and scorn hicks, the "Trafficke and travell" Lyly mentions are culture-shaping concepts in the late 1500s apply no urgent force on the geography of the play *Hickscorner*. This play seems to introduce geographical information in much the way the *mappaemundi* do, to encourage stasis rather than travel.

Whatever emerging awareness of the new global elsewhere is seen in this medieval drama, by the end of the sixteenth century, "Trafficke and travell" had become an urgent force indeed, and the response in various dramatic texts was vigorous and specific. *Hickscorner* never demands that an audience sustain an abstract conception of a global elsewhere because the text never attempts to convey, nor even briefly relies on, a sustained representation of that elsewhere. In contrast, a cartographically "pictured" representation of global traffic and travel is detailed with map-like accuracy in Ben Jonson's *Volpone*.

> Sir Politic: Sir, to a wise man, all the world's his soil.
> It is not Italy, nor France, nor Europe,
> That must bound me, if my fates call me forth.
> Yet I protest, it is no salt desire
> Of seeing countries, shifting a religion,
> Nor any disaffection to the state
> Where I was bred, and unto which I owe
> My dearest plots, hath brought me out; much less
> That idle, antique, stale, grey-headed project
> Of knowing men's minds and manners, with Ulysses;
> But a peculiar humor of my wife's,
> Laid for this height of Venice, to observe,
> To quote, to learn the language, and so forth. (II.i.1–13)[39]

Here, in a first line that bears similarities with the traveler's boast that begins Hickscorner's speech, Jonson conveys a sense of Europe that is fully represented in a way that was not conceivable for the author of *Hickscorner*. The nations of Sir Politic's speech align and cohere to form the abstract image of a map. This is Jonson's Europe, "conceived and grasped as picture." Though he will not be "bound" by any one country, Sir Politic is acutely aware of the abstract boundaries that separate spaces represented in cartographic practice. He protests that he has not lost affection for the "dearest *plots*" of land in his home nation, even though he left them when he traveled south to "this *height* of Venice." Not only does Sir Politic understand how local spaces are subdivided for acquisition and taxation, and how global spaces are subdivided by lines of latitude ("heights"), but he also expects the members of the audience to be casually familiar with these terms of abstract spatial demarcation as well. In the context of Jonson's explicitly map-like picturing of early modern Europe, Sir Politic's plan to acquire fashionable modes of behavior for his own long-term profit is a self-conscious use of representation to facilitate appropriation. The character has used the map-like picturing of Europe to appropriate the tastes and fashions of Italy for his own advancement: a comic (because unsuccessful) attempt at "conquest" of the continent. Indeed, this scene relies for its comic effect on a cartographic awareness of space among its audience.

This instrumental application of map-like picturing practice marks a critical difference between *Hickscorner* and *Volpone*. The representation of an abstract elsewhere in *Volpone* is extraordinarily clear. Unlike Hickscorner's litany of locations, which would never have been located anywhere other than the place of theatrical performance, the above speech as performed by an actor playing Sir Politic would have drawn the postmedieval audience away from the *here* of the platform stage towards the sustained representation of a real-world space anchored in the *elsewhere* of theatrical narrative.[40]
By 1604, the medieval understanding of urban space as a territory to be performed, even by a monarch, was well on its way to being superceded. Carlson argues that:

> No longer was the princely visitor greeted along this pathway by symbols of the city's wealth, power, and prosperity; he was met instead by monuments and allegorical paintings and tableaux reflecting his own significance. The city was still used as a theatre space [. . .] but became rather the scene for the display of princely power, at which citizens were present by sufferance—as spectators only. (20)

The shift in power described here by Carlson cannot be seen as a permanent usurpation of space by the sovereign, but rather as a temporary, strategic appropriation of the city. Certainly, this is the kind of royal performance demonstrated by James and the new urban spectacle offered by Jonson, Dekker, et al (see Chapter Three). In addition to a new structure to civic performance, Carlson rightly notes that the subject of the urban "drama" itself had changed. No longer was the coronation procession an opportunity for the monarch to perform (for) the city, but rather the early modern urban procession—certainly James's—became an opportunity for display as well as for an overwhelmingly (though not entirely) monovocal performance. The platforms and scaffolds on which the actors performed in the 1559 entry provided either the most basic physical support for the actors, like the platform stage or medieval "mansions," or the most schematic visual reinforcement of the hierarchical import of a given pageant. As will be shown in Chapter Two, James's pageant stations displayed an entirely different order of mise en scène.

An important corollary to this shift in civic scenography, the dynamic spatiality that characterized the medieval town continued to influence spaces into the early modern period. This space and its practices had its influence on Elizabeth and James's entries alike—however dissimilar those entries may have been in other respects. But the space of the medieval town "eroded and began to perish" with the emergence of the idea of the early modern city (Phythian-Adams 106).

Early modern space emerged, in conjunction and contention, with medieval space. This emergence is traced in the professional theatre, in public performance, and even in visual discourses of the city. It is to this last category that this study now turns, a survey of the canon of London representations circa 1600, with reference to their medieval precedents. These precedents are essential to understanding the hybridity of map images that integrate performance assumptions into their visual representations. Even in the space of the map, performance adheres as a dominating force in postmedieval London. For a brief time, then: "[t]he map thus collates on the same plane heterogeneous places, some *received* from a tradition and others *produced* by observation" (de Certeau 121, emphasis in original). This heterogeneous collation of tradition and innovation is the subject of the next chapter.

Chapter Two

Pedestrian Mappings: Performance and Map Images of Medieval and Early Modern London

The earliest extant printed view of the City of London is a woodcut by the Westminster artist and engraver Winkin de Worde. [Fig. 2] In de Worde's woodcut, circa 1497, London is portrayed as it often is in word and image: a city of spires behind its famous wall. In this image, the city seems to be represented from the west, an appropriate perspective for de Worde: he was a protégé of Caxton, who took over the latter's woodcutting and printing shop in Westminster (Hodnett 7). Thus, to get to the bookstalls in St. Paul's Yard, de Worde would have had to walk along the Strand (still a relatively undeveloped thoroughfare at the end of the fifteenth century) to Ludgate and the southwestern entrance to the City. The endpoint of this pedestrian route would seem to be the site depicted the 1497 woodcut.

In the immediate foreground of de Worde's image, one can see the beginnings of suburban development. The Temple area[1] was among the first urbanized developments under the jurisdiction of the City of London that stood outside the traditional medieval boundaries set by the City walls and the Fleet River.[2] By the 1490s, London's official limit was set at Temple Bar, a location often associated with civic and royal ceremony.[3] This may well have been the point to which de Worde walked to sketch the burgeoning medieval town before him.

Beyond the wall, the image shows a tangle of buildings and a medieval "skyline" dominated by spires. The many churches and towers of London are the frequent subject of visual and written representations of London. Of the three most prominent church spires, the one just to the right of the center of the image is of particular interest. This is the only spire in the image with a visible point of origin. It ascends from an polygonal church structure located in the middle ground of the image. And in the upper right corner of the image, a cluster of six slender spires rises from a single square building. This mostly obstructed square structure would seem to indicate a location at some

Figure 2: London. W. de Worde, 1497.
Museum of London

distance from de Worde's Temple Bar point of view—an early English effort at perspective. These structures invite speculation about their identity. Is the church visible in the foreground Temple Church, located geographically closest to the City wall? Is the central spire that of St. Paul's Cathedral, the structure that features prominently in virtually every early portrait of London? And the spire to the left, the only one to terminate in a cross, might that be St. Peter's Cornhill, the chief religious site in the eastern part of the City? And the cluster of spires to the right would seem to suggest the rectilinear White Tower at the heart of the Tower of London, a structure that appears in images of London almost as often as St. Paul's.

However tempting such speculative attempts to fix location may be, this image participates in medieval practices of urban representation, and as such it does not rely on exact visual accuracy in its execution of what might be termed a "visual encomium" of the City of London (Frangenberg 45). Roy Strong suggests that such images provide examples of "a lost sense of sight," demonstrating how late medieval Londoners "actually *saw* things" (43). But Lucia Nuti argues that the "look" of an image is not a question of *perception* but of *representation*.

> If the representation of a town [. . .] is at issue, the most trustworthy and significant image of it will undoubtedly be the one that matches most perfectly with the visual culture's mode of relating the observer to the object. (98)

Thus, in the case of the de Worde woodcut, as in the case of other pre-modern urban images, trustworthiness and significance are conveyed by "an image of the city as a symbolic structure, focusing on what makes [the city] typical, not specific and particular" (B. Klein 22). In the case of an image determined by the visual mode of medieval European culture, a viewer cannot reliably identify monuments and sites in this image, for though it may "incorporate authentic information," de Worde's image of London is not meant to be a visually accurate portrait of the city; its urban meaning is in its *inaccuracy*, through which London is seen as a "generic civic space" and located in relation to the space of a wider, international territory. Even the physical position of the observer is in question here, as there is no one point in the city that corresponded with such a view, crowded as it is with "as many buildings as possible in a single image" (B. Klein 22). Though an influential force *on* medieval and postmedieval map images, performance will remain an elusive trace *in* such images.

The strategies used in the medieval illustration of cities are typified by the city images in the *Nuremburg Chronicle*, edited by Hartmann Schedel, which first appeared in print in 1493. Whether de Worde, in 1497, was familiar with Schedel's work, this image of London would seem to participate in the same representational strategies. Kathleen Biddick observes that the *Chronicle* is widely regarded as "a quintessentially medieval artifact" (2000, 224), however Biddick's project is to "read the *Nuremberg Chronicle* against the grain of current scholarship that insists [. . .] on its medieval exemplarity" (232). Proceeding from her rereading of conventional views of the *Chronicle*, Biddick argues that the principal strategy at work in the *Chronicle* is a practice that she terms "becoming collection" (236). If medieval universal histories produce theology-determined accounts that unify the events of the Old Testament with those of the author's present in a point-by-point teleology, what Biddick calls *collection* is a narrative process that brings together historical, geographical, and ideological information in a single image. Thus: "To collect is to exclude time, to use synchronicity as a way of producing the space of collection" (234). The "spatial effect" of collection in the images of the *Chronicle* is one that displays affiliations with other medieval map images. Though the *mappaemundi* seek to unify the world in an image bound by the body of Christ (explicitly so in the case of the Hereford Map), each *mappamundi* serves as a kind of visual container for a diverse quantity of individual images. The practice of *collection* relies on an accumulation of data and representational strategies, to the exclusion of historical time. Schedel's *Chronicle* is such an accumulation, and though Klein notes that these images are unified in their visual treatment (22), each stands alone as an image of urbanity.

Schedel's collection (in Biddick's sense) of urban images serves a grand function. John Gillies, in his study of Shakespeare and geography, briefly explores the "order of city and world," an early modern duality that turns on the conceptual and rhetorical relationship between the Latin terms *orbis* and *urbis* (6).[4] Thus, even global representations like the Ditchley portrait or an early modern innovation like the world map, might be said to participate in discourses of the city. Following an associative logic similar to that of Gillies, Klein argues that in the *Chronicle*: "the globe is imagined precisely through the lived space of the city" (24). But Klein also observes that Schedel's cities are "fully fixed and determined locations" (29). Though Schedel's global imagination does indeed rely on cityspace, these images are hardly "fully fixed and determined": as with de Worde's London—in which no citizens are represented, only the oversized birds that circle the City's steeples—the cities of the *Chronicle* are suggestive of a flexible idea of location, rather than a fixed representation of a clearly defined site; this locational flexibility would seem to be a side-effect of the system of *collection* that produced the images.

Yet Schedel and de Worde's images participate in what I consider to be an even more quintessentially medieval representational system, the system that I term "pedestrian performance." Pedestrian performance was a medieval practice that relates the individual to public space via the experience of performance and the representation of that experience. Thus, pedestrian performance need not be solely experienced in a physical procession, but could as well inform a map or other image. As a result, while collection produces images that devalue or exclude *historical* time, the same images may include the *personal* and *social* time of pedestrian performance.

De Worde's image is a microcosm of the practices of late medieval visual culture that were increasingly prominent throughout Europe. The towers are not exact because the image is not meant to be a "simply realistic" depiction of the London skyline circa 1497 (B. Klein 22). Rather, de Worde's image is an encomium to "London-ness," and as such it presents an incompletely deter-mined image of the urbanity that makes London part of a larger collection of urban spaces. While the image is not historically distinct (the London of the image cannot be specifically dated nor its landmarks identified with surety) yet De Worde's late medieval city view synopsizes the author's personal, pedestrian relationship to London without a concern to isolate or anchor the city in his-tory. Though the city's geography is defined by its long-standing walls, Lon-don's conceptual terrain is equally well-defined by long-standing traditions of social practice. Packing his image with interpretive ideals of a social space was of greater concern to de Worde than visual accuracy.

Such an emphasis on the ideal over the merely "accurate" was, in many ways, Schedel's aim in his *Chronicle*, too: the images of the *Chronicle* do not consistently bare significant visual relationship to the physical appearance of the cities that are their ostensible subjects. Schedel's book seems calculated to collect examples of a European conception of the urban, a visual litany of places whose sum effect is the space of Europe if not its history. Perhaps this is the intention of de Worde's view as well, to represent a conception of medieval London, to record in a single image London's past and present, regardless of temporality.

The task of describing the relationship between performance and city views would be made much easier if the etymologies of the words *chorog-raphy* and *choreography* were as close as they seem at first glance. Instead, the Oxford English Dictionary provides two distinct word origins for these close homophones. The more familiar term, "choreography," is derived from ancient Greek; its literal meaning: "writing dance." "Chorography" is also a Greek-derived term, but its meaning is significantly different: literally, "writ-ing the region." During the late middle ages, this latter term came to be asso-ciated with a range of illustrative practices that focused on the production of local map images. Plots of private or church-related property holdings join images of town and cities in the category of chorographic illustration. Cho-rography was traditionally distinguished from cartography by the practice of the map maker. If the individual practitioner can personally "view" a region and make an image of that region based on observation, then the product of that practice is chorography. While uses of cartographic terms were flex-ible, by the sixteenth century, "a view or a plan of a city or of any other local

area produced in the context of geography was often called a chorography"
(Frangenberg 41). If however, the region to be mapped is so extensive that
individual observation alone is inadequate, and a map image is composed
using a combination of skills that extend beyond portraiture, then the product of this practice is cartography. Among sixteenth-century cartographers,
these map-making skills would have included surveying and mathematical
conversions and projections derived in part from Ptolemy's *Geography*.

Before Ptolemy's work was rediscovered in Constantinople at the end
of the thirteenth century, cartography was largely "the province of artists
and theologians" (Edson 165).[5] The personal experience of space was never
entirely removed from the map-making process. Even the seemingly inex-
act *mappaemundi* were produced according to a combination of theological
direction and information drawn from personal experience—an amalgama-
tion of Christian ideology and the collation of information drawn from travel
and chorography (Woodward, "Medieval" 288).

The desire that my wishful thinking seeks to satisfy in imagining a
shared word origin for *chorography* and *choreography* is a desire for an etymology that can offer linguistic support for the phenomenological association
between the practice of dancing and the practice of mapping. Choreography,
in its earliest usage, is the practice of recording the movements performed
by the dancing body. The local mappings recorded by chorography similarly invoke a personal, embodied performance. Cosgrove defines mapping
as the practice of recording "a graphic register of correspondence between
two spaces, whose explicit outcome is a space of representation" (Mapping
1). But space itself is a quantity to be produced: Nick Kaye observes that for
Tschumi the production of space is "always already subject to the event of
location; always already subject to performance, to its realization in practice"
(Kaye 51). The theory that I for which I have sought easy support in a fan-
tasy etymology is one that I will pursue at greater length in this chapter: an
understanding of postmedieval urban map images that is suspended between
performance and representation.

In this chapter, my investigation of the history of the space focuses on
representations of London, and relies on Peter Burke's claim that "images,
like texts and oral testimonies, are an important form of historical evidence [that] record acts of eyewitnessing" (14). Accordingly, the maps and
city views that will be the focus of this chapter rely on spatial practices that
record the personal, physical experiences on the part of the map-maker. The
activity of making a map can be seen as a mapping performance, and such a
performance produces a space of representation that preserves a trace-obvi-
ous or subtle-of performance in the image itself. Each of the maps discussed

below is the product of variously entangled practices that draw on medieval spatial traditions and the emerging concepts of early modern representation. These images engage with location in a way that structures a relationship between the map-maker and that which is represented in the map image. My consideration of postmedieval map images will draw on this medieval tradition of performance-determined mapping. For Catherine Delano-Smith, chorographies are descriptions of space that include an element of history in the account of landscape as well (186); it may be that a record of the passage of time in the increasingly abstract and geometrical medium of cartography provides the clearest trace of the medieval conception of space in early modern map images.

The phrase "map image," already used throughout this chapter, is derived from Harley, who proposes that "the map image is a structured [. . .] representation of selected spatial information, which when placed onto a storage medium becomes a map" (*Tudor* 41). The breadth of Harley's definition of a map image exceeds the conventional, contemporary idea of a purely abstract plane projection. This open concept of what might constitute a map image recalls the revolutionary redefinition of "map" posed by Harley and Woodward. Indeed it expands on that definition by the inclusion of "a storage medium"—an open ended term which could range from cave walls to compact disks.

Throughout this chapter, the subjects of discussion will be termed "map images," though they may not resemble maps as we know them today. Moreover, it should be kept in mind that "[w]hen seeking the meaning and purpose of medieval maps, one cannot assume that maps were used then for the same purposes or had the same meaning as they do today" (Edson viii). As Harvey argues: "It simply did not occur to people in the middle ages to use maps, to see landscape or the world in a cartographic way" (*Medieval* 7). Though my goal is to consider the map images of "Shakespeare's London," this study begins with map images of the middle ages, considers the ways in which it *did* occur to people to use map images in this period, and traces the influence of medieval practices of mapping on the hybrid representations and pedestrian performances of postmedieval London.

Postmedieval city views variously entail a degree of performance. The performance function of such views is in each case a residual effect of the uses to which map forms were put in the medieval period. Unlike the cities of Schedel's *Chronicle*, the London discussed here is not unitary: in line with Dana Arnold's injunction, the London of this study will be "re-presented as a constantly changing and developing entity evading the static definitions of deterministic histories" (128). Ironically, many of the images considered in this chapter seek to do exactly the opposite: to represent London as a static and definitive index of the city's history.

THE ITINERARY AND THE TRAVEL PERFORMANCE

Matthew Paris was a prolific medieval historian and cartographer. From 1217 he was a Benedictine monk at St. Alban's, north of London in Hertfordshire; other particulars of his life are in doubt (Vaughn 1). Paris's biographer Richard Vaughn notes that despite his name (presumably assumed when he took orders), Paris was probably English and not educated "at Paris, or indeed any other university" (1). In fact, there is no evidence to suggest that Paris ever left England at all. This last point is important because Paris's most notable accomplishment is a travel itinerary (c. 1252) that records primary and alternate routes for traveling from London to Rome. [6] [Fig. 3]

On the basis of this itinerary alone, Harvey refers to Paris as an "imaginative genius" (*Medieval* 8), for though written itineraries had been used in travel for centuries, Paris was the first known "to convert the written itinerary into a strip map, setting out graphically the route from London to Rome with thumbnail sketches of the places on the way" (8). Delano-Smith concurs, "[w]ritten itineraries had been commonplace in the thirteenth century" (150): often called "pilgrimage maps," these written guides "depicted the routes in a linear fashion rather than following the actual terrain" (Hanawalt and Kobialka ix). In fact, as Harvey notes, "[t]ravellers in the early middle ages never had maps to guide them," at least not maps in the modern sense (*Medieval* 9). Christian Jacob goes even further, advising the modern map-minded reader that "[t]aveling, exploring, seafaring, war-making, ruling and founding remote colonies did not necessarily imply the use of maps" (Jacob 26). Delano-Smith's theory that "[w]hatever early maps were used for, it was not for finding the way in the manner in which most people today use topographical maps or road maps [. . .]" makes Paris's itinerary all the more remarkable (142).

Each column of the itinerary is meant to be read from bottom to top, so the itinerary proceeds from London through Rochester and Canterbury to Dover, on the left hand column; on the right, routes are provided from both Calais and Boulogne to Reims and Beauvais at the top right. The itinerary continues like this, displaying sketches of landmarks and showing alternate routes, until the final page on which Rome is represented in a more elaborate view. This last page includes fold-out images of Rome attached (again, by hand) to the main piece of paper. This final map image combines rough illustrations of Roman monuments with textual descriptions of the

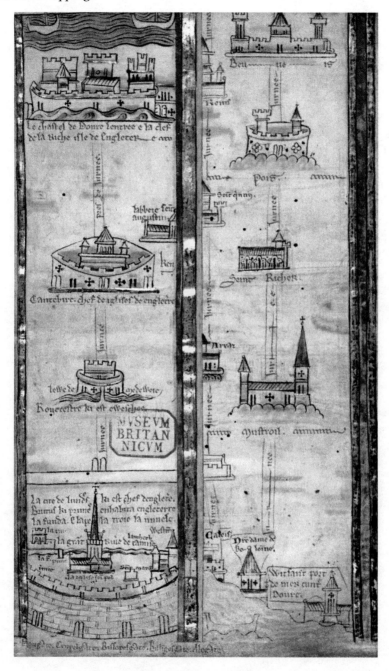

Figure 3: London to Rome itinerary, the first of four pages. Matthew Paris, c.1252.

city.[7] Paris's itinerary is not only an unusual artifact of medieval European mapping production: the starting point on the first page of the itinerary is a small portrait of London-the oldest existing image of the City.[8] [Fig. 4]

Even in this small map image, Paris's work is as specific as the view in de Worde's woodcut, and equally idiosyncratic. Paris had a personal familiarity with the city he illustrated in his itinerary. Paris lived in an Abbey northwest of London. Though there is no indication that he himself traveled to Rome along the route set out in his itinerary, Paris does demonstrate first-hand knowledge of London. In this map image, the city is shown from the north, and many of its features are labeled in Anglo-Norman. London's ancient city wall is in the foreground. Its gates are listed from east to west, but the gates depicted on the wall are evenly dispersed rather than topographically accurate, and the labels below the wall are not intended to correlate with the image. The river Thames ("*la grât riue de tamise*") is illustrated

Figure 4: Matthew Paris. London to Rome itinerary, inset.

in the middle ground, with "lambeth" and Westminster labeled but not illustrated in the distance. Within the space of the City itself, two architectural features dominate: the Tower of London and most prominently St. Paul's Cathedral. In common with de Worde's woodcut, Paris's illustration of London is not meant to provide specific information about the city, but rather to *collect* London in a single urban image, the image of a city suitable to be compared with the great medieval metropolis that is the endpoint of this itinerary: Rome.

Few geographical relationships can be determined from this itinerary, such as where there is a great wall, where there is water, and only rough proximity among locations. So while Paris's map-broadly conceived as a "map," following Harley and Woodward's re-definition-provides limited concrete geographical knowledge, it does serve to facilitate a spatial understanding of concepts and processes, specifically a comparative idea of location along an urban axis of great importance to medieval English Catholics. In this the itinerary serves as an *aide memoire*, valuable to those who, like Paris himself, "dreamed of pilgrimage, but remained at home" (Edson 14). But Paris's itinerary also serves a more active function: if an *aide memoire* is a text that one consults after the fact or in the absence of travel, then this visual itinerary also served as part of an *ars apodemica*, a prolegomenon to the art of travel.[9]

In contrast with the *mappaemundi*, Paris's itinerary explicitly invites its user to travel. This map makes no attempt to represent an overall territory, rather it presents a series of stages along the route from one place to another. No advice for how to get from one point to the next is provided. However, it is clear that one is intended physically to execute the "travel performance" implied by this itinerary. The structure of this document "directs [. . .] a particular series of events" (Corner 233), much the way a piece of dramatic literature serves as a script or directions for theatrical performance.

A city view in the context of Paris's itinerary was a representation of a place, a visual representation of a concrete destination. The location represented in an itinerary necessarily implies performance: this is a place to which one must travel in a given period of time in order to perform successfully a given journey. The sketches of cities provided in Paris's itinerary serve as landmarks, and each stage along his route is marked with the word "*journée*," a French word meaning roughly "what one might be able to do in a day." This spatio-temporal use of *journée* in medieval travel provides the etymological source for the contemporary English word "journey." The arrival at each of the landmarks represented by the thumbnail sketch on the itinerary signaled the completion of each stage of the pilgrimage, the end of the day's journey. The views in Paris's itinerary are not decorative, not provided for abstract admiration. They are functional and as such they do not stand alone: they are information that facilitates a particular *travel performance*.

As Harvey makes explicit, medieval travelers "never had maps to guide them" (*Medieval* 9). Instead they used itineraries. Travel itineraries were almost exclusively written instructions for proceeding along a succession of intermediate locations to a final destination. Harvey notes the dearth of extant examples of medieval travel itineraries: "Not many of these itineraries survive-probably most were written on scraps of parchment or paper and thrown away once the journey was over" (8). Cosgrove concurs:

> Fewer maps intended or used for practical purposes of navigation or location-finding remain, and still fewer of those sketched for immediate practical ends such as navigation, battle or field research, which are exhausted in the execution of their purpose. ("Introduction" 14)

Paris's "strip map" was an extraordinary exception to this rule, an exception that constituted the emergence of what was for medieval Europe an innovation in mapping that combined directional writing with city views and map legends. Delano-Smith suggests that "Paris's decorative graphic itinerary was probably unique in its day. It may have remained so, in England at least, until [. . .] 1675" (151-2). The scarcity of examples of this kind of map may have to do with the way in which they were used, or, in other words, the prevailing cultural concepts surrounding map use. Medieval culture did not produce maps that provided flexible geographical knowledge independent of a predetermined travel performance. Maps were made to serve a particular function, and when that function was performed, the maps were discarded, not because the map itself had lost value but because the map only had value in relation to the specific travel performance to which it was an accessory. When the performance was completed, the geographical knowledge that the map could provide was, in Cosgrove's term, "exhausted." In this sense, the use value attributed to maps can be seen to resemble the overwhelmingly provisional value assigned to theatre scripts in the medieval period and at the outset of the early modern. Very few such scripts remain because cultural significance was overwhelmingly assigned to performance, rather than to textuality. Cosgrove's phrase is as applicable to medieval dramatic literature as to medieval maps: they were "exhausted in the execution of their purpose."

Medieval itineraries were meant to be performed. Movement through the world is presented as a movement among cities, towns, and monastic micro-urbs: even a church is represented in Paris's itinerary on the same scale as the City of London. The locations that punctuate Paris's *journées* "serve to conceive of the globe as a massive social space" (B. Klein 29), a space in which *urbis* and *orbis* participate in a shared order of social and spatial meaning. "*Orbis*," as Gillies points out, "or the bounded 'world' directly recapitulates the sacred drama of the bounded city" (6). That the medieval subject thought of the *orbis* / *urbis* dualism as a relationship to be performed is evidenced in the "invaluable staging diagram" that accompanies the so-called Macro play *The Castle of Perseverance* (Bevington vii).[10] This map image shows a space demarcated for a public theatrical performance, with an emblematic castle at the center of a circular playing area. The image shows a space that evokes both an urban agglomeration and a medieval view of the world. Indeed, the *Perseverance* illustration resembles the individual map images of Paris's itinerary, though not the itinerary's overall structure. Moreover, the circular spatial scheme set out by the *Perseverance* image reciprocates, and even seems to reference, the *mappaemundi*. On this image, a place for god, the "*Deus [s]kafold*," is to the east, while the boundary of the world, the "*Mund[us] skaffo[ld]*," is located to the west. The idea made visual in the *mappaemundi* is prepared for performance in *Perseverance*: a theological conception of the space of the world is presented in a single, human-scaled space, one that is both conceptually and physically accessible to the audience and to the agents of theatrical performance, the actors.

With its emblematic castle, its sketched suggestion of a moat-like perimeter of some kind, and its overt relationship to performance, the space of the *Perseverance* diagram demonstrates remarkable visual and theoretical filiation with other medieval map forms. This diagram served as the frontispiece to a text that was intended for theatrical performance,[11] just as Paris's illustrated itineraries were produced in the service of travel performance.

Regarding itineraries: if an *aide memoire* is a text or image used after the fact to help recall (or, "re-*collect*"?) an event, then a script is a text or image that is used in advance of an event, to aid in its performance—be that it a theatrical performance or a travel performance. The introduction of theories of performance to the history of cartography provides valuable tools for the reconception of the uses of maps and map images in medieval and postmedieval Europe. While maps and map images that were once considered merely erroneous "abominations" have been embraced by the field (Harley, Delano-Smith, Harvey), numerous aspects of the culture and history of maps and mapping in this period remain unclear to the cartographic establishment. A theory of medieval mapping that asserts the need to read maps with an eye for the performance of space, as well as its representation, goes a long way towards reconciling the *mappaemundi*, Paris's itinerary, and numerous individual map images with a cartographic record marked more by lacunae than by extant examples of medieval maps.

Performance theory can assist in an investigation of the way in which space was used, produced, and imagined before visual and textual representation came to dominate European culture. De Certeau theorizes this pre-modern space, asking the question: *"Voyeurs or walkers"*? (92). Though the periodizing at work in de Certeau's theories is suspect, as previously discussed in the introduction, the process to which he alludes is one that will be on display in the examples that follow from the sixteenth and seventeenth centuries: one way of conceiving the historical transition from medieval to early modern is to consider the emergence of *looking*, of *voyeurism*, as the principal strategy for constructing (physically as well as conceptually) urban space; this representational voyeur superceded the space and the practices of the urban walker—though briefly they went hand-in-hand.

In a brief survey of sixteenth and seventeenth century map images of London, Andrew Gordon "seeks to return to the birth of that totalizing moment which de Certeau speculatively locates in the sixteenth century" (69). Gordon's often strong analyses are limited by a theoretical apparatus that follows de Certeau's broad misreading of the relationship between medieval and early modern spaces. Gordon's "belief in the city as an *inherently spatially performed* entity" is his first misprision, followed closely by his insistence that the city "was enacted before it was visualized, it walked [sic] before it was drawn" (70, emphasis). Gordon errs in collapsing the diverse history of space into a single practice that follows a "totalizing moment"; he offers no sense of a "before" to counter de Certeau's "after." And while performance may be inherently spatial, the space of the city is not "inherently [. . .] performed," as demonstrated by hundreds of years of spatial practice in the modern era that have rendered the Western city as an urban "representation," as merely "an optical artifact" (de Certeau 92). As with the valuable but incomplete work of Mullaney, I will draw on many of Gordon's insights, but I must the incomplete theorization of the history of urban space in this essay. There is no totalizing moment at which the medieval "before" can be distinguished from an early modern "after": multiple concepts of space could be found coexisting in concert and in opposition, determining the transitional space of the postmedieval period. The early modern voyeur emerged in the sixteenth century, but only gradually displaced the medieval walker / performer. The spaces in and of London would come to be determined by that voyeur, spaces which had previously belonged to the walker. Contrary to those who see a "totalizing moment" of transition, as Gordon does (69), the pedestrian practices associated with medieval urban culture continued to obtain in tension with "Renaissance" displays and lookings—forming together the hybrid spatiality of postmedieval London. It is the joint operation of these cultural strategies that makes a consideration of urban illustration from this period valuable.

In Paris's illustration, London is shown from the north. Though the city shown here is as imaginary as that of the de Worde woodcut, it shares with de Worde's image the trace of personal performance. This is the view that Paris himself would have seen while on his own limited travels, the direction from which he would have approached the city, traveling from St. Alban's in the north. In the sixteenth century, it will become increasingly conventional to represent a view of London as seen from the south. Or perhaps I should say: what becomes conventional is *a view*. In images from closer to 1600, the subjective medieval collection is superceded by perspectival voyeurisms: London will increasingly be fixed as an object to be regarded, an abstract representation of space. In this illustrative abstraction and objectivity, London becomes seen not as a place *for* representation but a representation *of* space available for appropriation; just one thing to be placed among others. The spatial practices by which a trace of performance intruded upon representations of London obtained throughout the sixteenth century. And if, as Klein suggests, "geographical texts and images also 'produce' space" (*Maps* 10), then the tension between performance and representation was indeed a productive one in the postmedieval spaces of sixteenth-century London. In this section, I contend that city views invite a virtual pedestrianism in ways in which other representational media do not.

"EYEWITNESSING" AND PERFORMANCE

The image of London included among the poems of Charles, Duke of Orleans (c. 1500) represents London "from" a point just east of the Tower, but the image is composed of several overlapping prospects such that no single point of view could be that "from" which the image, however exaggerated, could have been seen. [Fig. 5] The Thames is shown in the foreground, immediately south of the Tower of London. The White Tower is prominent here, with many figures showing a bustling activity inside and out. But the Thames is also shown in the background: London Bridge is shown, impossibly, both from the east and perpendicular to the south front of the Tower. In between can be seen the arcaded wharves of

Figure 5: London. From an edition of the poems of Charles, Duke of Orleans, c. 1500.

Billingsgate (Schofield 122), in a view consonant with neither that of the Tower nor of the Bridge. John Schofield notes: "Charles was captured at Agincourt and imprisoned in England from 1415 to 1440" (*Building* iv). Accordingly, Charles himself is, in all likelihood, the figure represented in the Tower seated at a desk. In the context of a miniature included in a collection of poems, this figure with pen and paper would seem to be represented in the act of writing the micro-history "stored" in the *collection* of this image of London. Whether or not illustrated by Charles himself, this image shows London in relation to the imprisoned Duke, a spatial construction based on "memory, recollection, and association" rather than a concern for visual accuracy (Kline 2). What Naomi Kline has said of medieval mapping in general holds true for this image in particular:

> The map could be explored as a 'picture' of the world and also as a 'portrait' of one's own conception of the world-that is, it can be considered within the personal context of artistic memory and of medieval thought. (2)

While certainly not a world picture in the Heideggerian sense, the Orleans image is a portrait and a map image—perhaps, portrait *as* map image. In either case, it is not meant to be relied on as a representation of the actual. As Burke writes:

> Whether they are painted or photographic, what portraits record is not social reality so much as social illusions, not ordinary life but special *performances*. But for this very reason they offer priceless evidence to anyone interested in the history of changing hopes, values or mentalities (*Eyewitnessing* 28, emphasis added).

Each of the urban portraits that follows is in itself a special performance: each seeks to communicated the idea of London that captures a global history in a local space; but as well each of the following map images demonstrates strategies of performance as part and parcel of that space. In the decades immediately bracketing 1600, the process of excluding the trace of performance from representations of the city accelerated, linking the work of the authors of city portraits (and the authorities they often represented) to efforts to define and control London and its topography.

As an example of urban power and control, the portrait of the coronation procession of Edward VI is a representation of a civic performance, a royal entry. This, the so-called "Cowdray portrait," is also a portrait of London itself; a forced perspective collapses the space of the city and includes the area across the river in the field of vision.[12] To the east, the Tower, the Bridge, and St. Peter's Cornhill are all grouped together to form an idiosyncratic topographic nexus of royal, civic, and religious monuments. The portrait also collapses the urban space between St. Peter's in the east and St. Paul's to the west in order to make the ceremonial axis of the city[13] the central focus of the image. The soon-to-be-crowned Edward is represented at the center of this map image, beneath a canopy carried by four knights, just to the left of the spatially displaced but ceremonially significant Eleanor Cross (Hyde 37).

St. Paul's Cathedral is to the right of the image, its spire, struck by lightning in 1561 and subsequently dismantled, is shown intact.

The Cowdray Portrait is a reduplication of performance. Not only is it a portrait of the city of London, and therefore, after Burke, in itself a "special performance," but the portraitist's primary goal was to record the public performance of the royal entry of Edward VI prior to his coronation. Edward's entry, like Mary's, Elizabeth's, and James's which followed him, was an occasion for performance by the City for the new ruler, and also performance by the ruler for the City and its citizens. Edward is shown on display and in performance, and so is London: the goldsmiths have their wares on display, banners hang from the buildings, and the streets are lined with Guild members, their heads appearing above the rooftops of Cheapside. In such detail can be located the special significance of this portrait (of) performance.

As Strong has said: "Topographical exactitude was not part of the [Tudor] way of thinking [. . .]" (41), but it must be noted that "all representations of cities are partial and provisional," not just those of the Tudor era (Balshaw and Kennedy 19). This provisional status of representations is not because of the way mid-sixteenth-century Londoners "actually saw things" (Strong 43), but because the representational strategies of postmedieval urban portraiture "brought together in an impossible spatial relationship" places and concepts that were not adjacent or even present (Strong 41-43). Strong suggests that images such as the Duke of Orleans in the Tower and Edward's entry challenge the idea that they are useful "as the eye-witness record of a single event" (Burke 43), but Burke's understanding of "eyewitnessing" makes room for images that record not only events but the particular cultural context in which the representation was itself performed.

As in the Orleans urban portrait, the Cowdray Portrait too shows a figure, Edward VI, in the act of performing his own location. But his performance is represented in the context of the portrait, a space structured by the artist's performance of "memory, recollection, and association" that produced this representation of the new king as well as of London and its spaces (Kline 2). Indeed, as James Howgego points out: "the artist has attempted to introduce the dimension of time by showing the arrival at Westminster as well as the departure from the Tower" (5). The representation of this image acts to memorialize the performance of Edward VI's coronation and to collate the spaces in which the event was performed, thus combining the medieval concept of collection with an effort at the "Renaissance" concept of perspective, as the landscape recedes in the distance. What can be said of the spatial compression in the Cowdray Portrait that associates the Tower, the Bridge, and St. Paul's can be said of the portrait as a whole: it performs an act of *re-collection.* This event and the spaces in which it transpired are performed, remembered, and grouped in this image.

FREQUENT TRAVELER: A RE-COLLECTION

The map images that follow participate in further reduplications of performance and its representation throughout the end of the sixteenth and the start of the seventeenth centuries. The three most famous and influential map images of the Elizabethan and Jacobean periods will be discussed: the 1572 view of London from Braun and Hogenberg's *Civitates Orbis Terrarum*, John Norden's 1600 "Double View of London and Westminster," and C.J. Visscher's "Long View" of 1616. These three images are so frequently described, reproduced, and anthologized that I have come to regard them as the main texts in what has become a critical "canon" of early modern map images of London. Moreover, in Helgerson's terms, these images "are bound by a dense net of intertextual relations" (347). Despite their frequent mention, these maps and map images are rarely discussed, rarely located in their cultural context. These map images deserved to be discussed together because they so insistently refer to each other. My goal is to explore the intertextual relations that link these images, and to evaluate these maps as not just cultural products but culturally productive.

I conclude this survey of map images of London by stepping beyond (or, briefly expanding) the temporal boundaries of this study to glance at two images in which the spatial concepts emerging circa 1600 achieve a belated realization. These two images, both by Wenceslaus Hollar, perform the divorce between the heretofore closely associated media of the urban plan and the city view. One of these images will be considered at the end of this chapter, the other at the end of the last chapter, where it suitably helps bring a close to this study.

The three famous images published between 1572 and 1616 share a number of common features, not the least important of which is a shared source. Each of these maps bears features that demonstrate its association with the so-called "copperplate map." [Fig. 6] No complete copy of this map remains in existence. However, of the approximately fifteen to twenty copper plates from which the map image was printed, three plates have been discovered.[14] All three plates show signs of considerable wear, suggesting that many printings of this map were made. Two of these plates are contiguous, showing an area to the east of the City, from Shoreditch to the Bridge. The third plate shows an area in the west of the City, from Aldersgate and Greyfriars south to the Thames, with a pre-1561 St. Paul's (its spire intact) prominent in the center of the plate. The authorship of the copperplate map "has so far eluded all research, as has almost everything else about its production" (Delano-Smith 190). From evidence available on these three plates, studies have concluded that the three maps I discuss in this chapter—along with the "woodblock" or "Agas" map—all at least derive substantial information from the copperplate map, when they do not copy it outright.[15]

The recent discovery of the third copper plate is critically important for the understanding of this map and its related series of map images. At the bottom of the plate, amid a handful of rowboats shown on the Thames, the royal barge is shown "being towed upstream towards Whitehall Palace by a galley and steered with a long sweep. The Queen is surrounded by a guard of halberdiers" (Fisher x). Although "the barge is depicted without a coat of arms" it bears "the caption '*Cymbula Regia*' (The Royal Standard) that signals the unambiguous inscription of monarchic presence onto the surface of the map" (Gordon 76). Various attempts to date the copperplate map suggest that it presents London as surveyed at or shortly after the time of Elizabeth's coronation, in the late 1550s. Based on this dating, Harley suggests that the copperplate map "may in fact have been engraved to mark a special occasion, such as the coronation of Queen Elizabeth" (*Meaning* 29). From the point of view of London's urban and cartographic historians, the discovery of an additional plate in the copperplate group adds substance to the speculations that the copperplate map was an "ur-text" that supplied important source material for contemporary cartographers for nearly a hundred years. From the point of view of this study, the discovery anchors this image of the spaces of London to a trace of royal performance.

Elizabeth's journey on the Thames is included on each of the following maps, in one form or another. Though the changes in the architecture and topography of London are haphazardly updated in these maps, the image of Elizabeth shown on the copperplate source is continually reproduced. It becomes part of a collection: each map image includes, and is some part determined by, the influential force of royal performance. In these map images, the trace of performance faded over time as the imprint of representation became more forceful and exclusionary. However, for a time, Elizabeth would remain a frequent traveler on the Thames, her perpetually incomplete journey attesting to the significance of performance in producing the space of the city, even in the form of a printed map.

In 1570, Abraham Ortelius inaugurated a new way of looking at the world. Though his projection of a sphere on a two dimensional rectangle looks familiar, it caused a sensation in a Europe that had only recently seen a gradual decline of the *mappaemundi* in the popular imaginary. Whereas

Figure 6: The most recently discovered (1996) of three known plates from the copperplate map, circa 1560. Museum of London.

the *mappaemundi* fixed the body in relation to a religious conception of the world, Ortelius's map of the world displaced the body entirely in favor of an abstract view of global space.

Ortelius's collection of maps covered the known world, but was regarded by its publishers as incomplete without specific knowledge of the places in which the world's people lived. While Ortelius's *Theatrum Orbis Terrarum* was in production, Georg Braun and Franz Hogenberg "sent draftsmen all over Europe to record views of cities" for a series of companion volumes, *Civitates Orbis Terrarum*, or "The Cities of the Whole World" (Alpers 68).[16] Cosgrove remarks that the collection of city images in the *Civitates*, published from 1572-1617, "mapped Europe's claims as the location of *civis* and thus civilization" (*Apollo's* 133). The very first image in this weighty collection of Europe's great cities was, at the time, a relatively small medieval town on the brink of a population explosion.

The image of London included in the *Civitates* is "the best-known of early maps of London" (Glanville 19). Based on internal evidence, the Braun and Hogenberg image shows London at the end of the 1550s, shortly after Elizabeth I became Queen of England, and shortly before the birth of Shakespeare. Since the discovery of the third plate in the copperplate map, the presence of the Queen's barge (carrying her coat of arms on the Thames) in the Braun and Hogenberg map strongly supports prior comparisons of "the spelling and incidental detail on this map with the anonymous Copperplate Map" that lead to the conclusion that the Braun and Hogenberg image is "a reduced copy of the complete Copperplate Map" (Fisher v).

Following the uniform orientation of Ortelius's maps, London is viewed from the south, and in contrast with the *mappaemundi*, and even Paris's work, spaces that were conceptually determined by theological paradigms, here London's most important cathedral, though prominent, is just one church among many. [Fig. 7]

Unlike the strategies by which medieval map images engages with their viewers, there is no direct expectation of performance addressed to the viewer of this map, no destination to be reached or religious theme to be contemplated. However, there are two frames of visual signification here which taken together actively reference the viewer. In the foreground is a group of figures meant to be taken as representative of London's wealthy citizens. This framing device—and the group is quite literally framed by the margins of the image—presumes a location for these figures that includes "the viewer conceptually within the landscape" of that location (Woodward 4). But the space of the city "behind" these figures is radically

Figure 7: London. Braun and Hogenberg, from *Civitates Orbis Terrarum*, 1572. © The British Library. All Rights Reserved.

different: one could not see the city in this view from the location of the foreground figures. Rather, the space of the map image of London "does not presume a located viewer" (Alpers 74). This *ichnographic* view resembles the abstract "God's eye view" of the Ortelius world map. Frangenberg defines ichnographic views as geometric outlines of a space, though often "ichnographic plans dating from the second half of the sixteenth century, however [. . .] are enriched with portrayals of buildings in elevation" (42) as is the case in the Braun and Hogenberg view of London.

This image attempts to reconcile the "impossible," nearly vertical "map view" of London in the background with the landscape space in the foreground.[17] The incongruous, foreshortened landscape serves as a stage for the Londoners who are represented there, and also as a vista from which, Klein suggests, "the city opens up to its visual appropriation from a point of view conceptually removed from any possible spatial experience of the human body" (34). After seeing the multiple spaces and times represented in the *mappaemundi*, it is not surprising to see a single map image contain a number of representational planes. Alpers suggests that what unifies images like this despite these separate frames of reference is that, "place,

not actions or events, is its basis, and space, not time" is its exclusive subject (91). Were such exclusivity the case, this map image would serve no
significance other than to announce London's "[c]ivic chauvinism" (Hyde
11). However, "town maps, perhaps more than any other of the map genres
[. . .] serve many interests beyond the strictly practical" (Delano-Smith
214). This representation of space, like the space of the city it represents,
incurs a debt to performance.

The costumes of the foreground figures locate the Braun and
Hogenberg image in time. That time frame is intended to be specific,
rather than the time made indistinct by the action of collection in many
medieval images. Nevertheless, this representation of space is a representation of history as well. The quartet of men and women represent the
wealth and power of London's merchant elite, and in so doing demonstrate that London "shared the civilized values of other great European
cities" (Harley, "Meaning" 29). The most central figure, a wealthy merchant, gestures to his left; he may be introducing the two women there,
or perhaps he is introducing the map viewer to the alternate space of the
city view beyond. "Sartorial in its emphasis," Biddick calls such representations of "typical" citizens "'local ethnography,' that is [. . .] various
views and perspectives on local aspects of gender, age, class, dress, fabric,
hair" (236). But "even without depicting historical events, geographical and chorographical illustrations can still be subservient to history"
(Frangenberg 44): by appropriating the copperplate map, the draftsman
of the Braun and Hogenberg view[18] has included, perhaps inadvertently,
more than just the suggestion of busy river traffic. In this image as well,
Elizabeth's barge is shown on the Thames.

The representation of the event of the queen's travel on the river,
framed by the stage-like landscape and its theatrical disposition of
characters, doubly inscribes London as a space that is located in time and
determined by performance. Gordon notes that this presence is included
"not to locate the map as a direct record of the coronation of Elizabeth,
but to establish the reference within the map to the city as a space for the
performance of ceremonial authority" (76). However, Gordon's insistence
that "the ceremonial city" is a space determined only by the performance
of royal authority is difficult to support. Though the image is indeed
framed "within the twin poles of monarchic authority—the royal palace
of Whitehall and the Tower of London, symbol of royal authority within
the city" (76), the bulk of the image is centrally given over to the civic
space of London. Moreover, the frame to this image is surmounted by
three important non-geographical figures. The central titling for the

image locates England in relation to London: "*Londinum Feracissimi Angliae Regni Metropolis.*"[19] This titling is flanked by the Tudor coat of arms to the left and London's coat of arms to the right, suggesting "the power that through the system of patronage brought [this map image] into existence" and also "the relation of that power to the land" as depicted in such maps (Helgerson 330). This image, then, demonstrates a balance of power in the performance of the space of the city: royal and civic forces in mutual operation.

Lastly, the image's foreground space, which Gordon does not discuss, frames the entirety of London in relation to a kind of stage space, recalling Mulcaster's description of London as "a stage wherein was shewed the wonderfull spectacle, of a noble hearted princesse" (Mulcaster 16). This description seems even more appropriate to the *Civitates* image, "wherein" the map of London serves as a spectacular backdrop to the theatrical disposition of foreground figures and the "princesse" herself behind them.

Even more explicitly than Braun and Hogenberg's London, John Norden's map image of London presents an image of historical space determined by performance. In 1600, John Norden (c. 1547-1625) engraved a panoramic city view of London and Westminster, seen (as was increasingly conventional) from the south.[20] [Fig. 8] This document jointly displays England's rapidly expanding civic and economic metropolis and alongside it, the burgeoning suburb that was the seat of England's political power.[21]

London and Westminster, respectively, share the space of this view, though a singular term like "view" seems inappropriate. Norden's engraving, entitled "The City of London," collects so many separate sites, images, and emblems that it pushes its ostensible subject to the margins. The City of London itself occupies less than one fifth of the total height of the image, pressed against the upper border of the view, immediately below the title "*Civitas Londini.*" As in the Braun and Hogenberg image, the words of the title are flanked by the coats of arms of Elizabeth and the City of London. The main west-east thoroughfare for goods and traffic, the river Thames, dominates the center of the image; views to the east and west are radically foreshortened, placing emphasis on the area of London immediately adjacent to the Bridge; and Norden's image places emphasis on the suburb of Southwark, huge in the foreground, with its notorious brothels and theatres. The chief religious structure in Southwark, St. Mary Overy (now Southwark Cathedral), is the most prominent church in the image; St. Paul's seems by comparison an insignificant landmark.

Figure 8: *Civitas Londini.* John Norden, 1600.

Immediately below St. Mary Overy, in the heart of Southwark, a framed cartouche bears this text:

> This description of the moste / Famous Citty LONDON. Was per-
> formed in / The yeare of Christe. 1600. And in the / Yeare of the
> Moste Wished And Happy / Raigne of the Right Renowned Quene
> ELIZABETH. The Fortye And Two. / Sr. Nicholas Moseley Knight
> Being Lorde / Maior. And Roger Clarke And Humphrey / Wylede.
> Sherifes of the Same[.][22]

Flanking this inscription, Norden includes two very different inset maps: on the right, a map more or less copied from Braun and Hogenberg's *Civitates* image of London; to the left, a rather different prospect of the nearby City of Westminster.

Norden, in *Speculum Brittaniae*, his 1593 atlas of Great Britain, "was the first English map-maker to inset a map of an important town within the borders of a county map" (Delano-Smith 189). His facility with inset maps is on display in this city view, for not only does the separation between the maps reinforce a distinction between London and Westminster, the differ-ence in appearance of these insets multiplies the representational strategies at work in Norden's mapping. The map of London, framed and inset to the right, is lifted from the *Speculum Brittaniae*; it is densely labeled, with a tiny key noting important locations. The map of Westminster, to the left, is radi-cally different in the style of inset; indeed, it may be unique in this regard. Rather than being represented within the conventional frame of the inset map, the space of Westminster is shown beneath the landscape of London, as though the paper of the map were peeled back to show another map beneath it, or, in an evocation of Renaissance anatomical illustrations, as if the surface of the land itself were cut and an "interior" Westminster revealed. Few loca-tions in Westminster are noted in this view.

"*Banke Syde*" and its theatres are prominent in the foreground of the *Civitas Londini* (View).[23] Norden need not have gone to the trouble of including Southwark in an illustration that was already potently engaged in representing urban relations between London and Westminster. As studies of other city views indicate, that which is included or excluded in a view of a city is as telling as the image of the city itself, and Southwark would seem to have strong associations for Norden. While Southwark had been officially part of greater London for centuries, this oldest of London's suburbs had a vexed (and vexing) relationship with the City itself.[24] Though the jurisdic-tion of London reached into Southwark, this suburb and its liberties were in

many ways "out of bounds," and the theatres were part of the boundary-defy-
ing culture of Southwark. Norden clearly felt that this culture was so essential
to any representation of London that he claimed—impossibly—Southwark
as the location from which this "view" was seen.

On the image itself, a small figure can be seen standing in the tower
of St. Mary Overy. Immediately above this figure is the legend "*Statio prospectiva*" (View).[25] The view of London in this image is rendered from an
impossible point of view high above the city and to the south. However, con-
tradictorily, the "*Statio prospectiva*" legend above the tower would seem to
claim that the tower of St. Mary Overy is the point from which the perspective of the image is located, possibly even representing the artist himself in
the tower of the church. Norden's image of the city would seem to participate
in the "bird's eye view" school of map images, a position reinforced by Delano-Smith, who notes: "In Norden's town plans, the angle of view is always
oblique, with the result that, although the buildings are represented pictori-
ally, they do not wholly obscure the street pattern" (188). Norden wants to
locate himself in Southwark, and to locate Southwark as the conceptual and
visual epicenter of the image, even though other view points would need to
be used to render the area south of the Thames, including St. Mary Overy
and the figure itself. There is an ironic contradiction here: in his enthusiasm
for representing the site of his performance of an illustration at St. Mary
Overy and the perspective point from which the city was seen, Norden has
included that point in the image, thus ensuring that it could not have been
the perspective point from which the city was seen!

Given Norden's use of the term "performed" in his "description" of this
image, and his attempt to record in visual form the event of his illustration
itself, an element of performance would seem to be invoked in the very
structure of this representation. Not only does Norden's legend explicitly say
that the engraving was "performed" in 1600 (View), but the map image also
includes an image of the civic performance that regularly represented the city
as "an autonomous mercantile civic space" (Gordon 81). The most prominent
of the multiple images on this map is located at the bottom border, where
Norden represents the Lord Mayor's Show, the public theatrical performance
that officially introduced each new mayor of London. And though the image
of this pageant is set outside the frame of the map image, Lord Mayor's Show
has a corollary within the map space itself. In the same spot on the river
where Elizabeth can be seen on her royal barge in the Braun and Hogenberg
map image, Norden has placed a similar image. A small ship is visible, as
is its label: "The gally fuste," or galley foist, the official barge of the City
of London, often used as an accessory to the Lord Mayor's swearing-in

ceremony in Westminster (View). Elizabeth-as-frequent-traveler is invoked by omission: Norden's substitution of the galley foist for the royal barge is an intentional assertion of civic over royal authority, authority that is asserted in urban performance. The galley foist's journey to Westminster and back is the boundary-crossing extension of the boundary-defining performance of the Lord Mayor's Show shown elsewhere in the *Civitas Londini*.

In this complex portrait of an early modern urban agglomeration, multiple sites of power are visibly on display, most explicitly the court and the city. Janette Dillon has usefully explored "the visible mobility of relations between court and city" and the ways in which these relations are "represented within the domain of theatre" (Dillon 15). But Norden's image does more than merely picture the sites of power that Dillon takes as her ostensible object of study: Norden's view is as much a depiction of representational spaces as it is a survey of social topography. The practices of cartography, urbanism, and performance are as much the objects of Norden's view as are the views of two neighboring poles of royal and civic power, and these practices contribute to the overall spatial effect of Norden's collection of representations. And it should not go unnoticed that, while court and city are undisputed sites of power, the dominant location in this performance-laden image is the site of the theatre. Perhaps in this image Southwark is surreptitiously offered as an alternative site of power; certainly it is offered as an alternative site for the production of the image itself.

Norden's collection of disparate images is a kind of spatial collage reminiscent of the multiple ideas, times, and places collected in the *mappaemundi*. Norden's map image takes on historical dimensions, recording not just the appearance of the city, but the multiple locations of London's urban power. And the geographic space of these sites is emphatically underscored by a reminder that municipal power is something to be performed: the image of the Lord Mayor's Show takes up more of the image's total surface area than does the representation of the City of London itself. If one were to consider the ratio of geographical space to performance space as represented by Norden in this image, the idea of "Civitas Londini" would seem to be determined more by public ceremony than by any mere physical territory. Ultimately, this image must be seen as a map of London's topology as much as any topography.

Norden's "performance" of London and Westminster is remarkable not for the metropolitan region it represents, but for the way it is represented. Norden's elaborate "cut" draws attention to Westminster as "different," using the practice of cartographic representation itself to *map* that difference. Biddick argues that certain strategies in the city views of the *Nuremburg Chronicle* perform the equivalent of representational "plastic surgery" on the landscape (232). In the case of postmedieval mapping, certain omissions or inclusions "cut" both the city being represented and the medieval representational tradition against which the postmedieval urban portrait reacted. Such a "cut" is made remarkably manifest in Norden's *Civitas Londini*. In effect, Norden is not only representing space, but in some measure time and culture too. In revealing the suburb of Westminster beneath the "skin" of London's terrain, Norden is indicating a passage of time, in the course of which a new and newly important town has emerged where previously there had only been an isolated cathedral and an enclave of royal accommodations.

Moreover, Westminster is not actually located on the plot of pasture land that Norden chose to excise; it is in fact further west. So in effect this surgical image serves as an elaborate inset which locates in the map a place that would otherwise be farther afield, out of the frame. By bringing Westminster so viscerally into contact with the "flesh" of London, Norden is powerfully suggesting the emergence of a new phase in the history between city and court, a suggestion that would seem to have dual implications. First, that it has become difficult to represent London without Westminster; second, that Westminster is being *drawn* toward the east, caught in the gravitational pull of London, a city bursting at its seams with citizens, many of whom were similarly drawn to the City.

In his reading of this map image, Gordon locates the idea of (royal) performance in the central portrait of London, overlooking the space produced by the interaction of the collected elements of Norden's image. London is not represented here as a singular, fixed urban identity. In fact, by suspending the name of this space between the royal and civic coats of arms, by invoking Elizabeth's power as the Thames's frequent traveler yet substituting the Galley Foist in her place, by dedicating the map image to Elizabeth while portraying the Lord Mayor's pageant as a visual anchor for the image, Norden represents London as a flexible space of multiple identities to be determined by the subjectivities and authorities of those in performance. The strategies of collection that structure Norden's representation confer upon performance the force to vie for and the authority to determine the space of London.

At the time of Norden's view, London was a city in which an ineluctable spatial growth was in constant tension with reluctant traditions of social practice. It is this tension which is most clearly illustrated in this map image. Norden's prospect is a complicated cultural artifact, one in which mapping can be shown to reveal important evidence about the conception and representation of cities in England in this period, and particularly about the popular idea of London and its real-and-imagined spaces. This map image is a *gallimaufry*, in Lyly's term: a hybrid space of visual and performance strategies.

A final note on the physical history of the Norden image: John Bagford records that he and Samuel Pepys both saw a copy of Norden's map displayed at Dulwich College in London. "Mr Secretary Pepys [. . .] was very desirous to have purchased it," Bagford noted, "But since it is decayed and quite destroyed by means of moisture on the walls" it would seem that he did not do so. This anecdote suggests an explanation for the very small number of surviving copies of Norden's and other map images from this period: they, like medieval itineraries, were "exhausted in the execution of their purpose," in this case the private display of a representation that collected the public spaces and civic performances of the postmedieval city (Cosgrove, "Introduction" 14). Like the performances this image collects, printed versions of this view did not necessarily aspire to permanence: they were discarded following the exhaustion of their value as decorative, domestic art.

To reiterate a point that I made at the outset of this section: this discussion does not set out to describe a "progression." The genealogy of London's representations in this period is organized by association, not a putative evolution. Although the images discussed here might seem to narrate a progression toward a visually accurate "picture" of London, I do not mean to suggest that the history of postmedieval images of London is an inevitable story of improvement, nor that the images discussed here were the only images from the period. Rather, what I try to chart in these canonical examples is a change in the values and uses that were attached to images of the city.

In the year of Shakespeare's death, the canon of urban representations of London marked a watershed. In an emergence as profound as Matthew Paris's coordination of urban representation, international space, and travel performance, the first instance of a divorce between representation and performance appeared in a major map image of London. The visual culture of northern Europe exerted its influence on an image of London that achieved to a large degree the exclusion of performance from the idea of the city in representation. Published in 1616, Claes Jans Visscher's panorama is titled simply, "London." [Fig. 9]

The lost "ur-map" of London, known only from the evidence of the three copper plates, had an influence on Visscher's "London," as had Norden's "Civitas Londini," though these two older map images are in representational form rather different from Visscher's panorama. The images in this chapter are grouped together because of their quotational relationship, their insistent references to each other. Though in its representational strategies Visscher's panorama is distinct, in its referential relations with the copperplate and

Figure 9: *London*. Claes Jans Visscher, 1616. Guildhall Library, Corporation of London.

the Norden images, it is part of this group. Of the three major map images from this period, Visscher's is the least "hybridized" in its form. Although continental practices of abstract representation dominate in this image, because of its quotational and referential dependence on Norden and the copperplate map, traces remain that link this image-a true panoramic portrait-to postmedieval representations of urban space as something still to be performed.

Visscher's Panorama of 1616 was not "performed" on the spot, as Norden claimed of his map image; it was performed instead in Visscher's workshop in Flanders. In fact, "there seems to be no evidence that he either worked in or visited London" (Shapiro 27-8). Howgego and Shapiro both reinforce the point that Visscher, for all the apparent detail of his image, "has no independent authority" for the minute particulars of the London he illustrated (Shapiro 31), and Hyde notes that "Visscher's source would appear to be Norden's prospect" (45). In its production then, Visscher's image of London would seem to be the first *representation* of this city, in Diamond's use of the term: "the making visible (again) of what is lacking or what has disappeared [. . .]" (85). Diamond's definition of representation is strongly consonant with Alpers's discussion of the "mapping impulse" in Northern European art during the seventeenth century, when: "the map allowed one to see something that was otherwise invisible" (67), as maps still do. In this case, Visscher produced this representation in the absence of the city itself.

More than merely eschewing a self-figuring "*Statio prospectiva*" gesture or a declaration of personal performance, like those of Norden, Visscher produced a representation of the city that is entirely without a located or locatable point of view. Although St. Mary Overy and the bridge are prominent in the foreground, the image is seen from multiple perspectives located above the southern reaches of Southwark. Visscher's panorama is not an act of "eyewitnessing" per se. Like Paris's itinerary, Visscher constructed a map image without ever personally traveling to the location illustrated in the image. However, whereas Paris's itinerary presumed that the map would precede or produce a particular performance, Visscher's map image is by contrast the substitution for, or surrogation of, performance. No one need visit early seventeenth century London, not even the illustrator, to "use" this image: it stands alone as an object to be appreciated visually.

Visscher's London would seem to be the least performed / performing of the three major images from this period: only the flights of angels and cherubim supporting the title banner and the coats of arms suggest anything beyond the representational. Alpers notes the gradual displacement of "the usual framing devices [. . .] which serve to place us and lead us in, so to speak, to the space" in comparable, contemporary urban portraits in the northern European tradition (74). The framing devices such as those that determine the spaces of the Braun and Hogenberg and Norden images of London are here absent. The representation of London's streets and architectural projections extends to the limits of the four sheets on which this image is printed. Rather than, for example, the frame to the Braun and Hogenberg that locates London in relation to the space of the viewer and in which the viewer is conceptually associated with the frame in contrast with the space of the city, here Visscher locates the entire city in relation to the space of the viewer. The absence of multiple spaces, locations, and frames in this image is what chiefly differentiates it from the other map images considered here, and in this unification of the space of representation Visscher effected a divorce from the practices of collection.

Traces of performance, however, are located *within* the representation. This, more than other images of London, is an inhabited location: the streets of the city and the surface of the Thames are teeming with Londoners. Chimneys belch smoke, flags flutter, sails bulge with wind, and the decapitated heads of criminals leer at the roofs of Southwark from Bridge Gate. Even the late Queen Elizabeth makes an appearance. This map image—a *representation of space*, in Lefebvre's strict sense—includes representations of urban subjects busily performing the quotidian practices of everyday life.

The Lord Mayor's Galley Foist is gone, and Elizabeth is once again in her accustomed location on the Thames. She continued to be the river's most frequent traveler, though by 1616 she had been dead for more than a decade. The royal barge, surmounted by Elizabeth's coat of arms, is heavily guarded by more than a score of soldiers in five adjacent boats. The queen and her attendant vessels ply the river heading east from Westminster—or do they? Close examination of the small royal flotilla reveals an anomaly: though the royal barge appears to be heading toward the west, the individuals shown on the boat pulling the barge appear to be rowing in the opposite direction. Despite his obvious mastery as an illustrator, one is forced to the banal conclusion that Visscher had rather little experience rowing a boat.

I linger on this detail not to challenge the reputation of a master engraver's craft, but to highlight the degree to which even the quotational trace of performance is confounded in this image. Elizabeth's perpetually suspended journey is in effect "misquoted." Visscher associates the space in his image with the archive of London's spaces by drawing on the image of the Thames's frequent traveler, but he does so inaccurately. This inaccuracy relegates performance to an ineffectual residue: this space cannot be performed, and the image of Elizabeth and her waterborne entourage is, in this representation, a quaint anachronism—or more appropriately an "aspatialism," for it is not merely out of time (the queen was, after all, dead) this royal performance is also out of place in the inflexible space of representational fixity.

The fixity of Visscher's representation would prove to be precedent-setting: the elimination of collection eliminated the flexibility of a space represented as one to be performed. This precedent was reinforced in subsequent images of the city. No discussion of the city views of London would be com-

Figure 10: London. Hollar's "long view," inset. Guildhall Library, Corporation of London.

plete without a consideration of Wenceslaus Hollar's long view. While the date for this image falls outside the rough parameters of this project, Hollar's portrait of London is clearly a participant in the discourses of performance and visual representation characteristic of the other images studied here. The image is strongly reminiscent of the Norden image from decades earlier. The forced perspective to the west in Hollar's view recalls that of Norden *Civitas*. Importantly, the performance of Hollar's image is represented in the image itself, and in a way in which Norden might well have admired. As has been noted, Norden labeled St. Mary Overy as the "*Statio prospectiva*," though it could not have been the point from which the entire map image was drawn. Hollar, by contrast, actually produced a map image that represents the city as drawn from a single location, not coincidentally, the same point from which Norden's miniature figure waves at the viewer.

There is only one location from which Hollar's "long view" could have been performed, from a point of view in Southwark at the top of the church of St Mary Overy. The perspective relationships among the objects in this panorama clearly locate Hollar's physical position during the time at which he performed the preliminary sketches for this work. The foreground images increase in size and are illustrated from an increasingly oblique angle as they get closer to the property of St. Mary Overy, stopping just short of including St. Mary Overy itself in the image. [Fig. 10] Despite this exclusion, the place of the illustration's performance is nevertheless clearly suggested: it is in fact allied with the point of view of any reader of this image. The very tower in which the artist stood to make this image is a strongly felt absent presence, a point just "off stage," as it were, from the contents of the image itself. Hollar's view of London, like those before it, is a representation of space. However, this image is remarkable because Hollar represents in his view the trace of his actual performance of the view itself. In its inclusion of Hollar's personal "view" and activities, Hollar's long view is a postmedieval "afterimage": this view traces its author's pedestrian performances, locating Hollar himself in relation to his object of representation. In this act of self-location, Hollar's map image recuperates a measure of the space of performance represented in the foreground of the Braun and Hogenberg view, even while the image makes a strong contribution to the "realistic" (i.e. non-performance inflected) representations of the city.[26]

The view of London represented in Hollar's map image could not have been seen all at once. This panoramic vista is, in that sense, visually impossible. It forces perspective to the west, making Westminster dwindle in the distance- surely not an accidental choice. By contrast, London bridge and the buildings of Southwark loom large in importance, just as they loom large in Norden's map image.

Hollar's view clearly refers to Norden's. Where the latter includes a legend that explicitly locates the "performance" of the view, Hollar includes that same performance information through implication.

As interesting as Hollar's "long view" of London is, it stands outside the genealogy of images from early modern London's visual culture archive. As an index of just how far removed Hollar's image is from the early modern city, in the inset above, Wren's Monument to the fire is visible at the extreme right side of the panel. The Monument offers visual testimony to the fact that Shakespeare's London had been burnt to the ground by the time Hollar made this image—an image, ironically, influenced by traditional representations of a city that had been destroyed by the time this image of it was made.

Visscher's abstract, long-distance performance provides the endpoint to the canon of early modern map images of London. With the emergence of Visscher's image comes as well the emergence of London as a fixed identity. De Certeau has described this emergence as: "the creation of a *universal* and anonymous *subject* which is the city itself" (94). This representation, this "picture" of a city, gains a use value that did not adhere to the medieval city.

> "The city," like a proper name, thus provides a way of conceiving and constructing space on the basis of a finite number of stable, isolatable, and interconnected properties. (94)

Thus, the representation of London that Visscher performed, at a great geographical and personal remove from the physical object of his study, is not so different from the performances of Ortelius and Mercator, whose representations also depicted abstract images unavailable to the human eye. Accordingly, Visscher's representational product could be described, in Mercator's words, as an "*oculus mundi*": a "global vision" of London.[27]

Chapter Three

The Boredom of King James: Representing the Urban Subject (15 March 1604)

London was in many respects a place of ruins. [. . .] The convent of the Poor Clares, known as the Minories, was destroyed to make way for storehouses; the church of the Crutched Friars became a carpenter's shop and a tennis court; the church of the Blackfriars was turned into a warehouse for the carts and properties of the "pageants." [. . .] There are many other examples, but the salient point remains that after the Reformation much of late Tudor London was in a ruined condition [. . .].

Peter Ackroyd[1]

"THE KING OF BEASTES"

Two days before his royal entry into the City of London, James I and the royal family arrived at the Tower of London, where they were to stay in the royal apartments until their formal progress through the streets of the City on the 15 March 1604, after which they would return to Westminster. Edmund Howes records the tourist's pastimes with which James occupied himself during his sojourn in the Tower.[2] James and "the Royal Party" were given a tour of the Tower (Nichols 320), which included an inspection of "all the Offices, Store-houses, and the Mint," and in the latter location "both the King and Queene coyned money" which they promptly gave away "to divers persons there present" (Howes 835).

After this review of the facilities, James inquired after the exotic animals kept in the Tower menagerie, particularly the lions: "[H]e asked of their being, & how they came thither, for that in England there were bred no such fierce beasts" (Howes 835). James appears to have voiced concern to his entourage, concerned that a creature as noble as the lion

could not be found as a native of the British Isles. Though his anxieties were confirmed, those present with the king went to no small length
to provide James with assurances of the nobility of Britain's indigenous
beasts, despite the lack of lions.

> [N]everthelesse Abraham Ortelius, and other forraine writers, do
> affirme that there are in Englande beasts of as great courage as the
> Lyon, namely, the Mastiffe Dog. Whereuppon the King caused
> Edward Allen, late servant to the Lord Admirall, now sworne the
> Princes man, and Master of the Beare Garden, to fetch secretly
> three of the fellest dogs in the Garden; which being done, the King,
> Queene, and Prince, with four or five Lords, went to the Lions
> Tower, and caused the lustiest Lion to be separated from his mate,
> and put into the Lyons den one Dog alone, who presently flew to
> the face of the Lion, but the Lyou [sic] suddenly shooke him off, &
> graspt him fast by the neck, drawing the dog up staires and downe
> staires.
>
> (Howes 835)

The king pursued this entertainment for some time, with ultimately
three dogs being introduced into the lion's den. All three dogs were more
or less handily dispatched, even when the second and third dogs attacked
the lion simultaneously. Eventually the lion retired to an interior room to
avoid further harassment. Howes's account suggests that the lion's flight
was prompted not by fear of another attack so much as by exhaustion
and annoyance (836). When the king's amusement with the lion-baiting
was concluded, the dogs were retrieved, and the king's son, Prince Henry,
provided the denouement to this drama.

> The two first dogs dyed within a few dayes, but the last dog was
> well recovered of all his hurts, and the yong Prince commanded his
> servant Ed. Allen to bring the dog to him to Saint Iames, where the
> Prince charged the sayd Allen to keepe him, and make much of him,
> saying, hee that had fought with the King of beastes, should never
> after fight with any inferiour creature. (836)

This account of James's spontaneous, private lion-baiting, conducted on
the 13th of March, 1604, is interesting for the way in which it locates in a
single site an intersection of the competing forms of power at work in the
first year of Stuart London.

One way in which this intersection could be described is through a consideration of the social forces which come into contact in the course of this event. The tripartite juxtaposition of "Theatre, Court, and City" has become conventional in the contemporary discourse of literary history: Janette Dillon's work on the subject takes this formulation as its very title.[3] Dillon has usefully explored "the visible mobility of relations between court and city" and the ways in which these relations are "represented within the domain of theatre" (15). The trialectics of theatre industry, urban power, and royal authority were acutely on display during James's sportive violence at the Tower,[4] though the "domain of theatre" is not invoked in the way that Dillon's project would suggest. James's fascination with the idea of the lion was surely as much a product of selfish concerns with his impending royal entry as with any personal zoological interest in "the King of beastes." The fact that James went to see the lions after visiting the mint is telling. In all likelihood, the coins being pressed on that day were newly prepared with the image of the king, perhaps the "laureate bust" coin prepared for James's accession (Goldberg 45). Thus, during his visit to the mint, James may well have had direct contact with a miniaturized representation of himself as an Augustan monarch. Coining the image himself, he would have performed a literal, if reductive, act of self-fashioning. This act is even more interesting when read in conjunction with the anxiety that James voiced about the lack of lions among the catalogue of indigenous British predators. Together, these two incidents suggest that what was really being baited in the Tower on the 13th—along with several hapless beasts—was a symbolic order. James arranged for the abstract idea of kingship to be quite literally "dogged" by a creature closely associated with British national identity, the mastiff. All in all, the afternoon offered a profoundly allegorical outing for the royal family.

Two days later, James would be publicly celebrated as "The First King of Great Britain," and the significance of this new status did not go unnoticed by James himself.[5] It would seem that while amusing himself and his entourage with real world sports at the Tower, James was also testing the compatibility of the two abstract terms that were united in his reign: "King" and "Britain."

However, this allegorical combat over the relative merits of royal authority and national identity was conducted within the controlling sphere of a different authority. The Tower marked the southeastern limits of the City of London, and had stood for hundreds of years as one of the most identifiable landmarks of the medieval city. Though an enclave of royal power, the London-ness of the Tower is as unmistakable as James's reason for coming to the Tower on the 13th of March. Though the ostensible purpose of the upcoming pageants was an elaborate welcome prepared for the new king by his loyal urban subjects, there was no small measure of obligation on James's part. As reviewed in Chapter One, by the time of James's accession, London's strength as an economic center was unrivalled in the British Isles. Even for a seasoned monarch with absolutist designs, the power of the City was not to be taken lightly. The Tower, though a royal residence and an enclave of the king's privilege, was nevertheless located within the walls of the City of London. And though James may have stood outside the jurisdiction of the City while he was in the Tower, he was well within the conceptual boundaries of his nation's social and economic capital.

The third variable in this algebra of social forces is invoked by the surprising inclusion among the royal entourage of the famous actor Edward Alleyn. Alleyn's presence at the Tower that day is surprising because of the relative positions of power which separate the new monarch from the common player: James is given residence in one of the most distinctive and ancient landmarks of the city, and will soon be welcomed as the main character in a theatrical event that will position him as central, literally and figuratively, to the life of the city. Alleyn, however much his fortunes may have risen in the world through association with Philip Henslowe and Christopher Marlowe, still remained by contrast with James a mere entertainment entrepreneur whose business interests, in Mullaney's words, "occupied the margins of the city" (22). And though Alleyn, too, will play a central role in James's entry pageant, and though his business interests had recently been elevated by the patronage of the prince, his role in the Tower on the 13th is that of "Master of the Beare Garden," little more than a keeper of ill-tempered dogs.[6] However, in the context of this account of James's pre-pageant pastimes, Alleyn serves as a representative of London's theatre industry, another element in the triumvirate of (unequal) powers on display in the Tower.

My project is not directly concerned with a consideration of the political tensions between London and Westminster in the period circa 1600, nor the social tensions defining the lives of players or the people of London. Though these political and cultural currents have been the common currency of innumerable studies,[7] this project places its emphasis on a different set of forces, forces that were in evidence during James's private entertainment in the Tower of London. These latter forces would be much more potently (and intentionally) on display two days later when, on the 15th of March, James conducted his official, spectacular entry into and progress through the streets of London. This other set of forces, though not entirely divided from the conventional alignment of forces described by Dillon, cannot be located in social and economic demographies so much as in representational and spatial practices. On this occasion, the Tower served as an intersection for a complex set of cultural coordinates, as revealed in the off-handed suggestion (recorded by Howes) that initiated the lion-baiting entertainment: the reference to Abraham Ortelius.

By the time of James's accession, Abraham Ortelius had become an international sensation. His *Theatrum orbis terrarum*, published in 1570, was "hugely successful commercially," as Cosgrove notes, "reprinted four times in its first year, regularly updated and translated into six languages by 1612 [. . .]" (*Apollo's* 130). With the *Theatrum*, Ortelius had "not only produced the first Renaissance atlas, but invented the very idea of the atlas" (Gillies 70). Ortelius's *Theatrum* would serve as the model for all subsequent cartographic collections, including the 1595 *Atlas* of Gerard Mercator.

The invocation of Ortelius during James's visit to the Tower is important because it indicates the ways in which the king and his courtiers pictured themselves and their relationship to a wider world. James's emblematic combat between the lion and the dogs was consciously conducted in relation to "Abraham Ortelius and other forraine writers" (Nichols 320). The idea of Britain, of *location* in general, was presented to the king as a cartographic idea: To be king of a particular place is to have a relationship with maps and the descriptions of place that maps employ. This scene in the Tower can be seen to have been performed on the conceptual terrain of Ortelius's *Theatrum*. Consequently, this event in the Tower takes on a representational dimension. James and the animal combat which he arranged are positioned on a cartographic nation-stage, much like the Elizabeth of the Gheeraerts portrait, in which the queen is shown standing on a globe. In this portrait, previously discussed [Fig. 1], the theatrical disposition of royal power in, or *on*, cartographic space represents the "otherwise invisible" relationship between Elizabeth's power and the place over which she wields that power (Alpers 67). A similar representational activity was performed by James in the Tower, though not one as enduring as Gheeraerts's portrait. The map on which Elizabeth stands in the portrait can only ever be "stage-like," whereas the sports in the Tower, supervised by none less than Edward Alleyn-master, as the contemporary reader is acutely aware, of more than merely a bear-baiting ring-invoked performance in a more direct mode. Though no literal map marked the floor of this playing space, nevertheless the royal baiting was played out on the stage of Ortelius's *Theatrum*. The idea of James as a monarch available for representation (as, for example, an image on a coin) is placed in the context of an international map image, and what followed was an exploration of the question, Where does King James *stand* in relation to the nations and cities assembled in Ortelius's "Theatre of the whole world"?

Yet the relationship between kingship and cartographic space represented on this occasion is less definitive than that represented in the Gheeraerts portrait. Helgerson notes that the innovation (and popularization) of mapping in sixteenth-century England "opened a conceptual gap between the land and its ruler, a gap that would eventually span battlefields" (332). In the space of this gap James can be seen to rehearse a relationship between power and location, and to do so via the intermediary figures of the combating beasts. James choose to stand just offstage from the global theatre that was mapped onto the space of the Tower; he allowed instead "the King of beastes" to enter Ortelius's representational sphere and do battle in his place. The power that James wielded in the scene in the Tower is a power over performance and representation: James could decide who was to perform and what was to be represented in the performance. In the case of the lion-baiting, James's own identity as "King of Britain" was performed, though James himself did not perform.

This chapter addresses the representation of space in one particularly influential public, urban performance. The specific focus of the discussion here is on the representation of urban space, a subject which was quite consciously the dominant feature of the civic pageantry prepared for the royal entry of James I into the City of London on 15 March 1604. This extraordinary event was a watershed cultural performance, the singular expression of a dynamic period of spatial development that challenged the relationship between the urban subject and the space of the city in early modern London. My examination of this city-spanning theatrical event serves to organize a consideration of the ways in which the city was being reconceived in both the real and the conceptual spaces of early modern England. In England, in London, in the years marking the turn of the seventeenth century, the work of this reconception was accomplished in representation and by representational strategies such as those deployed in this entry.

This reconception of space was marked increasingly by practices of visual representation that relied on strategies of perspective and display. These strategies are made manifest in the documents put into print by the three principal authors of James's pageant: Thomas Dekker, Ben Jonson, and Stephen Harrison. Jonson's text is the one most often discussed in relation to James's 1604 entry, no doubt a side effect of Jonson's high status in the field of literary history, relative to Dekker and the virtually unknown Harrison. Dekker's account receives less attention, despite the fact that his text provides a more complete document of the entry than does Jonson's. Harrison's account, too, has been neglected: the "artificer" of the entry, Harrison was by Dekker's own admission "the sole inventor of the architecture" designed and built for the occasion (Dekker 376). Not content merely to note that Harrison, as an author and a publisher, provides "the most extensive pictorial record of a street pageant in the Tudor-early Stuart era," Bergeron also positions Harrison as an influential "theorist, practitioner, historian, publisher, and cultural participant" (*Practicing* 175). Bergeron argues for the reevaluation of Harrison's contribution to James's entry, as a significant example of the rich tradition of "England's visual culture" before Inigo Jones (165). My discussion of Harrison will reinforce and extend Bergeron's argument. More than just an examination of Harrison's *Arches of Triumph* as an aesthetic landmark, a consideration of the cultural and material significance of the events and constructions that are documented by his text is an important feature of this chapter.

The three principal contributors to the royal entry of James I—Dekker, Harrison, and Jonson—have provided the three principal texts which serve as source material for the study of this entry. These documents are supplemented by a fourth text, that of Gilbert Dugdale. Dugdale's text "provides an eyewitness account" of James's entry, from the point of view of an audience member in the streets (Bergeron, *Practicing* 147), in this case a peculiarly avid audience member who may or may not have improvised his own contributions to the day's performances.[8] Dugdale's quirky and distinctive view from the margins adds a valuable voice to the discussion, one that is remarkable for how much it has in common with the voices and views of the "official" pageant authors. These are the four sources that will be considered in the following discussion of James's entry.[9] Each of these texts is expressive of the intersection of powers at work in this event, an event in which the new king, two dramatists, an "artificer," a citizen, and the municipal leaders of London all vied for a share of representational authority.

A lengthy consideration of a single theatrical event performed over only a few hours on one occasion only, this chapter is organized in several sections, focusing alternately on texts and performances. Though this section includes discussion of the performances supposedly documented by these texts, the emphasis is on printed matter. The second section theorizes the implications of the texts and performances discussed in the first section. Investing so much time on one day in 1604 may seem profligate, but I find this event richly representative of its cultural moment.

The aims of this chapter, though diverse, are unified by the practice of performance genealogies and the consideration of the role of performance revealed in a set of historical texts. Each of these texts documents the unpredictable conditions that marked James's entry, and in so doing each reveals its author's anxieties over the gap separating performance and writing.

The majority of scholarly work on James's entry has considered the literary features of the entry;[10] my focus will be on performance and the representation of space: the representational strategies used during the entry itself (including oral delivery of poetry amid the noisy chaos of the crowd), along with the textual strategies used to account for, recover, and erase performance in print. As such, my goal is the location of the performance counterpart to what Cosgrove sees only as "graphic": a mapping performance that serves as a "register of correspondence between two spaces, whose explicit outcome is a space of representation" ("Introduction" 1). For all the textual frustrations that they record, these four texts provide a record of the production of an incipient space suspended between the real and the ideal, a space represented in the streets of early modern London on 15 March 1604.

James's entry marks a nodal point in what Lefebvre calls "the long history of space." This event juxtaposes with particular clarity a space of representation and a space that is represented: in this case, the streets and architectural projections of London, on the one hand; on the other, the ornate architectural monuments and textually dense performances constructed for James which stood in stark contrast to the existing city space. These temporary constructions were composed of a series of representations of urban space, a series of spaces unified under the conceptual sign of "Londinium."

THE ROYAL SUBJECT

On 15 March 1604, James Stuart made his way through the streets of London. The occasion of his long-delayed arrival in the City was the king's decision to finally, grudgingly, participate in a city-spanning theatrical celebration of his relatively new kingship. A series of temporary triumphal arches was erected for the occasion, most of which were accompanied by a theatrical performance. The first of these arches was designed by Stephen Harrison after a concept by Ben Jonson, and it served as the gateway through which the king passed to begin his public progress through the city. This arch also served as a stage for Edward Alleyn, though this time he appeared not as the master of the bear garden but as one of London's foremost actors, playing the character of "Genius Urbis," the personification of the City of London.

The entry procession began with James's exit from the Tower of London "betweene the houres of eleven and twelve" (Harrison 333). The first entertainment that James would have encountered "was part of the children of Christ's Church Hospitall, to the number of 300, who were placed on a scaffold" near the Tower, where they sang for the king (334). But the first of the pageant arches to be the object of the king's eye awaited James in Fenchurch Street. After several blocks of weaving through the maze of medieval streets, James would have seen the "Londinium Arch." [Fig. 11] On the day of the entry, the Arch would have been concealed from view until the time of James's arrival in Fenchurch Street (though it had been on display uncovered for several days prior). Jonson notes that "[t]he whole frame was covered with a curtain of silk painted like a thick cloud" (383).[11] "At the approach of the King," this massive curtain "was instantly to be drawn" (383). Revealed beneath the curtain was a massive, ornate triumphal arch that Dekker describes as: "fiftie foote in the perpendicular, and fiftie in the ground lyne, the upper roofe thereof, one distinct gate, bore up the true moddells of all the notable houses, turrets, and steeples, within the Citie" (343). In describing his own invention, Jonson is both more concise and less specific: the uppermost part of the Londinium Arch "presented itself . . . like to the side of a City" (377). Bergeron's account gives the specifics that Jonson avoided, noting that the Arch "was fantastically decorated with the city of London carved in miniature on the top" (*English* 75) "miniature" being a relative term: the arch was crowned by a fifty-foot-wide painted portrait of the City of London. Jonson provided the name for this arch:

> [. . .] adorned with houses, towers, and steeples set off in prospective [sic]. Upon the battlements in a great capital letter was inscribed,
> **LONDINIUM;**
>
> (377)

Beneath this "prospective" rendering, "the battlements" of the arch were mounted with a formal cartouche bearing the title "Londinium," a second level of the Londinium Arch had two large chambers on either side, filled with musicians. These compartments flanked seven carved niches in which were placed small, emblematic statues. Below these, at the level of the arches themselves, were three full-sized niches. The illustration of the Londinium Arch shows Alleyn "with his arm raised in the central niche" in character as the Genius of the City (Gurr, *Playgoing* 9). Below Alleyn can be seen the costumed boy actor playing the only other speaking part in this pageant, *Thamesis*, the Thames River. But the most celebrated element of this arch was the enormous scale model of the City of London which crowned it. Though numerous spires reach up from the dense mass of houses and other structures packing the surface of the model, the easily recognizable form of

St. Paul's Cathedral dominates this representation of London's postmedieval "skyline."

This model of London offered James the spectacle of an idealized city, an abstract, Romanized space in contrast with the actual spaces of London. On this day, the latter space was filled with commoners crowding the streets for a glimpse of their monarch. James's entry procession is the first English civic pageant for which there exists a significant visual record, and the most remarkable and frequently discussed aspects of James's procession are the triumphal arches that were prepared by the pageants' "artificer," Stephen Harrison. This record is part of the particularly thorough set of published texts that document this event.

Others have provided significant re-presentations and narratives of James I's royal entry, so my goal here is not a re-telling of the event.[12] Instead, I want to focus on two aspects of this large scale triumph: James's performance, and the performance anxieties it produced in the three authors of the entry: Jonson, Harrison, and Thomas Dekker. A degree of chaos may indeed have marked the event, in the form of serial disruptions that seem to have been caused in no small measure by James himself. As a result, each of the publications associated with James's entry responds to this unanticipated chaos by restoring order to the performance, after the fact, in print.

Jonson and Harrison's Londinium Arch stands at the intersection of numerous avenues of early modern thought, urban experience, and cultural signification. As a physical object, it was an impermanent monument to both the past and the future of the city. This first arch represented London as reconceived via the city's Roman heritage, and in so doing the arch inaugurated a new (conceptual) space for the city. Indirectly, the arch demonstrated the power of London's theatre artists to mediate and direct the desires of London's royal and municipal authorities. But more visibly, the Londinium Arch served as a powerful precedent to "James's vision of a Romanized London," and the "frontispiece to the Jacobean era" (Baker 279, Parry 3), a potent visual signifier at the outset of the new king's reign.

Even a cursory consideration of Harrison's illustration suggests that the Londinium Arch was an object of considerable artisanal and artistic accomplishment. Bergeron's descriptions of the Londinium Arch are strongly positive, and even a cursory consideration of Harrison's illustration supports such statements as "highly embellished," "fantastically decorated," and "extravagant" (*English* 75, 78). However, the person who occasioned the effort on this and the other arches demonstrated considerably less interest than the artisans and artists may have hoped. The king's disinterest seems to have informed Dekker's anxious concern, expressed in a preface "To the Reader," not to

Figure 11: The Londinium Arch. From *The Arches of Triumph*, Harrison, 1604.
© The British Library. All Rights Reserved.

weary the king with "teadious Speeches." In these statements, as elsewhere in *The Magnificent Entertainment*, Dekker gives the distinct impression that he is working hard not to describe James as, quite simply, *bored*.

James I's bad behavior on the occasion of his own royal entry is infamous. The entry had been postponed for 10 months, from July 1603 to March 1604. Though this delay was initiated by a severe episode of the plague in London, it was due as well to James's fondness for hunting and antipathy to public appearances.[13] Historians and critics have often noted the king's sullen disregard on the occasion of the 1604 entry and at other public events, a critical tradition begun by James's contemporary chronicler, Arthur Wilson. Wilson's biography of James (1653) rarely lapses from unvarnished adulation for its subject, but one such lapse occurs early in the text.

Pausing to acknowledge James's abiding antisocial tendencies, Wilson notes that the king "did not *love* to be looked on" (12, emphasis in original). In describing this disaffection, Wilson draws, not for the last time, a distinction between James and Elizabeth: the new king "was not like his Predecessor, the late Queen of famous memory" (12). As Wilson further notes, James resented that on the occasion of his entry: "he must give his ears leave to suck in [the speakers'] gilded *Oratory*, though never so *nauseous* to the *stomach*." The passage continues:

> He endured this *days* brunt with *patience*, being assured he should never have such another [. . .]. But afterwards in his *publick* appearances (especially in his *sports*) the access of the people made him so impatient, that he often dispersed them with *frowns*, that we may not say with *curses*. (12-13, emphasis in original)

On the 15th of March 1604, audience members who anticipated an entry in the style of Elizabeth's, in which the monarch performed for and responded to the audience, would have found their expectations unfulfilled in James.

An anecdote from the days immediately prior to the entry further illustrates James's disposition. Based on an account provided by Dugdale in his text, *The Time Triumphant*, James intended to make a surreptitious outing to inspect the arches being built for his entry.[14]

> [O]ur heroicke King, hearing of the preparation to be great [. . .] was desirous for privately at his owne pleasure to visit them, and accompanied with his Queen in his coach, he came to the Exchange, there to see for their recreation; and thinkeing to passe unknowne, the wylie multitude perceiving something, began with such hurley-burly to run up and downe with such unreverent rashnes, as the people of the Exchange were glad to shut the staire dores to keep them out [. . .]. (413-4)

James, his presence discovered, sought refuge inside the Exchange, where the merchants were less frantic at his appearance. He praised the merchants for being "so well ordred and so civill one with the other," but James "discommended the rudeness of the multitude, who, regardles of time, place, or person, will be so troublesome" (Dugdale 414). The shock and excitement of those outside the Exchange might be understandable in response to such an unplanned first public appearance by the new king, but Dugdale supports James's rebuke of the multitude, saying simply: "it is his Highnes pleasure to be private" (414).

After scolding his fellow "Contrymen" for their "unreverent rash-nes," Dugdale provides advice for the people of London, suggestions for how to behave in the event of future chance encounters with the King: "when hereafter he comes by you [. . .] stand still, see all, and use silence" (414). This statement of protocol for the appropriate behavior in the event of spontaneous royal appearances serves as well for a description of the mode of reception that informed the construction of James's royal entry.[15]

Recent historians and critics variously note James's indifference on the occasion of his entry, often by way of comparison to Elizabeth's per-formance at her own entry. It may be accurate to observe, as Gail Kern Paster does, that "James disliked public shows far more than his politically canny predecessor" ("Idea" 48); and correspondingly, Bergeron observes that "James's role was much more passive" than Elizabeth's had been.

> This lack of responsiveness on James's part makes of the total theatri-cal experience something different from Elizabeth's coronation entry in which she engaged in a type of continuous dialogue with actors and audience. In London in 1604 the spectators had to settle for the mute presence of their sovereign.
>
> (*English* 75)

Nevertheless the difference between these two entries is not simply an issue of personal taste, certainly not naïveté on the part of James, an expe-rienced ruler who fancied himself an authority on kingship. Rather, this difference suggests a political design on the part of each sovereign, and the display of that design in performance.

Though "mute," James's presence was not uncommunicative: in a more strongly worded description of the sovereign's conduct, Parry notes that:

> James's haughty self-concern along with his dislike of crowds caused him to hasten tactlessly along the ceremonial way with a minimum of appreciation. He did not attend closely to the scenes or speeches, he did not address the people or show any evident delight. (21)

Though Jonson's two complex contributions paid particular "compliment to the royal intelligence" of this scholar-king, Parry concludes that "it is doubtful whether James had the patience to linger in thought before the display" (7). Peggy Phelan's description of the king, though, is the most succinct (and witty) of recent critical assessments: "James I, like many powerful men, had a short attention span" ("Numbering" 43).

However, it is in Goldberg's substantial study of Jacobean literature and politics that a critical insight into James's behavior is revealed. Goldberg's study explores "the unquestionable power of representation" (xiv). His comparison of these two famous entries opposes their performance strategies: "Whereas Elizabeth played at being part of the pageants, James played at being apart, separate" (31).

> Whereas Elizabeth kept hushing the crowd, attempting to make the progress totally a theatrical event involving the queen, her people, and their pageants, James stood aloof; for him to see was enough [. . .]. James displayed their subjection to his subjects, showed them their need for him and his aloofness from them. Indeed, his responses, insofar as he registered any, were negative, drawing back from his people, pointing to the difference, displaying boredom and fatigue, rather than Elizabeth's rapt attention. (31–2)

Just as it is difficult to imagine Elizabeth's enthusiastic display of affection for her people and her spoken responses to her pageants as entirely spontaneous, it is equally difficult to see James as merely the pawn of his own petulance. The detachment demonstrated by James is not merely the petulance of a self-involved king; James's conduct must be taken as, at least in part, a calculated performance. Thus, the king's self-display suggests that boredom itself served him as a representational strategy. James's boredom was an important aspect of the performance, perhaps the only aspect of the performance in which James himself actually performed.

I document James's boredom in order to illustrate the king's detached perspective on his own royal entry, as well as to mobilize some of the most significant issues pertaining to the spatial practices of early modern London. Stephen Greenblatt has famously observed that "[s]ocial actions are themselves always embedded in systems of public signification, always grasped, even by their makers, in acts of interpretation [. . .]" (*Renaissance* 5). James's boredom, whether a calculated pose or a sincere display of unaffected contempt, participated in the representational practices of his entry.

While the ostensible purpose of the work done by the aldermen, artists, and artisans of the City of London on this day was to create an "entertainment" that James would witness as a royal audience member, in the context of his self-fashioning performance, James himself was also very much on display. Bruce R. Smith articulates the complex audience relations in such a pageant.

> Regardless of how many thousands of bystanders were looking on, the real audience [. . .] was the monarch himself. What the mass audience saw in Renaissance pageants was a 'show' of the ruler watching a show. Built into the very social situation itself, then, was the juxtaposition of two planes of reality: the idealized world of the pageant and the real world of the human watchers. (225)

That James is situated in the context of this elaborate spectacle is the key to the self-fashioning properties at work in the performance. Critical valuations of self-fashioning, proceeding from Greenblatt's influential 1980 work, locate an author's "process of identity-formation" in that author's self-production in printed text (Montrose, *Purpose* 121). However, an important aspect of the power of early modern public pageants, such as that in which James appeared, was a capacity to act as self-fashioning *performances*. The occasion of James's 1604 entry served to present, and indeed *represent*, James to his audience. The theatrical performance displayed to the audience of Londoners was a complex one, variously composed of spoken text, painting, sculpture, written text (on the surface of the arches), architectural elements, and embodied performance. But however complex, the overriding goal of the event was to establish and make public James's new identity as "King of Great Britain," and to represent the power and authority inherent in this new identity.

   The new king was viewed in the context of his entry, and the audience's understanding of him informed by *their* relation to the entry. Orgel's 1991 study of court performance reinforces this point. That a pageant station like the Londinium Arch would have been seen by James was not the entire purpose of its construction: the royal performer "must be seen to see it" (*Illusion* 16). For this reason I suggest that James is both *presented* and *represented*. He was put on display for the audience of London, and his performance of an unwillingness to perform established in the streets of the city the king's power, status, and objectivity (presentation). Additionally, the *idea* of James and what James would mean in a cultural context was rehearsed in the course of the entry, a royal signification over and above the materiality of the king's body (representation).

   I describe James as "on display" rather than "in performance." Though he was both an audience for the event and part of the performance, James was nevertheless not an "actor" participating in that representation. As Goldberg stresses: "In James's entrance, he is the spectacle although hardly seen, and when seen, hardly offering himself to his viewers" (32). Instead, James allowed Alleyn to serve as his performance-surrogate, while James himself remained aloof. In the context of the emblematic, latinate pageant performances, Alleyn's Genius Urbis was available to the view of many while he was addressing himself to the king. At the king's bidding, Alleyn did what James would not: he performed. This *performance surrogation* makes a representational strategy out of what might otherwise be more casually termed "boredom."

Accordingly, James performed in much the same way that the arches did: he did not participate in the production of a "wonderfull spectacle" as did Elizabeth. Rather, James simply allowed himself to be observed; he made a spectacle of himself. James's "boredom" and self-separation from the events surrounding him constitute the representational corollary to Elizabeth's *platea*-like self-assertion in relation to her theatrical event. The spatial practices which allow one to perceive the world in instrumental terms as "other" to one's own space(s) can be seen to reflect the spatial practices of the *locus*.

As previously discussed, the spatial concepts developed by Weimann, particularly his much-quoted theorization of medieval performance practices, have led to a valuable vocabulary for the discussion of post-medieval performance. In this discussion, the terms *locus* and *platea* are key. Performance in the *platea* depends on an assertion of the "stage-as-stage" and the "cultural occasion" itself. The *locus*, by contrast,

> can be seen as a strategic approximation to the uses of perspectival form: it implicated the establishment of a topographically fixed locality. As in early modern cartography, the fixation itself, being in aid of knowledge and discovery, was instrumental in differentiating space and, thereby, separating the fixed place per abstraction from other localities.
>
> (*Author's Pen* 182).

In relation to Weimann's "instrumental" understanding of the representation of space, each of the arches that punctuated James's processional route can be seen to have constituted an imaginatively fixed narrative space that served as a *locus*, abstracting the space of the arch itself from the world of the audience and the "cultural occasion" of the entry.

James's accession procession was not a performance specifically *about* London. His entry was, instead, a sequence of visually dominated performances that, in sum, offered an elaborate representational spectacle of a re-conceived London. The practices of visually organized representation that emerged in late-sixteenth-century England briefly coexisted with the performance culture of medieval space. This coexistence produced hybrid spaces, performed and represented territories that relied on long-standing spatial traditions as much as emergent paradigms of space. The Londinium Arch is an example of the hybrid representational practices which would come to dominate London's discourses of theatre, visual culture, and urbanism. The model of London atop the first arch offered James the spectacle of an idealized city, "Londinium": an abstract *other city* in contrast with the space of the actual London in which the arch had been built—the latter, actual, space doubtless filled with commoners crowding the streets for a glimpse of their (bored) monarch.

The performance strategies on display in James's 1604 entry are the inverse of those that Orgel ascribes to the court masque. Orgel asserts that court masques as a form not only cannot be "dismissed as flattery" but that they are in fact "expressions of the age's most profound assumptions about the monarchy" (*Illusion* 40, 8). I would extend Orgel's argument to suggest that as often as the monarch turned to theatrical performance to authorize her or his rule, equally often did English audiences view all forms of theatre as expressive of the forms of power by which their lives were determined. The concepts that Orgel codifies for a particular instance are not exclusive to the court masque. Not only the masque but, more broadly, all monarchical appropriations of performance were profoundly expressive of the meaning of public power in early modern Europe.

Consequently, James's performance of public boredom was related to the court performance form, the masque. As Orgel describes masque performance:

> The climactic moment of the masque was nearly always the same: the fiction opened outward to include the whole court, as masquers descended from pageant car or stage and took partners from the audience. What the noble spectator watched he ultimately became. (*Illusion* 39)

James, though chief among the spectators in the streets of London, had no intention of becoming that which he beheld, one of the massed spectators of his entry. The goal of masque performance was to open outward and to *include* a specific community—the courtly elite. By contrast, the goal of performance in the case of James's royal entry was to remain closed and to *exclude* a general community-London's "preasing multitudes" of merchants and commoners (Dugdale 417). James's passive performance—or, performance of passivity—worked to create a distinction between the urban subject(s) and the objectified royal performer. In this case, objectification was a virtue, a privilege of royal power.

"TO THE READER."

The consideration of James's entry which follows attempts to navigate the vexed intersection of text and event by reading together the four published texts that discuss the entry, and by exploring the unavoidable conclusion that large portions of the material meant to be spoken during the entry were not performed, were in fact cancelled by James prior to or in the course of the performance.

I want to consider the "rhetorical occasion," in Logan's phrase, of the multiple publications that went to press following the event (251). These texts provide documentary evidence about the entry, but they do so in such a way as to signal their incommensurability with the event that they (ostensibly) document. Most explicitly, Dekker's text makes it clear that the material that he is publishing does not provide an accurate depiction of the events as they occurred. Instead, Dekker repeatedly states that he has composed an idealized version of the event, one that only occasionally offers an indirect glimpse—via apologies or corrections—of the entry as it had been performed and as he witnessed it. In fact, the impetus for publication of each entry text seems to proceed from its author's distinct perceptions of the event. Dekker is the only author to come close to stating that actual performance of the entry was so different from his expectations that he was prompted to publish his text in response. Jonson, Harrison, and Dugdale, all join Dekker at the print house, each variously moved to print by his own performance anxieties.

Julie Stone Peters makes the "very simple historical claim" that: "after print, performance was never the same" (4). While I make no effort to resist this claim, I must insist that it be seen as dialogic: print certainly had an effect on performance, but performance had an impact on print in this period as well. The relationship between these two early modern media was a variable, ambivalent one. The dialogic relations between performance and print bear strongly on the four records of James's entry into London, especially so given the critical history of the Jonson and Dekker texts. Each of these texts has been regarded, at different times by different authors, as "the text of the performance," an oversimplified conclusion to be sure. Relations between text and performance, as John Rouse has noted, are "subject to a fair degree of oscillation" (146).[16] While most audiences and readers conventionally think of theatre in terms of "productions 'of' a preexisting play text [. . .] [e]xactly what the word *of* means in terms of theories and practices is, however, far from clear" (Rouse 146, emphasis in original). As Weimann argues:

> For performers to use a text, even in the service of its mediation, is always an act of adapting it to materially given circumstances; the assimilation, therefore, is to something that is neither fully contained nor anticipated in the written representation itself. (*Author's* 17)

Dramatic performance is never a simple iteration of written drama.[17] The case of James's entry and its multiple, unreliable documentations begs Rouse's dramatic question: what is a "production of" really *of* anyway? Anthony Dawson, discussing editorial conjecture, describes the complexity of the early modern textual situation: "printed versions derive directly or indirectly from manuscripts, which, in turn, subtend and in sme cases derive from, perhaps represent, performance, though the only way we 'know' this [. . .] is through examining the printed versions" (33). Since manuscripts of Dekker and Jonson's pre-performance writing do not remain, readers of these texts must speculate critically about the after-the-fact relationship between these authors' quasi-dramatic publications and the performances that preceded them. The question is, what do these documents of a performance actually *document*?

Dekker's publication in particular is suspended between performance and text. Although this publication does indeed include the speeches that Dekker wrote for the occasion, it is not merely a "script." Rather, Dekker's text is an attempt to document the performance itself. Even more remarkable, Dekker informs his reader that this act of documentation is not transparent or objective. Dekker's address "To the Reader" (see below) explains that the motivation behind the creation of this text is an intent to re-write the performance. Dekker re-presents the events of 15 March 1604, "not as they were" but rather "as they should have been" (338). As a result, Dekker's text cannot be taken for granted as a reliable source for the events of the day. When the belief that this text is a transparent historical document is factored out, what remains is a text formed by the pressures exerted on it by performance.

Dekker provides a particularly complex example of the early modern "bifold authority" of text and performance, one in which the negotiation between these two forms of cultural production takes place not in performance but in print. While some form of script or scripts can be presumed to have preexisted the performance of James's entry, Dekker's printed text is written in response to—rather than in anticipation of—the performance.

Though much of contemporary critical discourse still considers only the one-way relationship between a preexisting dramatic text and a performance "of" it, Weimann's understanding of the text / performance relationship is conditioned by "mutually overlapping and interpenetrating" cultures of orality and literacy (*Author's* 9). Reading Dekker's *Magnificent Entertainment*, the reader encounters an author deploying text to mediate the contingencies of performance, adapting the "materially given circumstances" of performance in print. The uncontained, unanticipated conditions of this event were the preconditions of Dekker's publication.

Fredson Bowers states that Dekker sought the services of five different print houses "for maximum speed in producing a coronation *souvenir*" (231, emphasis added). Dekker's haste to make public his version of the event is reflected in the publications of Jonson and Harrison as well, a haste that I suggest bears a greater significance than Bowers admits. More than just a "souvenir," each of these texts seeks to recover a measure of its author's agency. Whatever each of these commoners may have imagined in advance, their intentions were overwhelmed on the day of performance by the peremptory authority of James. James's authority in performance was in tension with the representations of that authority, in text and architecture, by the three commoners. That tension is recuperated, even redoubled, in print.

In this overt tension between royal performer and documenting author(s), these texts are different from Mulcaster's document of Elizabeth's entry. Mulcaster's text was calculated to reinforce an idealized perception of the Queen and her performances during her entry. Though Mulcaster's text should not be taken for a "reliable, transparent, and objective record of the event," his text is "so insistently representational" that Mulcaster's clear intent was for his reader to believe that the text was indeed a reliable account (Logan 276).[18] The texts published by Dekker, Jonson, and Harrison in response to James's entry are not so insistently representational; rather, their own subjectivity is manifest.

As much as the written texts and visual display of James's entry served to fashion the new king's identity, so too did they serve in the identity formation of the king's subjects who labored in the execution of the performance. This condition reflects Greenblatt's claim that self-fashioning is a "resolutely dialectical" practice (1). Subsequent to the performance of the king's entry, each of the three artists who were together responsible for the conception, poetry, and design of the extravagant pageants rushed to record in print "an idealized account of the royal entry which was in actuality a rather chaotic affair" (Parry 4). Each of these accounts stands as a kind of monument to its author's own self-identity, as represented in relation to the author's contributions to the construction of James's identity. Though not all of the texts overtly record the king's boredom, each text indirectly documents the author's confrontation with James.

Dekker's text is a calculated response to the chaos of the "affair," a text that clearly seeks to restore order to the performance by reproducing it in print. James's influence on the performance of the entry is recorded at the outset of Dekker's printed text.

To the Reader.

> Reader, you must understand that a regard being had that his Majestie should not be wearied with teadious Speeches, a great part of those which are in this booke set downe were left unspoken; so that thou doest here receive them as they should have been delivered, not as they were. (338)

Dekker's opening caveat emphatically problematizes the relationship between texts and events in literary history. His address "To the Reader" serves as a suitable preface for all three of the collaborators' published documents: he makes it clear that these texts are an effect of performance.[19] The numerous critical studies of James's entry that offer text-based "readings" of the event are ultimately troubled to the degree that they fail to incorporate, let alone acknowledge, an understanding of the opacity of the performed event, however rewarding may be the product of a literary interpretation that privileges the published document to the exclusion of other considerations.[20]

Dekker was, as Graham Parry notes, "the principal pageant master" for the entry (9), and it was to Dekker that the most important portion of the pageant was assigned. Lawrence Manley describes this part of the route as "the City's main ceremonial route" ("Sites" 44). As Manley observes of Dekker's contributions to the entry: "[T]he series of pageant stations along this route defines a ceremonial crescendo, as the king passes from the 'great hall' of Cornhill to the 'presence chamber' of Cheapside to the 'closet' or rather the privy chamber framed by the passage from the Little Conduit into St Paul's Churchyard" ("Sites" 44). Though Dekker did not set this traditional route, he describes the entire progress in relation to an architectural conceit (synopsized by Manly in the preceding quote). According to this conceit, the audiences of the entry pass through a metaphorical sequence of increasingly intimate interior rooms, until finally joining the king in his private "presence chamber," before exiting London—the city as a whole reconceived as a "royal palace"—at Temple Bar. In order to reinforce his authority over this event, Dekker has composed his text to be read as the "official" record of the entry, in which he applies defining terms even to pageant stations that he did not compose.

Though Dekker's account was not the first to arrive at a London printing house, it is the most complete record of the day. Occasionally, Dekker provides his "Reader" with some restrained guidance regarding the relationship between the published text and the actual, performed event of James's entry. Most notably, early in the text, Dekker records the brevity of James's attention to the Londinium Arch. Dekker concludes his (already terse) coverage of the Londinium Arch:

> Too short a time (in theire opinions that were glewed there together so many houres to behold him) did his Majestie dwell upon this first place; yet too long it seemed to other happy spirits, that higher up in these Elizian fields awaited for his presence. He sets on therefore (like the sunne in his Zodiaque) bountifully dispersing his beames amongst particular Nations [. . .]. (344-5)

In what may be a subtle aggravation of their rivalry, Dekker notes that James gives little attention to one of Jonson's arches, and moves on toward Dekker's arches in the same way that the sun moves across the globe (forecasting the tropes of global mapping in Dekker's own New World Arch).

For Dekker, the principal purpose of his text of the *Entertainment* was to provide its author a belated compensation: it is an attempt to reconcile in print the inadequacies of the performance by reconstructing the pageant performances "as they should have been," favorably displaying his own work.

Dekker writes his re-presentation of the event in the present tense, describing each pageant station and its associated performances from the point of view of James himself, even indicating the direction in which James should turn his gaze for the fullest appreciation of each arch. Such narrational "stage directions" relate the reader to the point of view (in a literal sense) of James himself. This relation of reader and royal spectator, along with Dekker's "To the Reader" confession, make this a personal document in which Dekker records a public, royal event, but does so as the result of his own private and professional motivations.

Immediately following the "To the Reader" apologia that opens his account, Dekker spends four pages describing a theatrical scene intended as a prologue of sorts to the entire *Entertainment*, welcoming James on his arrival to the City two days before the actual entry procession itself. This theatrical scene was to have been "performed about the Barres beyond Bishopsgate" (Dekker 338). Mullaney notes that this kind of performance was a familiar civic form:

> In keeping with the conventions of the Roman Triumph as transformed and elaborated by the Renaissance, it had become customary for a monarch and his procession to pause outside the city gates, on the threshold of the community, at that tenuous point where royal domain shaded into civic jurisdiction.
>
> (*Place* 70).

In Dekker's account of this erstwhile civic welcome, the patron saints of Scotland and England, Andrew and George, arrive outside the Tower of London, coincident with James's arrival on the scene. There they are met by a female character, Genius Loci, who welcomes the two saints and praises the countries they represent, now united in James. Dekker's description of this unperformed scene is preceded by an acknowledgement: "*A Device (projected downe, but till now not publisht) that should have served at his Majestie's first Accesse to the Cittie*" (338, italics in original). Following the description, Dekker provides some reason as to why the scene may have been "projected downe," or not made public: "This should have been the first offring of the Cittie's love; and his Majestie not making his entrance according to expectation, it was (not utterly throwne from the altar, but) layd by" (341). Dekker seems to be choosing his words carefully, and perhaps also trying to assuage his own disappointment; as a result the distinction he makes between between "throwne from" and "layd by" is not entirely clear. Based on this line, and the ambiguous statement about James's failure to make his entrance as planned, it would seem that Dekker himself was surprised that the "Device" of Andrew and George was not performed, for, if its chief audience did not attend, one cannot perform an occasional event without the very individual who would have occasioned and authorized such a performance.

Though Dekker remains deferent, he places responsibility for the failure to perform on James. Wilson notes that James had just returned from his "private *recreations*" and "*hunting* exercises abroad," "banqueting and feasting" (12), which may suggest that he simply chose not to view the piece: rather than the condemnatory violence suggested by "thrown from" it may be that James simply rode quickly past the place at which he was meant to stop and witness this scene. In this way the scene may have been idly, even unknowingly, set aside or "layd by."

However nuanced his explanation for this cancellation, Dekker's second apology reinforces the impression that James was not a reliable audience member, or more appropriately, not a reliable co-performer. Dekker even invokes the language of the stage in his description of this mishap, describing James as though he were an actor who failed to enter on cue. This suggests that Dekker is well aware of the dual role that James was expected to play: chief among spectators, yet also the actor whose performance was essential to the theatrical enterprise. The peremptory cancellation of the civic prologue to the entry entertainment set a notable precedent for the subsequent performance.

Reading Dekker's qualifiers and explanations regarding the unperformed Andrew / George device, one is led to wonder how much of *The Magnificent Entertainment* itself was "left unspoken" or unperformed under similar, peremptory circumstances. James and his entourage may well have dismissed, or "layd by" a performance, simply by departing prematurely from the pageant prepared for them. Dekker's opening scene was "not publisht" in the sense that it did not receive the performance its author anticipated, and therefore was not available to the public until it appeared in print. I might be inclined to agree with Parry and Phelan, and dismiss James as merely callous and attention-deficient. However, there is agency in the king's boredom. However casual or passive was James's failure to enter on cue, this act "censored" the performance. Two days later, during the entry itself, if James simply rode past a pageant station, the performance prepared for that site would similarly have been "layd by" in his absence.

Indeed, James's presence was represented as "the animating force" that conferred meaning on the pageants, and in many cases brought them from dormancy to activity (Goldberg 32, 31). Clouds were lifted, fountains flowed, bleak landscapes were restored, and figures of blight banished with the arrival of the king. Such forms of theatrical representation have pragmatic counterparts: with the arrival of James, actors entered, speeches began, musicians played—these were occasional performances and James himself was the occasion. As a corollary, James's absence would have had a deleterious consequence on the performers. While there is no record of disruption at any other pageant station, we do have the text of Dekker's unperformed welcoming piece, written as if it had occurred in the same present tense as the rest of the text. This rhetorical device represents James *as present*; though James himself did not perform, where James was not, there was no performance.

Rather than the conventional, emblematic encounter between St. George and St. Andrew that Dekker had prepared for his arrival, James arranged his own entertainment on a similar theme: the brutal animal combat in the Tower was a performance more suited to James's idea of kingship and country.

According to the Stationer's Register, Jonson's record of his contribution to James's entry arrived in print before Dekker's. While Dekker's title was registered on 2 April 1604, Jonson's text was entered into the Register on 19 March 1604, just four days after the actual performance of the entry itself (Bowers 231). In another evidence of haste, "Jonson's quarto had been published in an uncorrected state, presumably to catch the topical interest" (Dutton 25), though Jonson made corrections and revisions to his contributions to the entry for inclusion in his 1616 Folio.

Although Dekker gives Middleton credit for the single speech that the latter writer contributed to the Entertainment, and effusively praises Harrison for his contributions, Dekker "does not mention Jonson by name, and a slight airiness may perhaps be detected in his very brief summaries of the substance of Jonson's elaborately written speeches" (Bowers 246). What Bowers describes as "slight airiness" certainly could be seen as evidence of the alleged quarrel between the two writers. Though Dekker provides a substantial description of the appearance of Jonson's pageant stations, he refers to Jonson's text in extremely abbreviated form: in both cases, Dekker provides only a short, paraphrased summary of the general theme of Jonson's pageant. Dekker might simply to be curtailing an account of Jonson's performance in order to save time and space, knowing that his "Reader" would have access to Jonson's contributions in that writer's own publication. However, Dekker makes no reference to Jonson or the availability of his already printed account. This omission is in contrast with the friendly credit given to Middleton and with Dekker's praiseful (if indirect) advertisement for Harrison's as yet unpublished collection of illustrations and texts documenting the latter's contribution to the *Entertainment*:

> But an excellent hand being at this instant curiously describing all the Seven [arches], and bestowing on them their faire prospective limmes, your eye shall hereafter rather be delighted in beholding those Pictures, than now be wearied in looking upon mine. (344)

Though here again Dekker declines to name one of the other contributors to the entry, the omission here is of a different sort. This is the omission of someone sharing inside information and building anticipation, not the dismissive summary that coldly serves as a place holder for the text of a rival author whom Dekker refuses to name. Whereas Jonson's text of the event asserts its own authority through a strategy of sweeping *exclusion* (see below),

Dekker pursued a strategy of limited *inclusion*. Dekker notes Jonson's contributions-along with those of Harrison and Middleton-but does so only in the most limited of ways. For example, Dekker does mention, in strongly positive terms, Alleyn's performance as Genius of the City: "His gratulatory Speech [. . .] was delivered with excellent action, and a well-tuned audible voyce" (344). This statement is notable in that it is the sole piece of evidence that would seem to confirm that at least one part of the *Entertainment* was performed and could be heard by James and others in the audience of Londoners. But even in this context, Dekker, who goes out of his way to provide a complete document of the event (however idealized) at every opportunity, does not quote directly from Jonson (whose text was widely available, should Dekker have wanted to quote from it); instead Dekker merely paraphrases in a single sentence the general idea of each of Jonson's two pageant texts, abruptly concluding each paraphrase with "&c"—the only uses of "etceteras" in the text (344, 374).

Jonson's text stands in contrast with Dekker's *Magnificent Entertainment*. Though both provided "permanent record of a transient show" (Parry 7), the latter reads like the final element in an auspicious civic commission, concluding as it does with a record of the various "*Committees*" who served as "Overseers and Surveyors" of the preparations-further examples of Dekker's inclusive approach (Nichols 375-6). By contrast, Jonson's text, which he called *The Royal and Magnificent Entertainment*, includes only his own "devices," and reads rather like a spectacular "advertisement of his own advanced skills in iconography" (Parry 7). To give Jonson credit, two of the three arches he designed were prominently placed, and though not in fact assigned to the most important traditional locations in the ceremonial space of London, Jonson's arches have come to be regarded as the defining features of the entry.[21] Jonson conceived the devices and wrote accompanying text for the first and last arches within the space of the City of London itself, and as well the "Pegme in the Strand," an architecturally less sophisticated pageant produced by the City of Westminster (396).

Entered in the Stationers Register on 19 March 1604, Jonson's publication was the first of the four texts documenting James's entry to reach print. Perry suggests that: "it is not surprising that Dekker and Jonson and Harrison each published a detailed report of his own devisings so that they could be studied and deciphered at leisure" (Perry 3). "[S]tudy" and "leisure" seem not to have motivated Dekker, whose document begins by announcing its performance anxieties and textual frustrations, while Harrison accounts for his textual urges by reference to the ephemeral performance for which his arches were designed. In a dedication addressed to the Lord Mayor and the Aldermen, dated 16 June 1604, Harrison explains:

> That magnificent Royalty and glorious Entertainement, which you yourselves for your part, out of a free, a cleare, and verie bountous disposition, and so many thousands of woorthie Citizens, out of a sincere affection and loyalty to his Majestie, did with the sparing of no cost, bestowe *but upon one day*, is here newe wrought up againe, and shall endure for ever; for, albeit those Monuments of your Loves were erected up to the cloudes, and were built never so strongly, yet now their lastingnes should live but in the tongues and memories of men, *but that the hand of Arte gives them here a second more perfect beeing*, advanceth them higher than they were before, and warrants them that they shall doe honour to this Citie, so long as the Citie shall beare a name. (331, emphasis added)

Harrison's dedication to London's municipal authorities makes clear that the fleeting conditions of performance, particularly one-time-only civic performances, motivated his publication to find "lastingnes," and even a "more perfect being," in print. Dugdale, too, can be seen to position his publication as a record of his own fleeting, subjective perceptions along with the unofficial encomiums that he or some other Londoner performed (see below).

Contrary to Parry's opinion, which shares a measure of Bowers's oversimplified notion of the "souvenir," Jonson's work alone of the three makes no reference to the contingencies of performance. This exception was a consistent feature of Jonson's work, and reflects its author's enthusiasm for the print house. Kastan asserts that: "Ben Jonson was different. Writing within the same professional conditions as did Shakespeare, Jonson assiduously worked to become a man in print" (*After* 76). This work is what Loewenstein calls the development of Jonson's "bibliographical ego" (1). In his publication, Jonson is trying to present a stable text, whereas the publications of Dekker, Harrison, and Dugdale, by contrast, are trying to stabilize a performance.[22]

Kastan notes Jonson's display of textual anxiety in the opening epistle to *Sejanus*, where Jonson admits to rewriting the play to expunge the authorial interventions of the playhouse:

> Belatedly, Jonson becomes the play's sole author, systematically erasing the hand of his collaborator, substituting new lines never played, in order to present to his readers a text that is his own, one indeed 'Written

by Ben; Ionson,' as the title-page says, rather than the play that was actually played in London. (*After* 77)

It is no surprise then that in his text of the entry Jonson makes no reference to James's expurgations and unexpected behaviors. Jonson's concern is to erase the "chaos" of the day's events, even James's role as collaborator in the entry, asserting instead Jonson's own identity as sole author of the entry-an assertion that suppresses the authorial function of even the king himself.

In the context of Jonson's habits of authorial self-assertion, consider the full title that Jonson gave to the quarto of 19 March 1604.

B. JON:

HIS PART OF

King James his Royall and Magnifi-cent *Entertainment through his*

Honorable Cittie of London,

Thurseday the 15. of
March. 1603.[23]

It is likely, given a date of publication that so closely follows the date of the entry itself (just four days later), that Jonson anticipated his own desire to see the erudite language of his pageant poetry in print, where his latinate emblems and references would have a more apt audience among readers than amid the throngs. Jonson may have been at work throughout the months in which the entry was delayed, preparing his manuscript for print well before its performance.[24] By the time of the entry itself, of course, James had already held his coronation. Though Jonson's 1616 title records the traditional order of events—certainly the order of events as they had been performed at Elizabeth's royal entry and coronation in 1559—it does not record the events as they actually occurred in James's case (the delay that caused consternation for the City and its brigade of entertainers did not inhibit James from taking power). Further, the "1603" date on the title page implies preparation for the first date planned for James, and a later emendation to reflect the actual date of the entry: the bottom of the page clearly reads, "Printed at London by V.S. for edward Blount, 1604." Perhaps this dating is the residue of a first draft of the *Entertainment*, one which may have been begun as soon as James's succession was proclaimed but before the unconventional ordering of the royal ceremonies (coronation before entry) was determined. The dates of print and performance on the title page of Jonson's quarto straddle the time between James's coronation and his access to the City of London, and would seem to suggest advance preparation for print on Jonson's part.

Jonson's printed text provides an extremely detailed account of his own contributions, though not a minute description of the appearance of the three pageants that he provided; for a significant description of the visual aspects of Jonson's contributions to the entry, one must turn to Dekker and Harrison. Not surprisingly, Jonson places an emphasis on the poetry which would have accompanied the triumphal arches, inaugurating a "*poesis*" over "*pictura*" bias that would mark, and mar, Jonson's relations with court performance for years to come.[25] In the way that it privileges writing over spectacle, print over performance, Jonson's *Royal and Magnificent Entertainment* is even more persistently addressed "To the Reader" than is Dekker's text.

Consider the title itself. Though abbreviated, Jonson's name appears on its own line, in a boldface, italicized type that is bigger than the type in which the words "King James" and "London" appear. Only the words "HIS PART OF" appear with greater visual force. That Jonson should see fit to place his own name by itself, with great typographical emphasis, on the first line of a text prepared for James's royal entry and paid for by the City of London, demonstrates not only remarkable audacity but an impetuous desire to assert his authorial identity in textual form; indeed, by assigning greatest prominence to the titling of the "PART" itself, Jonson makes the writing itself the headlining star of this publication. Dutton notes that Jonson "adopts for the first time here the distinctive spelling of his name, Jonson without an 'h,' by which he is known to posterity" (23). The introduction of a distinctive, idiosyncratic name for himself only reinforces the significance of this work in Jonson's self-image.[26]

In the case of a civic event that engaged both royal authority and that of the City, in a medium that—by virtue of its material conditions of performance—placed an even greater emphasis on *pictura* over poetry than did the masque, on his title page Jonson can be seen to be erasing a greater set of collaborators than would adhere to any product of the playhouse. As Joseph Loewenstein has claimed more generally for Jonson: "Publication completes the displacement of the performers both as a representational and as an economic fact" ("Script" 271–2). In this case, Jonson's assertion of authorship over *Sejanus* seems trivial by comparison to the erasure of king, collaborators, performers, and performance in *The Royal and Magnificent Entertainment*.

There is only one point at which Jonson makes an elliptical reference to the performance event itself, but this point is a particularly telling revelation of the author's textual anxieties. Following his description of the Londinium

Arch's physical appearance, and immediately before the text of the dialogue between Genius of the City and Thamesis, Jonson includes an extended passage in which he offers a theory of representation.

> *[T]he symbols used are not, neither ought to be, simply hieroglyphics, emblems, or impresses, but a mixed character, partaking somewhat of all, and peculiarly apted to these more magnificent inventions, wherein the garments and ensigns deliver the nature of the person, and the word the present office. Neither was it becoming, or* [sic] *could it stand with the dignity of these Shews, after the most miserable and separate shift of the puppets, to require a truch-man, or, with the ignorant Painter, one to write, "This is a Dog," or "This is a Hare;" but so to be presented, as upon the view they might, without cloud or obscurity, declare themselves to the sharp and learned; and for the multitude, no doubt but their grounded judgments did gaze, said it was fine, and were satisfied.*
> (383, italics in original)

Particularly in relation to the Londinium Arch—surmounted as it was by a realistic portrait of the City of London, which was placed above a staged dialogue between allegorical figures—Jonson's statement provides some explanation for the "mixed character" of the representation at work in this and other arches. Jonson draws on aspects of the English emblematic tradition, while also dismissing any presentational devices, such as explanatory titles or an interpreter ("*truchman*"). He is well aware of the "state and magnificence" and more specific architectural features that are "proper to a Triumphal Arch" (383), yet he does not hesitate to adorn classical Roman forms with names and designs drawn from London's geography, or indeed even with a representation of the city itself. The classical examples that Jonson references (both textual and architectural) do not admit realistic representations of city images into the visual "rhetoric" of the arch form. And Jonson's statement would not likely be an after-the-fact justification for an arbitrary creative process: as already noted, Jonson's text appeared in print so soon after the entry itself that there would have been little opportunity to adjust the manuscript, confirming that this theoretical passage must have been prepared in advance. In fact, this passage is a carefully considered articulation of Jonson's plan for the arches, and for the Londinium Arch in particular. What Jonson describes as "mixed character" provides a suitable description of the representational strategy of this and other arches, a contemporary theoretical statement about spatial hybridity.

Notably, despite the efforts of these two writers to articulate themselves in print, the Dekker-Jonson entry rivalry found its conclusion, not in textual authority but rather in a municipal one. By mid-May, Dutton notes:

Jonson's publisher, Edward Blount, was forced by the Stationers' Company to surrender all the remaining copies of his stock to Dekker's publisher, Thomas Mann Jr. The legal basis of this is unclear, unless Dekker was able to argue that his commission from the City authorities to publish an account of the day's proceedings precluded Jonson's right to print his own contributions [. . .]. (25)[27]

A rivalry that had begun in performance and was pursued in print ultimately was decided by the authority of the City, the very authority with which Dekker had allied himself. At this early point in his career, Jonson was "attempting," as Joseph Loewenstein has observed, "to extricate himself from the confused literary market of the public theaters and to insert himself into what might be called a [. . .] patronage market" ("Script" 270). Though his publication was curtailed, given the prestigious court commissions that were soon to follow, it seems that Jonson succeeded in entering the "patronage market," despite his setback in popular publishing. To the degree that the publication of his part in the entertainment supported his subsequent work for an elite clientele, the confiscation of the remaining copies may have been more or less immaterial to him.

Bergeron notes that: "No English pageant previously studied is so dependent on triumphal arches as this one, and they are highly embellished architectural achievements, the details of which are fortunately preserved in Harrison's drawings" (*English* 75); and elsewhere: Harrison "'performs' in his book a work of art the likes of which the country has not seen before" (*Practicing* 179). Nor was the historic significance of his achievement lost on Harrison himself. His dedication of his *The Arches of Triumph* to the Lord Mayor and the aldermen of London states:

> I would not care if these unpainted pictures were more costly to me, so that they might appear curious enough to your Lordship and Worships; yet in regard that this present age can lay before you no president that ever any in this land performed the like, I presume these my endevours shall receive the more worthie liking of you. (331)

To his due credit, the illustrations in Harrison's text provide a sense of the extraordinary emphasis on the visual in James's entry, as commanded by the arches and their accompanying pageants.

Given that we know nothing of Harrison's career beyond his contribution to the entry and his publication of "the most extensive pictorial record of a street pageant in the Tudor-early Stuart era" (Bergeron, *Practicing* 168), it is difficult even to begin to estimate his role as an "author" of the arches in a reliable way. Harrison's contribution to the entry is known from his own publication and from Dekker's generous reference to him at the conclusion of *The Magnificent Entertainment*:

> Stephen Harrison, Joyner [. . .] who was the sole inventor of the architecture, and from whom all directions, for so much as belonged to carving, joining, molding, and all other worke in those five Pageants of the Citie (Paynting excepted) were set downe. (376)

Dekker's phrase "the sole inventor of the architecture" strongly implies that Harrison made a significant contribution to the physical features of the entry. In D.J. Gordon's study of Jonson, Jones, and the masque, the words "inventor" and "invention" emerge as terms indicating creative responsibility for "the whole dramatic fable" and not just for building the physical expression of that fable (81). Though Dekker's use of the term "inventor" may have been more loose than that of Jonson, what is known of the flexible production conditions that surrounded both public and coterie theatrical production in the period suggests that Harrison's contribution may have taken many forms: executing detailed instructions; or, elaborating on limited, general remarks from a dramatist; or, even initiating the conception of one or more of the arches himself. Based on a study of *The Arches of Triumph*, Bergeron argues that the illustrations[28] and descriptions in Harrison's document "indicate a sophistication that we usually associate with Jones and the masques" ("Introduction" 180). In the absence of more extensive, specific documentation, this acknowledgement would seem to mark the limit of what can be said of Harrison—his career in general and his contribution to James's entry in particular—without undue speculation.[29]

But in a departure from his usual mode of informed text analysis and discussion of the historical record, Bergeron interjects a theoretical claim on behalf of Harrison, asserting that in Harrison's designs, "[s]ymbol and reality meet in a real-world urban setting: art appropriates the setting that it occupies" (*Practicing* 180). The occupation of a specific site, the appropriation of its given identity, and the destabilization of a location's conventional meanings are all effects of the interaction that Bergeron briefly sketches: the conflict between the representational space of the city and the representation of (urban) space on display in the first of Harrison's arches. The representation of space in a "real-world urban setting" projected the desire to reconceive the existing space in terms of the spaces and concepts of the "Renaissance," concepts that "honored classical precedent and the aristocratic platform of its learned recovery" (Weimann, *Author's* 186), producing spaces that were as yet unrealized in the physical topography of 1604 London. This interaction of urban representation and real-world city contributed to, in Lefebvre's classic terminology, "the production of a space. Not merely the space of ideas [. . .] but a social and a mental space. An *emergence*" (260).[30] Though it was only one among seven pageant stations, the "Londinium Arch" stands as the most *productive* (Lefebvre's sense) of the arches prepared by the City for James's entry.

The hybrid representational form exemplified by the Londinium Arch draws on traditions of London civic performance while it appropriates "Renaissance" representational forms. For all the vigor of his engagement with the pressure of print, Jonson's theory of representation relies on visual recognition. Live performance is the presumed medium in which his hybrid practices of spectacle and civic performance are to be appreciated. It is "*the view*" of "*the sharp and learned*" that conveys information about the pageants. And even "*the multitude*" would find their limited appreciation for the shows of the entry in their "*gaze*" not their hearing. Jonson's awareness that the visual is essential to the medium of the civic performance is incorporated into this statement of his representational agenda, even though his own primary contribution to this performance was for the aural medium of oral performance. Jonson's expectation that some of his texts would not be fully appreciated (or even audible) in performance necessarily gains urgency in this passage on representation. Jonson describes the visual aspects of civic pageantry as the "*complimental part*" of the performance, the correlatives to the spoken word (383). Making that incompletely received text available to an audience as soon as possible has as much to do with Jonson's theory of representation as with his own vanity as an author: for Jonson, the "complimental" relationship between words and images was not guaranteed in the noisy chaos of civic pageant. Without both parts, the whole would fail to be meaningful. Only by making the verbal component of his work available to those who saw but could not hear on 15 March could Jonson ensure that the representational circuit would be closed.[31] The hybridization of visual and textual practices marks the Londinium Arch (even in its name), provides a guide to other arches in this entry, and serves as a paradigm of the hybrid spatial practices of this transitional period in London's history.

How are we to understand the particularly vexed relationship between event and text posed by any consideration of James's entry? An unknown amount of the poetic text written for the occasion was officially excluded in advance, and more was consigned to silence on the day itself when the king simply passed by locations where he was to have stopped. Moreover, the material conditions of such a city-spanning "mega-event" [32] would generate the noisy chaos of "a world of people" (Dekker 342), conditions that must have favored visual aspects of performance rather than oratory. Only on one occasion does Dekker specifically report the audibility of a performer: an actor of Alleyn's stature may have been able to command some measure of silence, enough for Dekker to speak of his "well-tuned audible voyce" (344). In general, though, Dugdale reports that "the noyse of the showe" was great (417). Those parts of the pageants which Dugdale can describe are based almost entirely on what he could see.

Dugdale's publication, *The Time Triumphant*, is valuable as an "eyewitness account" (Bergeron, *Practicing* 147), though apart from occasionally being able to hear "musique of all sorts" (416), Dugdale reports no speech that coincides with or even resembles any material from the published texts of Dekker or Jonson. In fact, the two speeches that Dugdale does provide are remarkable for their complete lack of resemblance to any of the poetry or performances provided by or described in Dekker or Jonson's texts. Dugdale gives the remarkably complete text of a performance by "an old man with a white beard, of the age of three-score and nineteen" (416); while in other cases, Dugdale can do no more than identify that "an Oration" was taking place in the distance (419). According to Dugdale, this performance by the "old man" was received no better than many of those reported by the professional playwrights: it was ignored by the king, who passed by, unseeing. Dugdale describes this incident:

> But the narrow way and the preasing multitude so overshadowd him [the old man], and the noyse of the showe, that oppertunitie was not favorable to him, so that the King past by; yet noting his zeale, I have publiquely imprinted it, that all his fellow subjectes may see this olde man's forwardnes, who mysit of his purpose by the concourse of people; beside the King apointed no such thing, but at several stays and appointed places. (Dugdale 417)

This coda follows eighteen lines of poetry delivered by the "old man," which is remarkable, given that Dugdale could provide not a single word from Jonson or Dekker. This situation is peculiar enough to prompt Nichols to conclude that Dugdale "was, probably, himself the 'old man with a white beard' [. . .]" (419 n1).[33]

Whatever the identity of the performer who delivered this text, Dugdale's elaborate justification for its publication is remarkable. Though Dugdale shows no remorse for the many speeches he did not hear, or heard but omitted from his record, he includes the full text delivered by the old man and shows great empathy for the fact that his "zeale" should have been overlooked by the king. In this qualification, Dugdale shares with the other authors an anxiety over the king's relationship to the performances. Editing, omission, exclusion, censorship, noise, boredom: whatever the reason a text or performance may have been overlooked on the day of the entry, Dugdale joined Dekker and Jonson in seeking recourse to print in response to royal oversight. Dugdale's explanation for seeking to record his experience of the entry in print would serve as well for Dekker and Jonson: Dugdale "publiquely imprinted" a text which had not received adequate acknowledgement when it was first publicly performed for James.

Dugdale's performance (whether he himself performed it, or has simply appropriated it in print) was neglected under circumstances similar to those of Dekker's planned dialogue: it was "layd by" because "the King apointed no such thing." Whether or not a given performance was planned in advance, the places and performances of the entry were clearly subject to James's will (and whim), as much in the case of Dekker, the pageant master, as in the case of Dugdale- a pageant admirer, an active audience member, but ultimately just another urban subject whose identity is produced in performances and texts that remain peripheral.

In the midst of this city-shaping theatrical event, other performers (famous and peripheral) may have been walking among the liveried servants and retainers of the new king. William Shakespeare, as a member of a theatre company newly renamed under the patronage of the king, would have been entitled—perhaps obligated—to walk the streets of London in the royal train.[34] He and Burbage could have exchanged critiques of Alleyn's performance, and discussed the relative merits of the contributions made by Dekker and Jonson—if they could have heard anything. Some of Shakespeare's own urban representations and spatial productions will be considered in the next chapter. At this point, it is enough to assert that Shakespeare himself would have seen at first hand the Londinium Arch, observed the architectural and textual monuments prepared for James, and walked the streets of a city "doubled" by this urban performance: a Londinium, suspended between the physical space of the postmedieval town and the representational space of an idealized city: "Londinium," a multivalent collection of London's real-and-imagined spaces.

LONDINIUM: CAMERA REGIA

In Chapter One, I set out to trace a genealogy of texts and performances that suggest the ways in which the city serves as the fragmentary repository of its own histories. One of the premises of *City / Stage / Globe* is that, though performance may have a material effect on physical space, the trace of that effect remains elusive. As Thomas Postlewaite has put it, "theater is an art form that disappears" (171), though Schneider argues that rather than disappearance, the condition of performance might be better described as given to "messy and eruptive reappearance" (103).[35] This study seeks to theorize the disappearances and reappearances of postmedieval performance in order to better understand the emergent urban spaces in early modern London.

The Londinium Arch provides example of the ways in which each of these authors sought to transcend the constraints imposed by the various forces at work in this event and to re-negotiate his own agency as an urban subject. Though Dekker notes that Alleyn's performance was commendable (344), for an eyewitness in the audience on the occasion of James's entry, there is little doubt that the arches contributed by Harrison would have been the dominating force in the event. Not only would they have been less vulnerable to last-minute censoring than the authors' texts, or to the king's peremptory disregard as were the actors' speeches, the arches would likely have been more fully appreciated by the audience of this performance. Although "the preasing multitude" might have temporarily "overshadowed" an audience member's view of one of the arches (Dugdale 417), all seven of the arches were standing by the time of James's arrival in the City (13 March 1604) and remained standing even after he had passed on to Westminster.

James's accession progress was remarkable, and not just for the arches or the sovereign's indifference. Bergeron sees the 1604 pageant for James as "a pivotal moment in civic pageantry" (*English* 89) and "a turning point, unlike those that had preceded it and determinant of the form for those that follow" ("Introduction" 8). In a consonant observation, Sydney Anglo locates James's coronation procession in an entirely different historical and aesthetic category from Elizabeth's, the former owing "little to its Tudor and much to its continental forebears" (5). I, too, see the 1604 royal entry as setting a precedent for the future of politicized public performance in early modern London, a telling reflection of the cultural shift that would become so visible during the course of the Stuart reign. An incremental but important shift had taken place in the use and representation of urban space. An understanding of space that was beginning to appear on the continent when Elizabeth entered London had become, by 1604, an important new form championed in England by members of a continental cognoscenti, such as James and the artists who conceived his entry.

Amidst the sculpture adorning the Londinium Arch, James was met with a globalizing representation of his rule (not for the first time). The emblematic figure *"Monarchia Britannica"* bore "in her lap a little globe" inscribed with the words: "Orbis Britannicus" (Jonson 378, formatting as per original). This appearance of *orbis* in a performance structure otherwise dominated (visually as well as conceptually) by *urbis* is not surprising. The space represented here was "a world separated from the world" (Jonson 378), a microcosm of the macrocosm, a physical representation of the *orbis / urbis* spatial dualism. The Londinium Arch served as a stage for the performance of the commensual relationship between the space of the city and the space of the globe.

At James's approach, the sheet of clouds covering the arch lifted. When describing the revelation of this stage, Jonson is careful to note that the clouds lifting from the Arch are those of a London that had been longing to see its king, but the effect of this theatrical device would seem to be just the reverse: it was not the king who was revealed to London, but rather (a representation of) London that was revealed to the king. Though the meaning of this display in which clouds are seen to lift (and in which a massive sheet of cloth is actually lifted) may be ambiguously doubled, the power that it confers on James is unambiguous. Parry observes that many of the pageant arches "require[d] the presence of the King to release their message" (3), while Goldberg notes more forcefully that James was "the animating force" of the entry (32), a force clearly on display at the outset of the first arch in the entry.

Cosgrove has observed that arches were often used "to signify entrance to a distinct knowledge space" (*Apollo's* 294 n93), a practice that had become, by 1604, a commonplace of England's printed media.[36] Margery Corbett and Ronald Lightbown have made the definitive study of frontispieces in early modern English texts.[37] And in a productive essay, David Weil Baker has thought together numerous arches and their significance to the urban representations and self-fashionings of Ben Jonson.[38] Whether represented on the page or constructed in physical space, the architectural form of the triumphal arch:

> focuses vision—as does the proscenium arch, a related structure. The former, like the latter, is meant not only to be looked at but looked through, creating an urban *perspective*. (Dillon 147)

The viewer's gaze is directed by the structure of the arch to the territory that lies beyond the arch, and that territory is framed—visually and conceptually—by the arch. That which is seen through an arch is viewed in terms of that arch. In other words, arches not only focus attention on a particular space, they work to determine the way that space is understood. The function of an arch to condition the appearance and meaning of urban space is a representational function. Moreover, that representation of space is not temporary, even in the case of evanescent performances like entries and theatre.

Identifying "a temporal as well as spatial meaning" in what Jonson would call "prospective" forms, Cosgrove notes that: "looking forward, the sense of prospect [. . .] excites imagination and graphs desire, its projection is the foundation for and stimulus to projects" ("Introduction" 15). The temporal dimension of urban representation gives an otherwise impermanent performance the power to suggest lasting changes to the spaces in which it represents. De Certeau puts a question mark in parentheses when he tries to pin a general date on the emergence of new concepts of the urban in Western Europe: "Perspective vision and prospective vision constitute the twofold projection of an opaque past and an uncertain future onto a surface that can be dealt with. They inaugurate (in the sixteenth century?) the transformation of the urban fact into the concept of a city" (93-4). In the Londinium Arch, a representation of the city is shown in *perspective*, but the Arch itself invites a *prospective* view—of that fact-based, present-tense representation, as well as of a speculative future for the city itself. The word that Jonson used to describe the painting on the top of the arch may have seemed an early modern typographical error, instead provocatively suggests the dual work of image and vision in the city.

The representational capacity of the classical architectural form of the arch is multiplied in the case of the Londinium Arch. Not only does the Arch serve to re-present the urban space of London (especially the environs of Fenchurch Street) in 1604, the Arch itself offers a representation of London. The London beyond and beside the arch must be considered—"viewed"—in relation to the London *of* the Arch itself. Although such arches were "not only to be looked at but looked through," the image offered to the viewer-king, commoner, alderman, artist-by the Londinium Arch would not have been an expansive urban vista. Indeed the tangle of London's streets was particularly dense in the first twists and turns of the procession leading up to the first arch. As the epigram from Peter Ackroyd that begins this chapter indicates, postmedieval London was a hodge-podge of buildings—built, retrofitted, torn down, rebuilt—whose features and arrangement reflected immediate needs rather than an urban plan, least of all the classical forms increasingly current on the continent. Instead, the "prospect" of London represented atop the structure was the primary "view" of London on display, displacing the view *through* the arch onto a view *of* the arch. The portrait of London rendered by Harrison for James I's royal entry into the City of London participates in a tradition of London portraiture with a record that dates back more than three hundred and fifty years (as discussed in Chapter Two), though never before on such a grand scale. And, as with this tradition of city views, the portrait of London in James's entry is consistently associated with practices of performance. In the midst of a London overtly displaying its role as the ceremonial space for city-spanning (royal) performance, the first of the performances prepared for the king was a pageant arch about, and indeed *of*, the city.

The view that crowned the Londinium Arch is the most obvious representation of space associated with this pageant: a map image of the City of London was introduced as part of a theatrical event about London, performed in the streets of London. The classically derived architectural form of the arch was unlike any of the "vernacular" architecture that characterized the built structures in Fenchurch, their origins firmly in the medieval period. Moreover a structure that served to focus the visitor's view would have been starkly out of place in a city not constructed around vistas, avenues, and key buildings-in other words, *views*. The view through the Londinium Arch would have revealed only a bit more of the tangle of streets and half-timbered buildings. Though the postmedieval city could not yield to the views proposed by the Arch, the fact that the Arch directs its space into the unyielding terrain of the city anticipates development, *projects* not only into the city but, following Cosgrove, into the city's future.

The future of London projected by the Arch would seem to be suspended between a view of the City's present and an idea of its past. The "prospective" view of London is literally superimposed on a monument to continental, classical architecture. And it is this city in suspension—between past and future, real and ideal—that is represented in this Arch. It provides a speculative view of a classicized idea of London as reinvented via its ancient past: for this reason it is given the name "Londinium," the name given to the foundational Roman settlement on the Thames.[39] To pass through the Londinium Arch, as James it seems was eager to do, was to accept its liminal proposition: to cross a threshold into a new space, a conceptual space dominated by contemporary ideas of classical form, a space of vistas in the midst of congestion, a space that anticipated London's urban development in the near future.

The façade of the structure that introduced London's new conceptual space was the subject of some controversy among those who contributed to the entry. The controversial elements seem ludicrously minor, but reveal authorial engagements of greater significance. Beneath the cartouche bearing the title "LONDINIUM" there was another panel of text. As Jonson describes it: "in a less and different character," was written,

"CAMERA REGIA;"

(Jonson 378)

All three of the entry's main authors participate in a dispute over the phrase "Camera Regia." The phrase is Latin for "the chamber of the king"-"which title," Jonson notes, "immediately after the Norman Conquest it [London] began to have; and by the indulgence of succeeding Princes hath been hitherto continued" (378). Jonson's position, as noted above, is that the size of the latter text was smaller and in some significant way "different" from the text of the word "Londinium" (378). He justifies this distinction with reference to the Latin motto that runs centrally across the Arch, "Par domus haec coelo sed minor est domino," which Jonson paraphrases as: "though this City (for the state and magnificence) might (by hyperbole) be said to touch the stars, and reach up to Heaven; yet was it far inferior to the master thereof, who was his Majesty" (378). In his seemingly unmotivated justification of a relatively minor point of lettering on this monument, Jonson is particularly emphatic, though it does nothing to clarify the "camera regia" distinction.

Dekker's description of the same lettering runs counter to Jonson's. In his text, Dekker records that: "upon the battlements of the worke [the Londinium Arch], in great capitals was inscribed thus:

"LONDINIUM"
And under that, in a smaller, but *not* different character, was written,
"CAMERA REGIA"

(344, emphasis added)

Why would Dekker go out of his way to say that the lettering was *not* different? This issue would appear to be a typological battleground on which Jonson and Dekker continue their quarrel, arguing in print over the size and "difference" of a pair of words. Dutton suggests that Dekker is correcting the "inaccuracy" of Jonson's description (20), but Dillon suggests that the authors are engaged in a rivalry over the authority of the representation itself: "What the two inscriptions compare, after all, is the city *per se*, and the city in allegorical relation to the monarch" (139). Authorship and textual authority were the subject of all three published documents, much as royal authority was the subject of James's performance. Throughout his publication, Jonson is quite explicitly aligning himself with the authority of the king, but in describing "the chamber of the king" as "less and different" than London, just exactly what Jonson is saying about relations between royal and civic authority is unclear. Dekker praises the City and its leaders in his document, though without cutting his ties to royal authority; his distinction suggests a more equitable status between "Londinium" and "Camera Regia," one that maintains a hierarchy while not ruling out a kind of representational congruity—"smaller, but not different."

That neither author claims the space of James as greater than that of London is an unusual lapse in the immodest, hyperbolic praise that marked court performances for James—certainly the denotative content of Jonson's masques is praiseful to a fault. And in his text, Dekker consistently defends a degree of civic pride for his patrons. Might it have been important to Jonson that James imagine himself as, obviously smaller than a city, but distinct from the city? Might the implication be that James was "different" from London and therefore not a part of London: separate from its pressing crowds, unaffiliated with its lowborn leaders? And might Dekker have seen some civic benefit in aligning James with those same crowds and leaders, and so suggesting that the chamber of the king was not so different from the space of London after all? It is difficult to parse the meaning of this quarrel over type face and size without assuming a single, consistent bias on the part of each author-not a reliable assumption. But it is Harrison who took a decisive, if quiet, position in the "Camera Regia" quarrel, and who may offer another way of understanding the significance of this debate.

Harrison made the most emphatic distinction of the three official authors. Harrison's publication is clearly "the most biased in favour of the city" (Dillon 139), and in his publication, Harrison—who wrote the third account to reach readers, and the only one with visual art—did not include the words at all in his engraving of the Londinium Arch. [Fig. 14] Remarkable that, in a publication dedicated to the Lord Mayor, a visual detail recorded by the two other authors of the entry would be entirely omitted by the third, notably, the one artist responsible for actually executing this detail on the arch itself. The boldness of this position is hard to mistake. One might wonder if Harrison's willful act of editorial license and civic pride contributed to his subsequent disappearance from England's artistic and historical record.

While I agree with the associations that Dillon suggests about authorities, the question is not simply one of allegorical resonance or political affiliation. The text that appeared on the arch (at, by Harrison's measure, about eight feet in width) was an indication of authorship: of the arch, of its representation ("Londinium"), and of the city itself. Each version of the titling offered by each of the authors serves as a kind of signature, inscribing the face of the arch—and by extension, "Londinium" and London—with an indication of the source of its authorship and authority. While not definitively decidable, the question of titling on the Londinium Arch is a question of ownership over space: to reformulate Frye's question regarding Elizabeth, the question behind the Camera Regia quarrel is: Who represents London?[40] Orgel offers valuable insight into representational formulation, though in a different context: "An elaborate gold frame around a painting says something quite different from a simple black band, but what it says is about its owner, not about the painting" (*Illusion* 20). In the case of the Londinium Arch, deciding "ownership" of this frame was critical to deciding ownership of that which it framed: London.

In what was much more than a negligible cavil, each of these authors can be read as trying to determine representation and ownership, "framing" the debate after his own bias and in his own best interests-interests not necessarily consistent with other authorities represented in his text. Writing about "[p]ower and its representation" in officially-produced map images, Helgerson observes that: "maps do not, however, speak only of the source of their authority-that is, of the power that through the system of patronage brought them into existence-but also of the relation of that power to the land they depict" ("Land" 327, 330). Such relations of power and representation are crucial to estimations of the urban mappings performed by the Londinium Arch. This structure participated in practices of "urban mapping" traditionally "concerned with projects to secure the city as a single socio-territorial order" (Cosgrove, "Introduction" 16), and the debates among the authors reduplicate such concern. James's entry was about power, and his power in relation to London's power. Accordingly, the power to represent the city was contested in the three different interpretations of the "Camera Regia" legend on the Londinium Arch: lesser, equal, absent.

Mullaney argues that events such as royal entries served in the early modern period as "the rehearsal of cultures," reinforcing or reinventing— indeed, re-presenting—a culture's codes ("Strange" 73). Though the codes on display during his royal entry (social, spatial) tended toward innovation, James participated in a tradition that was equal parts British and continental.

> In keeping with the conventions of the Roman Triumph as transformed and elaborated by the Renaissance, it had become customary for a monarch and his procession to pause outside the city gates, on the threshold of the community, at that tenuous point where royal domain shaded into civic jurisdiction. Halting made the royal visitor more spectator than actor in the drama at hand [. . .]"
>
> ("Strange" 70).

The liminal nature of this "threshold" performance underlined the contestation of power and representation at work in the space of the Arch. The spaces of London were represented in and by this Arch, which served as a literal threshold, ambiguously straddling the spaces of royal, municipal, and theatrical authority over the city.

In fact, the representational value of the Londinium Arch itself was a point of contention: the meanings of this impermanent monument are not easily resolved. Baker asserts that "monuments include acts of erasure and substitution as well as remembrance" (266), and Dear argues that monuments "are conflicted sites of identity and power, culture and memory" (251). The urban memory associated with the Londinium Arch was not that of a historical past but a historicized present. Any site that invokes the *remembrance of things present* necessarily takes the form of representation. The Arch itself was a site of contest for identity, power, and social memory, a contest that was conducted in the terms of the last factor in my list of London's social forces: theatrical authority.

The theatre, as an emergent social force, was more strongly represented in the Londinium Arch than in any other Arch in the entry. Alleyn's involvement in the entry offers a determining factor: his fame would have added additional meaning to an identity already doubled in his roles as both the Genius Loci of the allegory and the king's surrogate in the performance. But another site with which Alleyn and his practice were associated was construed in the Londinium Arch: Southwark. London's entertainment district on the South Bank of the Thames is the absent presence in the Londinium Arch; much like the tower of St. Mary Overy in portraits of London, Southwark was the point from which the scene atop the Londinium Arch was viewed. In fact, Bergeron makes the persuasive claim that the London represented on the top of the Londinium Arch is viewed from approximately the position of the theatres themselves: "I suggest that the perspective from which we view the city on the arch corresponds to a position on the South Bank near the Globe Theatre" (*Practicing* 168). The Globe Theatre then becomes the second *orbis* associated with this *urbis*: by means of perspective representation, Shakespeare's place of representation is associated with James's / Jonson's / Harrison's / London's representation of space. The Londinium Arch offered a view of London from (roughly) the Globe theatre.

The absent presence of the Bankside theatre district suggests the vigor with which the various forces at work vied for authority in the space of this single impermanent monument. In the Londinium Arch, the spaces of the City's postmedieval geography were displaced by new architectural and spatial conceptions. And in the portrait atop the Arch, Greater London was displaced in favor of the traditional urban core. Yet that wider city was included in a practice of viewing that located the king, through substitution and perspective, in the place of the stage. When James regarded the Londinium Arch and the image of the city that surmounted it, that representation of the City made London available to the king for appropriation; this was the superficial theory behind the Arch: giving the city to the king. However, the location from which this representation of the City was conceived is the location of the theatres, a location that was in many respects outside the boundaries of the City proper (*propre*), and certainly not a site included in this portrait. James was pressured by this representation of London to conceptually occupy the place of London's stages in order to appropriate visually the image of the City represented to him.[41] Thus, the Londinium Arch performed a surreptitious representational appropriation of the king himself, displacing him into the spaces associated with the theatre artists who created the event.

So, although the City and the king may have been most visibly in contest in the space of James's entry, the strategies of the Londinium Arch display the power of London's thirdspace, the theatre, and the urban subjects who associated themselves with its practices. From the margins, James's urban subjects employed the place of the stage to temporarily determine the place of their king.

The Londinium Arch was both an impermanent monument and a lasting concept. It endures as a nodal point in the history of early modern London's spaces. For contemporary critical inquiry, the hybrid space described as "Londinium" provides a theoretical landmark by which to locate a productive conceptual intersection in early modern London. For the Londinium Arch straddled not only a narrow, medieval street in the City, it straddled as well a threshold across which traditional and emergent spaces briefly coexisted, suspended between representation and performance.

Chapter Four

"To See Caesar": Theatrical Performance and Shakespeare's Rome (*Caesar* and *Coriolanus*)

GUILDENSTERN: We're just not getting anywhere.
ROSENCRANTZ: Not even England. I don't believe in it anyway.
GUILDENSTERN: What?
ROSENCRANTZ: England.
GUILDENSTERN: Just a conspiracy of cartographers, you mean?

Tom Stoppard[1]

This banter from *Rosencrantz and Guildenstern Are Dead* provides a theatrical "play" on the idea of space as something both real and represented. When Stoppard's Guildenstern jokes that England just may be "a conspiracy of cartographers" (107), he hits close to the practices that lie behind the production of national space. It is apt that Stoppard's twentieth-century appropriation of Shakespeare should play on ideas of identity, representation, and the space of the stage. At the time Shakespeare conceived *his* Guildenstern, emergent spatial practices were (re-)conceiving the space of nations as abstracted from individual experience yet still indebted to concepts of physical performance.

At the time James came to power, his nation's popular culture was busily appropriating Rome as a valuable model for the reimagining of Britain as an empire and London as a city. Not only did Rome provide a precedent for those seeking to authorize and consolidate power, but it also served as a site of contest where existing social relations could be explored, reconsidered, and troubled. Caesarism was in the air, and Shakespeare's London "saw its problems mirrored in the wide glass of Roman history" (Wells 4), from the references to Rome that riddle John Stow's late Elizabethan *Survey of London*[2] to James's elaborately Romanate royal entry.

At the conclusion of his entry procession through the City of London, James encountered the second of two arches conceived by Jonson and built by Stephen Harrison: "The Temple of Janus." [Fig. 12] Situated appropriately enough at Temple Bar, the official western boundary of the City, this pageant saw the return of Edward Alleyn in his role as the Genius of the City. Alleyn's character ordered a Roman priest, played by another actor, to light his sacred fire not for a feast of Mars but for the triumph of James (Jonson 392). That Jonson composed James's entry in relation to Roman historical and literary sources may not have been forcefully apparent in his first arch: few words, most notably the Latin name for the city that the Romans founded on the Thames, would have provided textual testimony to the Londinium Arch's classical associations (though Harrison's design would have suggested to the well informed spectator a classical architectural source).

Unlike the Londinium Arch, the Temple of Janus was "a towering mass of classical scholarship" (Parry 18). Its surface densely inscribed with Latin text, the last structure of James's entry was less an architectural monument than a freestanding literary object.[3] Much of this text was quoted from Roman sources, though some was of Jonson's invention, notably the neologism emblazoned on the Temple's facade: "S.P.Q.L." (395). This abbreviation appropriates a Roman source in the context of James's London. The original Roman formula, "S.P.Q.*R*.," abbreviated "*Senatus Populusque Romanus*": "the Senate and People of Rome."[4] Though the new formula is never translated, following the first arch the reader of the Temple of Janus could assume that it introduced "the Senate and People of *Londinium*." With the substitution of an "L" for an "R," Jonson invented a new social category for a new space. So doing, Jonson not only recalled his previous invention, the Londinium Arch, he also implied (on James's behalf) that the crown's authority and London's people—even London itself—were framed by discourses of Rome.

After James passed through the Temple of Janus, a door in the Temple closed behind him, concluding the entry by concealing James from the assembled "People of Londinium," while at the same time revealing additional text:

IMP. IACOBVS MAX.
CAESAR AVG. P.P.

PACE POPVLO BRITANNICO
TERRA MARIQVE PARTA

IANUM CLVSIT. S.C.[5]

It seems appropriate that James, in passing from the City of London, should be celebrated as a new Caesar Augustus, "*imperator*" of a newly united Britain. While the word "imperator" has imperial implications, Jonson must have known its primary usage: indicative of a commander-in-chief or a victorious general. The implication is that James was not only displayed to London, but that in course of his passage, the king had conquered the city as well.

Not only were the language and imagery of James's entry Roman, the political designs of the king were equally imperial. Jonson's flamboyant new name for James, "Jacobus Maximus," would have been all the more appropriate in relation to Alleyn's last words, delivered from this arch at the limits of the City's domain. His valedictory included the line: "And may these Ides as fortunate appear / To thee, as they to Caesar fatal were" (Jonson 394). That James's entry was held on the 15th of March was a detail that could not have been accidental.[6] Jonson was careful not to associate James with Julius Caesar nor the Ides of March with assassination. Thus, the Ides of March served as a date from which was marked, not the death of a republic, but the beginning of an empire.

The "S.P.Q.L." blazon on the last arch gives a proper name to that empire, and locates the entire entry and all the people in attendance in a conceptual "Londinium." More than just a reference to London's Roman history, "Londinium" was the representation of historical space amalgamated with urban topography, a space in which a new city could be imagined in conjunction with the entry of its authorizing king. Goldberg has suggested that a "spectral kingdom of Augustus" was the masque-like "setting" for all of Jacobean politics (165). Jonson gave that kingdom a name. As James exited the Temple of Janus, the king left behind the "simultaneously real-and-imagined" city limits of Londinium.

From the geographical destination of Matthew Paris's itinerary (see above, Ch. 2) to the representational site of James's entry, Rome had served for centuries (in England, as elsewhere) as a forceful paradigm of urban space, and it would do so for Shakespeare as well. Gail Kern Paster speculates that: "Shakespeare is particularly drawn to those moments in the Roman past which brought the internal order of the city to a point of critical change, when one kind of city was giving way to another" (58).[7] On the occasion of the 1604 entry, Shakespeare's own real-world city was at a point of critical change, but Paster's formulation must be reversed in the case of early modern London: it was not the present that was drawn to the past, but the past that was brought to the present: "Rome" was introduced into the streets and even into the proper name of the city, where (in both cases) it was used to inaugurate a new space for London. The postmedieval town was on the verge of giving way to early modern urbanism, and representations of a Romanized London were deployed in the service of conceiving and convening that new cityspace.

Figure 12: The Temple of Janus. From *The Arches of Triumph*, Harrison, 1604.

In contrast with James's entry, in which the king was compared to Augustus, I will consider Julius Caesar and another famous Roman, Coriolanus—both, of course, title characters in Shakespeare's plays. The theatre practices inscribed in Shakespeare's texts mark these plays as related to but significantly different from the representational strategies at work in James's entry. I will begin with *Julius Caesar*, in which Richard Wilson sees "the scars of a material struggle" (40), and in which I too see the lasting marks of a cultural transformation.

LONDON CALLING

The imagery and language of James's entry introduced an idea of Rome into the space of London. The entry's triumphal arches were only the most visible examples of the event's Romanness, their architectural form drawn from Serlio, who himself drew from classical Roman forms.[8] Additionally, the arches were adorned with written quotations from a range of Latin sources. These quotations not only informed the entry pageants with constant reminders of Roman culture, they also worked to incorporate the *ideal* of Rome into the *idea* of London. In the representational strategies of the entry, a new conception of London emerged, a hybrid of early modern concepts of classical Rome and the material conditions of London's actual places and histories. In Lefebvre's terms, a new *representation of space* was being produced, one that offered a stark contrast with the *representational space* in which it appeared. In the interaction of these spaces, not only was Rome quoted in the context of London, but London was quoted in the context of Rome: the Londinium Arch and the Temple of Janus themselves bracketed the physical city, framing the early modern English streets, houses, and churches between classical Roman reference points. Like the image of the city on the first arch, all of London was temporarily defined in the space of "Londinium": a city suspended between the real and the imaginary, the material and the representational.

Marjorie Garber provides a productive way of thinking about the quotational uses of Rome in the texts and performances of Shakespeare's London. Garber observes that "the idea of Rome is itself [. . .] a quotation" (52). Her point is that there is no single, "authentic" Rome, but a series of things Roman, themselves abstracted from other sources. Correspondingly, the idea of Rome was not a daily presence in the city that James entered in 1604. Rather, an idea—"Rome"—was introduced into those streets by way of quotational sites and performances. Subsequent to this entry, the city was subject to the lingering quotation marks of the Romanate performance.

The result: in the streets of London during and after James's entry, as in the Roman plays of Shakespeare,[9] "Rome" was always already in quotation.

For Garber, the work of quotation is akin to the work of representation: something is introduced into a context where it had not been, and by use of quotation marks, a distinction between the two—the thing introduced and its new context—is maintained. As Garber observes: "Notice that we put 'in quotation' in quotation marks" (52). And notice as well, in the appositive that starts the preceding sentence and the parenthetical citation at the end of it, how carefully "Garber" is distinguished from its context, my sentences. Such usage is the source of Garber's authority, that she and her words are distinguished from "Hopkins" and my words; but this distinction is also the source of my authority. I, Hopkins, can deploy "Garber" in the service of my argument. Quotation as a practice sets up boundaries that distinguish between inside and outside for a particular purpose. Thus, quotation is a function of difference, and also a function of power.[10]

In James's entry, "Rome" is quoted in the context of London, introduced as an element of difference. This difference is the primary source of James's authority, the authority to represent a reconceived urban space and to animate that new space, in much the same way that the massive curtain was raised to reveal the Londinium Arch at the start of the first pageant. Even in much contemporary theatre, a curtain marks the border of difference; in the case of the Londinium Arch, the curtain served as quotation marks that separated a perceived city from one conceived in representation. The raising of the curtain removed the quotation marks, as it were, blurring the distinction between the real and the representational. This is, in Garber's phrase, the "use of history" to which the quotation of Rome was put in James's London entry (52): a new idea of London—associated with the urban authority of Rome—was made physical by the temporary monuments along the entry route and authorized in performance by the king.

In the course of his reign, James made periodic attempts to "reenvision and, to some extent, provide for the reconstruction of London as a city of permanent rather than easily razed edifices" (Baker 277). In a proclamation of 1615, James showed approval for:

> all Edifices, Structures, and workes which tend to publique use and ornament, in and about Our said Citie, as the paving of Smithfield [. . .] the reedifying of Algate [. . .] and the like workes, which have bene

erected and performed in greater number in these twelve yeeres of our
Reigne, then in whole ages heretofore. (Stuart 346)

As James observes in this proclamation, London had already become "the
greatest, or next the greatest Citie of the Christian world" (345), so his two-
fold goal was to limit *vernacular* construction and the growing sprawl of
London's suburban slums,[11] and to direct all building energies instead to
the beautification and "ornament" of the city (346). In a passage that paraphrases (a quotational form of appropriation) Suetonius's *Life of Augustus*,
James proclaims his Roman vision for London.

> We could desire and wish [. . .] that as it was said by the first
> Emperour of Rome, that he had found the City of Rome of Bricke,
> and left it of Marble, So that Wee whom GOD hath honoured to be
> the first King of Great Britaine, mought bee able to say in some pro-
> portion, That Wee had found Our Citie and Suburbs of London of
> stickes, and left them of Bricke, being a Materiall farre more durable,
> safe from fire, beautifull and magnificent. (346)

James exaggerates the extent to which this Roman vision had been accomplished. Though the paving of Smithfield was "performed" at his suggestion,
the renovation of the site of Bartholomew Fair could hardly have been seen
as the cornerstone of an Augustus-like re-creation of London. Nevertheless,
this municipal project served to reinforce in the physical terrain James's idea
that both he and London should be defined in Roman terms. The paved
Smithfield was a kind of physical quotation, the brickwork of which set off
a hybrid space where "Rome" and "London" tentatively met and meshed.

James had Roman ambitions.[12] His claim of imperial status was jus-
tified by his unification of a Great Britain, and the seat of his latter-day
Roman empire was London. In the Temple of Janus, London stood synec-
dotally for James's kingdom, just as Rome represented both city and empire.
James had Roman ambitions for London, too. His grand vision for rebuilding the city was only marginally applied to London's spaces in the course
of his reign, and even then only at the margins. Only after James's reign
would far reaching physical changes be applied to the city. But even in his
incomplete achievement, James displays *romanitas*, for Julius Caesar, too,
belatedly exerts his "will" over the city, bequeathing in his final testament a
civic space to Rome's masses. As Timothy Hampton describes Caesar's post-
mortem transaction:

The topography of the city passes out of the hands of patrician cliques. The statues of Caesar that dot the cityscape are now replaced by the 'walks' and 'orchards' through which the hero's presence surrounds and engulfs public consciousness. (225)

This civic space, however, does not come into being in the course of Shakespeare's play; though proposed, it remains a space deferred.

As I discuss in Chapter Three, the Londinium Arch, though only a temporary monument, was a space of conflict for urban power and representational authority. Erasure, substitution, and remembrance are at work in that arch, and may be seen to define Shakespeare's most determinedly urban plays as well, *Julius Caesar* and *Coriolanus*. In this chapter, both plays will be discussed in terms of the quotational performances that come to constitute the conceptual territory in which they are set. Borrowing from James's entry, I will use the term "Londinium" to describe and define the hybrid theatrical space of these plays.

The setting of these plays participates in the same kind of spatial suspension as represented in the Londinium of James's entry. To return to Diamond's definition of the term, representation is: "the making visible (again) of what is lacking or what has disappeared [. . .]" (85). The representational space of Londinium exists between the parentheses of Diamond's "(again)": a carefully constructed retrospective performance that locates discourses of the past in the present. Garber suggests that Roman representation is marked by paradox: "A quotation is *always* 'in quotation,' always *in*appropriate for its proper place" (52). To be inappropriate for the proper would seem to imply an inherently contradictory spatial relationship, but it is a contradiction that aptly describes Shakespeare's Londinium. These two Roman plays, emerging as they did in the context of postmedieval London, were themselves quotational. Moreover, they contain numerous internal quotations which provide points of juxtaposition between Roman source and postmedieval context. The goal of this chapter is to examine the most productive points of juxtaposition, where representations of Rome and performances in postmedieval London worked, together or in contest, to suggest a new space for Shakespeare's city.

At one of the most contentious points of *Coriolanus*, the tribune Sicinius, representing the plebeians, speaks out against Coriolanus, who is defended by the Senators. Sicinius warns the people: "You are at point to lose your liberties. Martius [Coriolanus] would have all from you" (III.i.193-4). The Senators try to shout him down, saying: "Fie, fie, fie! / This is the way to kindle, not to quench. / To unbuild the city, and to lay all flat" (III.i.195-7).

To which Sicinius replies: "What is the city but the people?" (III.i.198).[13]
Here, Shakespeare offers two views of the city. The Senators see the city as
a set of buildings, as physical structures supported by the people's submis-
sion to the will of their leaders. But the people see the city differently: they
see the city as a community of and for the people. According to this latter
view, the will of the people should *define* the city, not threaten to "unbuild"
it. Shakespeare seems to have introduced two irreconcilable conceptions of
civic authority. Coriolanus sides with the first one. The title character in this
play is a surly, unappealing war hero who is entirely unwilling to do anything
for his city except fight in its battles, and his unwillingness to make any con-
cessions ultimately brings about his exile from Rome. Ironically, after being
exiled, Coriolanus raises an army from among a city of people he has just
defeated, and returns, threatening to "unbuild" Rome himself.

Although Rome is a literal and metaphorical battleground throughout
both *Julius Caesar* and *Coriolanus*, it is never entirely clear how Shakespeare
wants the audience to answer what I feel is a determining question for both
plays: "What *is* the city?"

Montrose has suggested, as previously quoted, that Shakespeare's theatre is not merely an "inert product" of his culture, but "a source of cultural
production" (*Purpose* 109, "Shaping" 31). The consequence of this position, now widely accepted as "characteristic of New Historicism" (Wilson,
"Introduction" 5), is that Shakespeare's plays must be regarded as not merely
redundant reflections of their culture but as in fact productive representations that contributed to the conditions of Shakespeare's own culture. As
Wayne Rebhorn writes, in a now classic discussion of *Caesar*, "the play offers
a particular perspective on its context, seeking both to define the shape of
what it represents and to shape its audience's response to that representation
[. . .] thereby actually helping to constitute the very context of which it is
a part" (32). This understanding of the constitutional power of the theatre is
echoed by Jean-Christophe Agnew who, in describing the emergent commercial phenomenon in which Shakespeare participated, argues that the public
theatre did more than just "reflect relations occurring elsewhere; it modeled
and in important respects materialized those relations" (xi). Thus understood, Shakespeare's theatre can be seen to generate a product with the power
to bring about material change, and in the case of the urban-engaged plays
discussed in this chapter, this material change had an effect on the spaces and
practices of the city. That the city and its history had an influence on Shakespeare is hardly in question, but the critical corollary of this influence is more
challenging and, for this inquiry, more important: the representation of city
space in Shakespeare's plays influenced the physical space of the city. At a

time of particularly acute social dynamism in London, the public theatre played a part in deciding what the city was, and what it could become.

De Certeau contends that the space of the modern city emerged in sixteenth-century Europe, and that this new space was marked by an obsession with representing the city as a static, unchanging image: "The city, like a proper name, provides a way of conceiving and constructing space on the basis of a finite number of stable, isolatable positions" (94) For de Certeau, modes of visual representation-practices of looking and picturing-emerged in the early modern period as strategies for the stabilization and control of identity, be it the identity of an individual subject or of a city. The characters Caesar and Coriolanus can both be seen to struggle to stabilize their identities in representation: Caesar continually refers to himself in the third person.[14] Coriolanus is particularly concerned with fixing the meaning that he links to his newly minted "proper name." But the plays named for these characters are not hospitable to their eponymous Romans' representational fixations. Londinium is not merely an image, "picture-like to hang by th' wall" (*Coriolanus* I.iii.11), but a space to be determined in performance.

PERFORMANCE AND THE CITY

Richard Wilson suggests that *Caesar* is a play "*on the edge*": like the Londinium Arch, *Caesar* serves as a "gateway to a new order" (9, italics in original). For Wilson, this new order is a political one, anticipating the absolutist intentions of the Stuart monarchy. But this play is also on the edge of urban history and the midst of transition in the way the political was represented. *Caesar* dramatizes the "the theatrical city" as an institution in decline. The Rome in which *Caesar* is set is a city in which urban theatrical performances retain the power to determine civic identity. However, the determining authority of civic performance is far from uncomplicated, and those who execute such performances may not gain the authority they sought or be able to determine the city's political identity. Faced with the incremental decline in the capacity of performance to secure urban meaning in his culture, Shakespeare may be reproducing in this play the failure of the authority of Elizabethan political entertainment, and of Elizabeth herself. The product of this play is a backward-looking history, a recollection of the culture of public performance during a crisis of (urban) representation. Only in the unrealized civic spaces of Caesar's walks and orchards does Shakespeare anticipate what might come next, beyond the "edge" of London's immediate future.

The primary documenter of *London's* walks and orchards, private spaces and public monuments, is Stow. From the first sentence of his *Survey*, Rome is a point of comparison to London:

> As the Roman writers, to glorify the city of Rome, derive the original thereof from gods and demi-gods, by the Trojan progeny, so Geoffrey of Monmouth, the Welsh historian, deduceth the foundation of this famous city of London, for the greater glory thereof, and emulation of Rome, from the very same original. (33)

At the outset of this heterotopic walking tour of his native city, Stow forges a representational connection between the "famous city of London" and the idea (and ideal) of classical Rome. More than a mere association or comparison of the two cities, Stow begins his *Survey* by invoking the legendary genealogy of the two cities. Though Stow realizes that this genealogy's dubious associations with "gods and demi-gods" were invented in order "to glorify" the ancient city (33), such biased purposes are not dismissed so much as appropriated. In order to glorify his own late sixteenth-century city, Stow invokes the legendary precursor of Roman Londinium, as described by Geoffrey of Monmouth: Troynovant.[15] Only a few lines later, Julius Caesar is mentioned in comparison to Geoffrey of Monmouth:

> This [King] Lud had issue two sons [. . .] who being not of age to govern at the death of their father, the uncle Cassibelan took upon him the crown; about the eighth year of whose reign, Julius Caesar arrived in this land with a great power of Romans to conquer it; the manner of which conquest I will summarily set down out of his own Commentaries, which are of far better credit than the relations of Geoffrey of Monmouth.
>
> (Stow 33-34)

Clearly, Caesarism was afoot in London as early as 1598, a matter of months before the unusually secure date for Shakespeare's most famous Roman play (see below). Stow's *Survey* drew on and reinforced popular connections among Caesar, Rome, and the history of London. Shakespeare can be seen to pursue a similar project in *Caesar* and *Coriolanus*.[16] The discourses of "Rome" frame the space of these plays just as the discourses of "London" framed theatrical practice on Shakespeare's stage. As with the images that constitute the canon of London's pictorial representations, these plays "belong together" because they "are bound by a dense net of intertextual relations" (Helgerson 347), relations that further bind each play to the real world of spaces and events. Shakespeare's *Caesar* has become "one of the most quoted texts in debates about critical theory," and the play continues to draw and focus critical attention as do few others (Wilson 1). Critics frequently seek to establish and stabilize the subject or subjects that the play is "about": "*Julius Caesar* is not only a political play, but also a play of character."[17] "Time is the subject of Shakespeare's story in *Julius Caesar*."[18] "At its core, *Julius Caesar* is a play about reading and writing."[19] And as often as not in these stabilizing critical enterprises, the object of critical discourse that substantiates these claims is "language"; ironically, though, that discourse often seeks to analyze the instability of language as it is used in the text.[20]

Responding to the critical tendency to find in *Caesar* a wealth of meanings, each definitive, Wilson describes the play as "a text that dreamed the past as a museum" (1). Resisting the pull of such a lovely metaphor, I prefer instead to read the play, not as a "museum" of static, inert objects, but as a *performance archive*. I regard *Caesar* as a flexible text, whose meanings are multiple, processual, and provisional. In fact, *Caesar* is articulate in its consideration of the flexibility of identity in performance, and the strife that can result from attempts to represent a singular, inflexible identity in the public sphere.

Most prominent among the critical commonplaces associated with *Caesar*, is the consistent repetition of the information available about its date of performance. Swiss traveler Thomas Platter documented his attendance at a performance of *Caesar* at the Globe on 21 September 1599.[21] This documentation would also seem to secure the assertion that *Caesar* was the first play to be performed at the new theatre built by the Lord Chamberlain's Men, The Globe.[22] While discussion and debate over the dates and conditions of Shakespeare's plays in publication is lively, the critical discourse surrounding their performances is almost inevitably rather more slight. It is therefore of particular note that the performance history of *Caesar* is so insistently part of its critical history.

The importance of this play extends beyond "merely" the history of Shakespeare, to include the history of one of the major urban developments in London during this period: the rise and establishment of the public theatre.[23] Not only was the city a theatrical formation in postmedieval London, the theatre was an urban formation as well. Shakespeare's *Caesar* corroborates and collaborates with this dual urban / theatrical formation, not only as a product of urban space, but also as an agent producing that space.

Of the classical, Roman conceptions of the city and the world, Gillies observes that: "[t]he walls of the city and the borders of its territory are both telescoped into the edges of the ancient map [. . .]" (6).[24] This spatial correspondence between the micro and the macro was an inherent part of the idea that was represented in Shakespeare's Rome. Also inscribed in this urban history was the violent act whereby Romulus murdered his brother Remus as he leapt over the city walls. Following this act, the conclusion of the founding myth of Rome, the murderous brother gave his name to the city. Violence, ritually enacted, defined Rome's "proper name" in the postmedieval imagination as much as Rome's walls defined its physical territory (de Certeau 94).[25] In a city that had only recently slipped the traditional bounds of its own Roman-constructed walls, Londoners saw in Rome a reflection and often an authorization for their own city.

The opening of *Caesar* presents an urban scene richly expressive of the cultural anxieties and representational possibilities that worked to shape dramatic literature and theatrical practice in postmedieval London. In the very first lines of the play, the tribunes Flavius and Murellus castigate a group of "Commoners":

> FLAVIUS: Hence! Home, you idle creatures, get you home!
> Is this a holiday? What, know you not,
> Being mechanical, you ought not walk
> Upon a laboring day without the sign
> Of your profession? Speak, what trade art thou? (I.i.1-5)

The Commoners respond with irreverent puns that play on the guilds and professions by which they are named: "Carpenter" and "Cobbler" in particular. The comic exchange reaches its culmination when the Commoners finally confess their reason for assembling.

> COBBLER: [. . .] But indeed, sir, we make holiday
> *To see Caesar*, and to rejoice in his triumph.
> MURELLUS: Wherefore rejoice? What conquest brings he home?
> What tributaries follow him to Rome,
> To grace in captive bonds his chariot-wheels?
> You blocks, you stones, you worse than senseless things!
> O you hard hearts, you cruel men of Rome [. . .]. (30–6, emphasis
> added)

For an audience of 1599, this exchange would have begun in a space firmly anchored in the everyday placeworld familiar to the Elizabethan Londoners in attendance. Even before the first lines would have been delivered, some number of actors playing the parts of the Commoners must already have been on stage before the tribunes entered, otherwise there would be no mischief in progress to justify their outrage. Since the names and language given to these Commoners identify them with an Elizabethan population more than with Roman plebeians, one may well assume the "holiday" disruptions were forms of Elizabethan performance anachronistic to the representation of Caesar's Rome. Describing the performance of *Caesar* that he attended in 1599, Platter records that: "when the play, was over, [some of the actors] danced very marvelously together as is their wont, two dressed as men and two as women" (qtd. in Gurr, *Playgoing* 213). If, as Platter describes, something as incongruous as a jig could have followed a Roman tragedy, one must admit the possibility of nearly any kind of "holiday" behavior at its outset.[26]

Other more obvious juxtapositions like clocks, chimneypots, hats, and billiards can be found throughout Shakespeare's Roman plays. Though in 1910 MacCallum could assert that Shakespeare included these anachronisms "without any consciousness of the discrepancy" (85), I argue that Shakespeare's use of history (or indeed, abuse of it) was intentional. As Coppélia Kahn maintains, anachronism isn't the issue: "Through a kind of cross-pollination that isn't simply anachronism, Englishness appears in Roman settings, and Romanness is anglicized" (4).[27] Like the arches of James's entry, Shakespeare's juxtapositions of London and Rome are neither accidental nor incidental: they are strategic cultural hybridizations produced from the interaction of text and performance.[28]

Critical speculation about Shakespearean theatrical performance is indispensable to understanding the representational strategies employed in *Caesar*. The text of the play strongly suggests that the theatrical event would have begun before the point at which the text itself begins. In other words, performance by the actors would have begun before the beginning of the authorized and "authored" text attributed to the characters. This pre-textual performance would have taken place, not in any representation *of* space but in the representational space of the theatre itself, framing Shakespeare's *Caesar* by exposing the conditions of its own production with playful performances located not in a fictional narrative but in an actual location.

Wilson argues that this "exposé" would have made it clear to the real-world commoners attending the theatre that "they had no business to be there" ("'Is this a holiday?'" 57). However, I find it difficult to conclude that the tribune's address was an expression of "company policy" on the part of the Lord Chamberlain's Men (56)—after all, the dismissive tribunes would soon be "put to silence" for their actions (I.ii.285-6). Robert Weimann suggests alternative terms by which to consider the play's opening:

> [O]ne of the ways by which the Elizabethan theatre appropriated power
> was to challenge the representation of authority by an alternative author-
> ity of theatrical representation which derived at least part of its strength
> from vitalizing and mobilizing a new space for *Spass* [. . .].[29]
>
> ("Towards" 272)

The actors playing the Commoners can be seen to have opened up a playful contestatory space, one in which the real-world conditions of theatrical performance remained visible along with (and even in opposition to)
the representation of authority by Flavius and Murellus. While the tribunes may have chased the Commoners from the stage, the commoners in
the audience would recognize that all the actors on stage were commoners
like them.

On the occasion of the performance that Platter attended, by the time
Murellus was delivering his monologue on the state of the empire, a representational transition would have already begun. The "holiday" dialogue
that marked the opening of the play serves the dramaturgical function of
tenuously anchoring the performance in the concrete world of London,
1599. Subsequent dialogue leads the audience toward the abstract space
produced for the narrative: Rome. Before Murellus speaks, the scene is
dominated by characters recognizable as similar to those in attendance at
the Elizabethan playhouse, perhaps indistinguishable from them. Murellus' accusations make anachronistic reference to the quotidian business of
Elizabethan Londoners. His references locate the opening of the play not
so much in Rome as in the same London as the performance itself would
have taken place, and identify the speakers not so much as Romans but
as part of the crowd. Murellus interrupts the Commoners' playful banter,
and the space of comic performance—with its references to the world of
its audience and the space of theatrical production—gives way to the production of an abstract space far removed from that of the playgoers.

In the course of this representational shift, the audience is led across
a "threshold" separating the world in which the play is performed from
the world represented in the play. Writing about the liminal spaces at the
beginnings and endings of Shakespeare's plays, Weimann notes that when
such a threshold was being crossed in performance: "the impromptu,
pragmatic, and vulnerable interface between symbolic forms and material
stages was most irrevocably in question" (*Author's* 216). At such threshold moments, Shakespeare can be seen to negotiate in dramatic form "the
world-in-the-play and the playing-in-the-world," two spaces to be accom-
modated on a single stage (*Author's* 216).

"*LOCUS* AND *PLATEA* REVISITED" REVISITED

Shakespeare's *Caesar* reveals a class of issues related to changing conceptions and practices of space in late Elizabethan culture.[30] In the case of London, a gradual shift in the conception of space introduced hybrid spaces, and new ways of practicing the space of the city. These changes were closely related to "the historical shift" that Montrose has noted, expressed politically in local and national realignments; but this shift also appears in the reconceptions (and re-*per*ceptions) of (social) space. Recall that Klein finds in this period "a redefinition of contemporary spatiality: space defined in terms of the people [. . .] increasingly yields to its representation" (19). In the case of London, a gradual shift in the conception of space introduced new modes of spatial production, new ways of practicing the space of the city.

Dear finds that "the spatial form of the built environment reflect[s], and condition[s], social relations over time and space," arguing that "the built environment is both the product of and mediator between social relations" (39). In considering such relations, Cosgrove notes an increasing awareness, among "postmodern geographers" (such as Dear) and those influenced by their work, that "the relationship between societies and their environment as it is lived is as much a product of consciousness as of material realities" ("Introduction" 6). It follows that a change in "consciousness" will contribute to a material change.

Dana Arnold, in a study of nineteenth century London, writes: "the way in which a city can function and evolve as a means of expressing urban experience and social life can reveal modern ways of seeing" (xix). In the case of the London in which Shakespeare would have first presented *Caesar*, "modern ways of seeing" were not as dominant as in the London of Arnold's study; rather, these "ways of seeing" were in the process of being invented. Dear would locate in Arnold's choice of words an emphasis on visual perception; he notes that "[t]he Reformation was a rationalization of religious belief and practice that shifted the emphasis from sacramental experience to study of the word and text" (28-9). Dear directly associates this new value for the visual to changes in the use and form of the space of the city: "The roots and precepts of modern urban planning lie deep in the history of modernity, especially the rationalities characteristic of the Enlightenment and the hegemonies of science and the state" (110). This new "vision" for urban planning began shortly after *Caesar*'s premiere: the introduction of artificial perspective from the European continent would have an influence on the intellectual and artistic circles of England, an influence that would be felt all the more strongly in London over the course of the seventeenth century. This new "perspective" on representations of space, along with the "swelling scene" of global exploration and commerce, precipitated a revolution in the way that Londoners viewed the world and their place in it. At the end of the sixteenth century, the "modern way of seeing" that Arnold describes had just begun to take its place in the cultural consciousness of Elizabethan London, including written drama and theatre practice.

Scenes such as the opening of *Caesar* rely on a "double business" in the "purposes of playing" that invokes a "bifold authority" in representation. Such representational "doubleness" in theatrical practice has received extensive, profound consideration in the work of Robert Weimann. In *Author's Pen and Actor's Voice* (2000), Weimann considers the early modern emergence of visually determined representational strategies to offer a reconsideration of the terms *locus* and *platea*, which he first discussed in his foundational *Shakespeare and the Popular Tradition*. I wish to extend Weimann's reconsideration of his own study to show the meanings governing the space of the city reflected in the city's complexly represented other: the space of the stage. There, the interaction between the ideal and the real, the abstract and the concrete, were made as vivid and accessible to the city's inhabitants as in the space of a map.

Weimann's expanded consideration of the *locus* and *platea* performance conventions on early modern stages takes into account "the newly expanding space *in* (imaginary) representation and the recently institutionalized, material space *of* its performance" (*Author's Pen* 180, italics in original). Weimann frames the understanding of these terms in the context of considerations of representation in and of space. He re- defines *platea* as "an opening in the *mise-en-scène* through which the place and time of the stage-as-stage and the cultural occasion itself are made either to assist or resist the socially and verbally elevated, spatially and temporally remote representation" (181). The *locus*, by contrast, "can be seen as a strategic approximation to the uses of perspectival form: it implicated the establishment of a topographically fixed locality" (182). The players' occupation of the imaginatively fixed narrative space of the *locus* abstracted the theatrical performance from the world of the audience and the "cultural occasion" of attendance at the public theatre, establishing a *counter-occasion*: a represented event separate from the theatre and the audience around the platform stage.

Importantly, *platea* and *locus* must not be seen as mutually exclusive. The interaction of these spaces demonstrates a consonance between Shakespeare's theatrical practice and that of hybrid spatial constructs such as the Londinium Arch—an object that integrated performance with self-contained representational location. In 1599, the space of *Caesar*, a dramatic fiction set in Rome, would never have ceased to be associated, however tenuously, with the space of the stage from which that fiction emerged. For example: the Cobbler says that he has come "To see Caesar"; indeed, the audience members that he so closely resembles would have come to see *Caesar* too. In the Cobbler's punning phrase, "Caesar" refers to both the character *in* the representation and the representation itself, the "cultural occasion": a play at the Globe theatre.[31]

Beginning as it does in the space of the *platea*, the play suggests that the space of the stage would have produced an ambiguous intersection of London and Rome. *Caesar* initiates its discourse on the power of the theatrical in urban life with a scene that conflates the city *in* performance with the city *of* performance, inviting continuous comparison between the characters' Rome and audience's London.

Performance is an essential tool for engaging theories of space. Performance gives substance to written drama and activates the events that occupy theatrical space. But the spatial activity of early modern performance cannot be fully understood without engaging with representation. As Weimann's work has consistently demonstrated, representation is the key to understanding *locus* and *platea* as much more than merely a relationship between "upstage" and "downstage" portions of the playing area, as these concepts are often reductively mistaken. Such terms of stage location are, at any rate, anachronistic in a discussion of early modern London's platform stages, where audiences would have been located on three (and in some cases on four) sides of the players. By oversimplifying the understanding of *locus* and *platea*, scholars of early modern literature and theatre run the risk of underestimating the complex meaning-making at work on the Elizabethan stage.[32]

The representation of a fictional *elsewhere* in early modern theatre was supported by performers' adherence to the "prescribed roles" and "imaginary landscape" of narrative drama. In Shakespeare's plays, fictional agents operate and fictional events transpire in a location that is non-identical with the location in which the actual performance took place. (Ex. Rome is real, but Caesar's Rome was far removed in time and geography from Shakespeare's London, and mediated by Shakespeare's source texts and his own creative interventions.) It is with such representation of space that the *locus* is associated. But *platea* space is not merely a point "downstage from" the *locus*; rather, the *platea* is a space produced by early modern actors at any time at which they acknowledged the actual event of performance while performing in relation to a representational event.[33] There would have been no need to go "downstage" to produce *platea* space: a performing agent need only acknowledge that *there is a stage* to invoke the space of the *platea*, and even to do so from within the *locus* of representation, thereby hybridizing the topography[34] of the performance space. The strategy of negotiating the relationship between *locus* and *platea* provided Elizabethan performers (and writers) with opportunities to engage the audience, to comment ironically upon the action of the narrative, and (not unimportantly) to make a joke. In other words, the difference between *locus* and *platea* is found not in a particular stage location, but in a performance decision. The agency of the player was to be found in such decisions, in the negotiation representation and the representational. And in the purposes of *locus* and *platea*, the players of postmedieval London found, not a false dichotomy, but a multivalent source of representational authority and cultural productivity.

"IT IS PERFORMED"

While Jonson may have sought to locate his personal authority on the printed pages of *Volpone*, *Sejanus*, and *The Royal and Magnificent Entertainment*, among other early seventeenth century publications, theatre practice at the end of the sixteenth century still generally found authority not at the printhouse but at the playhouse, where location was only precariously anchored in the *elsewhere* of representational space. As exemplified in the scene that begins *Caesar*, the plays of Shakespeare were calculated to take advantage of the instability of representational space in the theatre. However firmly fixed the characters of Flavius and Murellus may be in the abstract setting of the *locus*, the scene does not advance until the Cobbler and his crew yield the real-world site of the *platea*. *Caesar* does not begin with an abrupt leap to Rome but with a gradual transition from the lifeworld of the London playhouse to the abstract cityspace of Shakespeare's representation. This transitional opening is an essential part of the play's representational strategies and of the meaning it wishes to make of the city in which *Caesar* was first performed. In the uses of *locus* and *platea*, Shakespeare and his players found a multivalent source of individual authority and cultural productivity, and through Shakespeare and his players the city incurred a debt to the stage.

Though the performance of Rome on the platform stage seems in stark contrast with the elaborate architectural pageantry of James's entry, this urban play participates in the cultural phenomenon of early modern hybrid space that I describe with the Latin word that Jonson appropriated for James, "Londinium." The space of Londinium serves as the unacknowledged *limen* connecting the abstract elsewhere of early modern representation with the real place of the stage. Much like the "distinct knowledge space" that Cosgrove notes is often opened up by arches (*Apollo's* 294 n93), public theatrical performance worked to introduce a distinct narrative space. While the idea of Rome may provide a paradigm of urban space in *Caesar*, it is through the gaps in this representation of Rome—the *platea*—that London's own spaces were produced.

Though the innovations in visual culture that would eventually reshape the city were emergent in 1599, Shakespeare's London was still manifestly a city of pageants and processions where, in Mullaney's words, "a community could chart, in its actual topography, the limits and coherence of its authority" (10). However, the authority represented in the streets of *Caesar*'s Rome (as in Shakespeare's London) was one whose coherence was more vulnerable to challenge and disruption than Mullaney's statement admits. In the opening scene of *Caesar*, Murellus continues to upbraid the Commoners, presenting the space of the city as a space for the display of authority, but also as a space where that authority is contested.

> MURELLUS: Knew you not Pompey? Many a time and oft
> Have you climb'd up to walls and battlements,
> To tow'rs and windows, yea, to chimney-tops,
> Your infants in your arms, and there have sate
> The livelong day, with patient expectation,
> To see great Pompey pass the streets of Rome;
> [. . .]
> And do you now put on your best attire?
> And do you now cull out a holiday?
> And do you now strew flowers in his way,
> That comes in triumph over Pompey's blood? (I.i.37–42, 47–51)

This speech establishes a discrete *locus*, a geographically and temporally specific representation, but one that presents an experience of urban space not unfamiliar to the audience of postmedieval Londoners who so recently saw themselves reflected in the *platea*-playing of the Commoners. The tribunes dismiss Commoners who have "come onstage to celebrate Caesar's military victory as they have celebrated Pompey's, but without distinguishing between victory over a foreign enemy and victory 'over Pompey's blood'" (Paster 69). The coherence of a "community" must be measured not only in the civic display but in its reception among the people, and the tribunes make it quite clear that both are in question.

The holiday against which Flavius and Murellus militate is the feast of Lupercal.[35] Their complaint is not with the holiday itself, but with Caesar's appropriation of it as an occasion for an urban triumph not unlike a royal entry. The character of Caesar is introduced in the midst of his entry into Rome, as he orchestrates his own city-spanning theatrical event.

> CAESAR: Calphurnia!
> CALPH: Here, my lord.
> CAESAR: Stand you directly in Antonio's way
> When he doth run his course. Antonio!
> ANTONY: Caesar, my lord?
> CAESAR: Forget not in your speed, Antonio,
> To touch Calphurnia; for our elders say
> The barren, touched in this holy chase,
> Shake off their sterile curse.
> ANTONY: I shall remember:
> When Caesar says, "Do this," it is performed. (I.ii.1-10)

In his performance of urban ceremony, Caesar displays a thorough understanding of the theatricality of the (political) stage. Not content to be merely the object of his spectators' view, Caesar actively performs in his Lupercal entry, and instructs Calphurnia and Antony in their roles. Caesar displays a flexible understanding of his own public identity—so much so that he attributes transformational power to the civic triumph, and wishes to make sure that Calphurnia is touched by that power. Antony's response, "When Caesar says 'Do this,' it is performed," positions him as Caesar's performance-surrogate, not unlike Alleyn's role in James's entry. But Caesar, unlike James, does not hesitate to join the performance.

In his subsequent exchange with the Soothsayer, Caesar shows his willingness to exploit personally the theatrical structure of his entry, stopping his entourage and hushing the crowd in order to hear his petitioner's cryptic message. Though Caesar ignores the Soothsayer's warning, this gesture is reminiscent of those performed by Elizabeth during her entry, in which she "played at being part of the pageants" (Goldberg 31). Caesar, too, is engaged with this performance and with the construction of the identity that it performs: his own.[36] Throughout the play, the discourses of power in the city are directly compared to the discursive space of the theatre. By continually referring to and metaphorizing theatricality, Shakespeare is also continually indexing the "cultural occasion" of the theatrical event itself. The city represented in *Caesar* is a theatrical space where authority displays itself to the people, but where it is also judged by those same people.

The scene that follows between Brutus and Cassius sets the scene for the theatrically framed murder to come. Cassius seduces Brutus to join the conspiracy, while in the background the city's people can be heard, joined in a "general shout" for reasons not yet known to the two onstage. Caesar's civic triumph has culminated, offstage, with Antony's offers of a crown ("coronet") and Caesar's triple refusal. Goldberg observes that "this is the only moment in all of Shakespeare when the backstage area is conceived of as one on which the action onstage depends, one continuous with actions onstage" (167). Indeed, at this moment the "onstage" space is "offstage" from the space of civic performance. Offstage shouts punctuate the onstage debate over Caesar's power, a debate that articulates the potency of public theatrical displays by which "new honors [. . .] are heap'd on Caesar" (I.ii.134).

In this scene, Cassius asks, "what should be in that 'Caesar'?" Throughout the play Caesar has insisted that he is "true-fix'd" (III.i.61) and has demonstrated an attachment to the fixity of his own proper name. This it seems is symptomatic of Caesar's "Colossus"-like self-representations, which Cassius fears. However, the conspirators overlook Caesar's willingness to perform, to conform his identity to political and social contingency; in other words, to accept that his identity is as often flexible as it is "fix'd." Cassius, Brutus, and Casca see in Caesar's increasing reluctance to put aside the crown, a man accommodating himself to the "style of gods"; they fear that in the course of the Lupercal entry the idea of "Caesar" will become synonymous with that of "Colossus" in the popular imagination

The dualistic use of urban space both for display (by those in authority) and for spectatorship (by the populace) is further expanded by a discussion of the reception of Caesar's offstage performance. Casca relates what he saw: Caesar fainted after being offered the crown.

> BRUTUS: 'Tis very like, he hath the falling sickness.
> CASSIUS: No, Caesar hath it not; but you, and I, and honest Casca, we have the falling sickness.
> CASCA: I know not what you mean by that, but I am sure Caesar fell down. If the tag-rag people did not clap him and hiss him, according as he please'd and displeas'd them, as they use to do the players in the theatre, I am no true man. (I.ii.258–61)

Here, coincident with the formation of the conspiracy, the discourses of power in the city are directly compared to the discursive space of the theatre. "Indeed," Drakakis notes, "in the play as a whole, one man's truth is another man's theatre" (83).[37] But the theatrical aspects of the drama do more than merely question the characters' veracity: Shakespeare invests in the theatre's "self-conscious role as an urban institution that not only reflects but produces urban meaning" (Munro 115-6) by continually referring to and metaphorizing theatricality.

When the conspirators take violent action, the discourses of the theatre are so strongly invoked that they suggest an infinite regress of the theatrical, a multiplication of violence in representation. Following the murder of Caesar—notably staged in Pompey's Theatre—is precipitated by Caesar's last, fatal insistence on the stability of his identity: "I am constant as the northern star" (III.i.60). Following the murder, it is Brutus's turn to orchestrate a public performance.

> BRUTUS: Stoop, Romans, stoop,
> And let us bathe our hands in Caesar's blood
> Up to the elbows, and besmear our swords;
> Then walk we forth, even to the market-place,
> And waving our red weapons o'er our heads,
> Let's all cry, "Peace, freedom, and liberty!"
> CASSIUS: Stoop then, and wash. How many ages hence
> Shall this our lofty scene be acted over
> In states unborn and accents yet unknown! (III.i.105-110)

Brutus's staging of the conspirators' public appearance is met with a reply that displaces the scene from civic performance to public theatre: Cassius's lines refer to Shakespeare's own production, in which, "ages hence" the murderers' "lofty scene" was indeed "acted over." These lines, delivered from the most narratively substantiated position of the *locus*, invoke the double vision of the *platea* in which both ancient Rome and contemporary London would have been equally in play on the stage. At this point, Shakespeare puts his entire play in quotation marks, reminding his audience that Caesar's death was not in fact actually happening in the past, but was being "acted over" in the present: performed again in an accent that would have been "unknown" to Caesar and in a state "unborn" in his Caesar's age-though in a location that he himself had claimed, and would later be named "Londinium."

In a theatrical crime scene that is itself "deeply dependent on the mechanics of representation" (Drakakis 82), the conspirators murder Caesar because they believed that he represented himself as greater than they. They have little opportunity to secure their representation, however, before yielding the scene to Antony, whose own re-presentation quickly displaces that of the murderers.' From the second line of his funeral oration, "I come to bury Caesar, not to praise him" (III.ii.74), Antony seeks to appropriate the version of history recently established by Brutus and the other conspirators, and to produce for the Commoners a favorable retrospective representation of Caesar. This is, in a sense, Caesar's last public performance: even in death, his identity remains available to theatrical interpretation, and Antony takes advantage of the performability of this late Roman actor and the flexible potential for meaning in his name.

At the outset of *Caesar*, the tribunes established and defined the *locus* in Rome, by disparaging the playful plebeians: "you blocks, you stones [. . .] you cruel men of Rome" (I.i.35–6). At the most critical point in Antony's oration to Rome's citizens, he flatters the plebeians with the same words: "You are not wood, you are not stones, but men" (III.ii.142). Antony's oration reverses the movement of the opening: Antony *"comes down from the pulpit"* and stands among the Commoners to read Caesar's will (III.ii.163 sd). Rather than asserting a *locus* distinct from the *platea* space produced by the Commoners, as Murellus and Flavius do, Antony moves from *locus* to *platea*. Antony is the only character in the play to perform in this way. Though this movement preserves the narrative fiction, Antony's gesture of inclusion nevertheless takes in London's groundlings along with Rome's plebeians. It is not above imagining that when he came *"down from the pulpit,"* the actor playing Antony may well have left the platform stage and joined the groundlings in the Pit. As Alessandro Serpieri observes, the theatre-loving Antony consistently demonstrates "mastery of every stage space" (Serpieri 128), including Shakespeare's theatre as well as Pompey's.

While the Commoners may have been chased from the stage at the outset of the play, Antony finds the authority to overturn the conspirators' victory by including the audience of commoners in his performance (III.ii.201). This victory was not the result of mere rhetoric, but of a performance decision. As discussed in Chapter One, the spatial theories of Tschumi are relevant here: the operations of dramatic text and live performance on the early modern English stage effected the careful agencing of (representational) space and (theatrical) event.

This effect is essential to the understanding of the theatre as productive, not merely a product. The play repeatedly describes the conspirators as anti-theatrical. Cassius in particular is singled out: "He loves no plays, / As thou dost, Antony" (I.ii.203-4). Cassius in turn vigorously condemns Antony as "a masker and a reveller!" (V.i.62), though it was he who advised Brutus against letting Antony speak at Caesar's funeral. Where Cassius fails to see the value of performance for entertainment, Brutus fails to see the full political potential of civic performance; he failed to recognize the flexibility of theatrical representation by which his own version of history was so quickly re-authored by Antony's oration. The military conflicts that follow are an afterthought: Rome was contested in performance. The city was lost and won in Pompey's theatre. Following the early example of Murellus and Flavius, those who fail to respect the authority of public performance are "put to silence."[38]

What is at stake in these representations is a version of history. The murder of Caesar and Antony's reading of Caesar's will are both representations of history framed by public urban performance.[39] Yet, these representational performances are themselves located (quoted) in the context of *other* representational performances. In *Caesar*, perhaps even more than in his history plays, Shakespeare overtly announces that his theatre is engaged in the production and reproduction of history.

The complex interplay of concrete performance and abstract representation, located as it was in the permeable representational space of "Londinium," created for the early modern audience an opportunity to compare "the limits and coherence" of the authority on display in *Caesar* to their own understanding and experience of power and its authorizing urban performances. I am not suggesting that the functions of such a consideration would be to stimulate resistance to authority among the theatregoers; I agree with Kermode that the political implications of the play are "ambiguous" and "difficult [. . .] to assess and interpret" ("Julius Caesar" 1146). But, without ambiguity, *Caesar* addresses urban authority, and does so in relation to the complex simultaneous coexistence of the stage on which the play would have taken place and the fiction that was represented there. Shakespeare relies on the relationship between the concrete and abstract registers of the theatre event to interrogate the relations of power in his representation of Rome, juxtaposing that *theatrical* relationship with his own *material* London and its authorizing urban performances.

"AUTHOR OF HIMSELF": RELUCTANT PERFORMANCE

In yet another of her studies of *Caesar*, Garber observes that "[t]he taking of the name for the man" can be seen to be a "thematically important element throughout this play, where Caesar is at once a private man and a public title" ("Dream" 52). Barton, too, remarks on the rhetoric of naming. She notes that "in later scenes [Caesar] resorts to [. . .] self-naming almost obsessively" (86-7). For Barton, the result of such obsessive "self-naming" is that the individual subject transforms himself into "a somehow externalized object," perhaps because "although this man is in many ways noble, he is also far too aware of the fact" (87). The character of Caesar, though "almost obsessively" concerned with fixing his political identity, nevertheless sees his authority as something to be publicly performed; he is also not unaware that his identity and his name itself should be mutable in a culture of city-spanning theatrical events with the power to reverse sterility, confer kingship, wreak havoc, and transform a republic into an empire.

When Garber concludes that "*Julius Caesar* is, in a way, the last play of its kind," she is identifying this text as partial evidence of the cultural shift taking hold in late Elizabethan England ("Dream" 46). I too view *Caesar* as among the last of its kind, for the way in which it shows events that simultaneously perform and represent the relations among the city, its rulers, and its urban subjects. Frye's discussions of the "competition for representation" in the latter years of Elizabeth's career demonstrate the conflicts between, on the one hand, the lingering sense that authority was something to be engaged through public performance, and, on the other, Elizabeth's increasingly concerted efforts to stabilize and define her identity in name and image.[40] In 1599, *Caesar* demonstrated the attrition of the cultural traces that linked medieval spatiality to late sixteenth-century London.

James's entry offers strategies of representation and performance (never mutually exclusive) that seem to consciously take the next cultural steps past the "last of its kind" status of *Caesar*. While the event displayed the doubled space of postmedieval London, the king himself retired into fixity: de Certeau's "*propre*" was James's ruling representational force, in name and image. James refused to yield the *locus* of his own representational identity. He refused to engage with the means of the entry's production, and instead remained "on display" in the stabilized London of his Latin-derived, Romanate representation.

At the outset of *Caesar*, a structuring question is posed by Murellus: "What conquest brings he home?" This demand can be seen to interrogate the play as a whole. Within the fiction of the play, Murellus questions the assumptions of power and the relations of monarch to community. "In *Caesar*, Rome is a city obsessed with the nature of individuality" (Paster 69); this obsession is introduced early and frames the relations of city and individual throughout the play. But Murellus' question opens up another field of consideration: the "conquest" of *elsewhere* is a practice distinctly opposed to the space of "home." The spatial dynamic that Shakespeare attributes to ancient Rome is in fact indicative of the "modern ways of seeing" emerging in Shakespeare's own time and place, ways of seeing that seek, in Weimann's words, "to set the image as an object before oneself and to set it forth in relation to oneself" (*Author's* 187). In other words, the "conquest" Murellus expects from a victorious Roman general is related to Heidegger's "conquest of the world as picture" (129). The spatial practices that allow one to perceive the world in instrumental terms as "other" to one's own space(s) can be seen to "double" and reflect the spatial practices of the *locus*, which in the theatre "was instrumental in differentiating space and, thereby, separating the fixed place per abstraction from other localities" (Weimann, *Author's* 182). *Caesar* then poses a double question: the play interrogates the authority motivating a conquest of space within the representation; and it questions the authority of representation itself, through strategic interruptions in the closure of that "abstraction," the play's represented location. By these interruptions, "the action is pushed further into that liminal realm already occupied by the theatre itself" (Drakakis 70). Thus, Shakespeare's Rome is a city in which power is contested both by the forces authorizing the representation of power and also by Rome's population—the latter being an audience not unlike the audience of the play itself, an audience well aware of the limits of representation.

If Shakespeare's *Caesar*—in which Rome's leaders use performance as the medium of deadly conflict—is the "last of its kind," then Shakespeare subsequently explored Rome via a play in which the city's leading citizen absolutely refuses to perform at all. *Coriolanus*, like *Caesar*, begins with a structuring challenge, the dramatic (urban) question: "What is the city but the people?" (III.i.198). Rather than taken at face value, this question is explored, troubled, and ironized throughout the course of the events that transpire in and near Coriolanus' Rome, a city far removed historically from Caesar's.

To recall Gillies's conflation of *orbis* and *urbis*: the "walls of the city" which were "telescoped into the edges of the ancient map" also served to delimit the physical and conceptual spaces of performance whereby individuals defined their experience of the city (6). While the setting of *Coriolanus* (1608), geographically, is the same city as that in which *Caesar* is set, historically, the latter play takes place hundreds of years before the events of *Caesar*, when Rome was a city whose power "did not extend much beyond its city walls" (Cantor 11). The theatrical setting that conditioned the performance of a political murder was framed, for Caesar (as for Remus), by the discourses of the urban. In *Coriolanus*, discourses of the city loom large, as well; the city in this latter case is one chronologically much closer to Remus's legendary leap and Romulus's foundational murder.

In the Rome of *Coriolanus*, the theatrical conditions that repeatedly invite, even demand, performance are met with derision and dismissal. Though this is the same Rome as that in which Brutus and Cassius stage their murder in a theatre, this city's greatest figure is only ever a reluctant performer.

Bryan Reynolds's interpretation of the ways in which performance reinforces the political content of *Coriolanus* provides a useful response to much existing *Coriolanus* criticism (111),[41] a body of work that, as with *Caesar* criticism, has often focused on language.[42] What these logo-centric studies offer to performance-oriented considerations of this play—and I count this chapter among the latter—is a consideration of the naming obsessions that periodically trouble the characters (and readers and audiences) of *Caesar*, but reach in the title character of *Coriolanus* an extreme form of identity dysfunction.[43] *Coriolanus'* aggressive self-fashionings are symptomatic of his anti-theatrical bias: Coriolanus refuses to play a role-to hazard his identity in performance-other than the one that he has determined for himself, and this refusal leads to unrest, exile, and death as he continually asserts his own representational "*propre*" over the performances that validate civic authority. Naming in *Coriolanus* becomes a species of representation.

Though theatricality is not so clearly marked as important to the representational economy of *Coriolanus* as it is in *Caesar*, nevertheless, conventions of public performance prove to be of the utmost significance in the play. However, Goldberg's study of "the politics of literature" often conflates spectacle and performance when in fact these terms, and the representational strategies they imply, are oppositional. Goldberg: "Just as Coriolanus will not display himself to the crowd, he denies us, his audience in the theater" (281). On the contrary, apart from the action of battle, mere display for others' visual inspection is the only form of representation that Coriolanus will accept for himself. When not at war, his preferred state is, as his mother fears, "picture-like to hang by the wall" (I.ii.11). This static picturing, this "singleness and unchangeableness of meaning that he aspires to," is reinforced by the epithet given to him in the course of the battle with the Corioles: "The name and the thing united inseparably, 'Coriolanus' will have one meaning only, at all times and in all situations" (Calderwood 80). Goldberg argues that Coriolanus adopts modes of self-display akin to those of Britain's new king: "Like James he depends on invisible and unrepresented confirmation" of his authority and identity (193). I disagree. Rather, James and Coriolanus both demonstrate a dependence on *visible* representation; though if anything, Coriolanus' dependence is even more extreme than that of James. In his withdrawal from (social) performance, Coriolanus collapses his public self-fashioning into a proper name and a fixed image. Contempt, like James's boredom, is Coriolanus' representational strategy of choice.

It is difficult for me to think about Shakespeare's *Coriolanus* without comparing the title character to James I. Coriolanus wants to be regarded as a hero, but outside the context of war, he feels, as Kermode observes, "reduced to a mere actor" ("Coriolanus" 1441). Coriolanus is reluctant to perform, and, unlike James, he offers no surrogate to perform in his place. As a result, there is no performance at all.[44] This lack of performance, it seems, is what truly threatens to "unbuild the city" of this play. By themselves, the people are a mob; without citizens, the physical city is an empty husk: in his refusal to contribute to the public performance practices that unify the city and the citizens, Coriolanus threatens the integrity of civic life itself. By comparison, the characters of Shakespeare's *Caesar* self-consciously play with civic authority as a force to be constantly staged. Although the historical events of *Caesar* occur roughly four and a half centuries after those of *Coriolanus*, Shakespeare's *Caesar* would seem to be the necessary precedent to *Coriolanus*: the latter play shows the political consequences, not of "inaction," but of "not acting."

For Coriolanus certainly cannot be accused of inaction. When he is not describing the people as the "scabs" on the body of the city (I.i.166), he can be found in the thick of battle—though even here he finds time to vent his "contempt for the lower orders" (Hill 185), upbraiding the plebian foot soldiers as the "shames of Rome!" (I.iv.31). When he is visible to the audience, Coriolanus is an aristocratic abuser, but when he performs the actions for which he is celebrated as a valiant soldier and the savior of Rome, he is not visible. As Goldberg points out, Coriolanus' "heroic capture of Corioles occurred behind closed gates" (192). Though this is the eponymous act after which Coriolanus is named, the act itself does not appear on stage. Consumed with martial passion, he invades the city single-handed as the doors close behind him. I am reminded of the end of James's entry, when the doors of the Temple of Janus close behind the king, leaving the people with the memory of his passage and displaying text that announces James's transformation with new, Roman names: "*Imperator*" and "Caesar Augustus." This moment at Corioles "indicts the desire to see that [the early modern] theatre audience shares with the plebeians" (Marshall 107). Though there is no writing on the doors of Corioles, Martius, like James, is separated from an audience of (London's) plebeians by the doors' closing and will subsequently emerge transformed and re-named.

Neither the citizens of Rome nor the members of the audience see Coriolanus perform the fighting prowess for which he is lionized, and in subsequent scenes Coriolanus will struggle to keep this event as veiled in peace as it was in war. This insistence on concealing his acts is what Michael Bristol calls Coriolanus' "calculated self-exclusion" (214). Coriolanus consistently rebukes those who praise his actions, though he accepts the name given to him as an outward sign of those actions. Though he will not tolerate others' attempts to define him in public, even when these definitions are well intended, he defines himself by his actions, and for this reason he is eager to take on a new name derived from those actions. So definitive is this re-naming that even the text of the play itself reflects the character's transformation: following his "battlefield promotion" in act one scene nine, the speech prefix for the character formerly known as "Martius" is changed mid-scene.

> COMINIUS: For what he did before Corioles, call him,
> With all th' applause and clamor of the host,
> Martius Caius Coriolanus! Bear
> Th' addition nobly ever! (I.ix.63-6)

Following immediately on this declaration, references to the character in the text do indeed "bear," and even enforce, the "addition": subsequently, Martius' lines are preceded by "Coriolanus."

Persuaded by his mother to accept an appointment as Consul, Coriolanus must first appear before the politicians and then before the people. In his most egregious display of public reticence, Coriolanus storms out of the Senate prior to the ritual recitation of his feats, declaring that he would prefer not "To hear [his] nothings monster'd" (II.ii.77). Less than one hundred lines later, the people waiting for him in the market recall that Coriolanus referred to them as "a monster" and "the many-headed multitude" (II.iii.11, 16). It would seem consistent to conclude that what Coriolanus finds equally monstrous in both cases is a multiplication of identity: not only the multiple identity that attends the many commoners who make up the singular "people" of the city, but as well the assignment of identity applied to him by the members of the Senate which would add their interpretations of him to his own self-perception, thereby "monstering" him with a hydra-like profusion of identities.

Though Coriolanus is attached to his new name (in both literal and figurative senses) for its power to monumentalize his own past, he will not sit by while his "nothings," acts which were performed in concealment, are retroactively made public at the discretion of others. Anticipating his own dread of performance, Coriolanus tries to avoid his obligatory public mortification as well: "It is a *part* / That I shall blush in *acting*, and might well / Be taken from the people" (II.ii.144-6, emphasis added). His dread of the appearance is not a simple distaste for the "monstrous members" of the people (II.iii.12), but rather a fear of the play-within-a-play conditions of public performance. In fact, he is assigned a role in this civic theatrical, and "assigned costume, lines, and action" too (Simmons 113). The costume, "*a gown of humility*," is

appropriate to the part he must play, but humility is not a role that Coriolanus would ever author for himself (II.iii.39 sd). Given that Coriolanus is
a reluctant performer of the part in which he has been cast, what Simmons
calls the "value of his performance" is easily manipulated after the fact by the
tribunes (113). Following his marketplace appearance, Coriolanus rushes off
to change his clothes so that he may know himself again (II.iii.147); mean-
while, Sicinius and Brutus re-present Coriolanus as "a traitor to the people"
(III.iii.66).

After this re-presentation, Coriolanus cannot recoup the change made
to his public identity. Though his mother implores him—"To have my
praise for this, perform a part / Thou hast not done before" (III.ii.108-9)—
Coriolanus can be only himself, "absolute" (III.ii.39). He is so insistent that
his identity cannot be changed that when he is pronounced "banish'd / As
enemy to the people and his country," Coriolanus' reply to the tribune and
to all Rome is defiant and absolute: "I banish you!" (III.iii.117-9, 123). In
this contradictory hyperbole, Coriolanus takes on himself not only identity
but location: when he leaves the city he banishes all those who betrayed his
immutable ideal of Rome. As Vivian Thomas puts it: "The flawless Roman
is exiled because Rome becomes flawed" (220), at least from the perspective of the one exiled. More than just his "projection onto Rome of what
he felt Rome was doing to him" (Cavell 252), Coriolanus' banishment
of the city conveys his belief that he that has remained stable while the
"monstrous" and mutable elements in the city have brought about intoler-
able change. Coriolanus' rebuttal is a myopic declaration of independence:
Rome is banished from him, not the other way around.

When Coriolanus next appears, the text conveys another kind of
"nothing," an inversion of nomination. In a textual gesture that recalls the
point at which his character attribution shifts from "Martius" to "Coriolanus," the exiled Coriolanus returns to the stage disguised even to the
reader: throughout the scene of his arrival in Antium, he is referred to
only as "a Roman" (IV.iii). After introducing himself to one of the Volces,
Coriolanus is left alone on stage. He uses the opportunity to address the
city itself:

> City,
> 'Tis I that made thy widows; many an heir
> Of these fair edifices 'fore my wars
> Have I heard groan and drop. Then know me not,
> Lest that thy wives with spits and boys with stones
> In puny battle slay me. (IV.iv.1-6)

This is Coriolanus' only solitary moment on stage, and he is the only character to speak alone in the play. Though he has adopted "mean apparel," he remains unquestionably himself. Indeed, given the opportunity for thoughtful soliloquy, instead he addresses a bellicose and condescending monologue to a city. Unlike Antony, who asserts his facility with performance by moving into the *platea* to win over the plebeians of *Caesar's* Rome, Coriolanus remains always in his own private *locus*, and even when alone he will address a city in the abstract, rather than speak to the city's people or to the people in the audience of the theatre.

Upon entering Antium, Coriolanus will not refer to Rome by name, referring to it instead by description: "th' city of kites and crows" (IV. v.42)—a dreadful image, reminiscent of de Worde's woodcut of London, in which the city is represented as a depopulated space regarded "from above" by carrion fowl and birds of prey. [Fig. 3]

Coriolanus is exiled from Rome because he refuses to perform, and he will bring about his own death through a similar refusal. Returning to Rome with a conquering army, Coriolanus is met by his family, who beg him to spare the city. He initially refuses, declaring: "Let the Volces / Plough Rome and harrow Italy, I'll never / Be such a gosling to obey instinct, but stand / *As if a man were author of himself,* / And knew no other kin" (V.iii.33-7, emphasis added). Eventually, though, Coriolanus gives in. At the request of his mother and his wife, he spares Rome, but for doing so he berates himself, again in anti-theatrical terms: "Like a dull actor now I have forgot my part" (V.iii.40-1). It is not so much that Coriolanus has merely found himself speechless, but that he has "forgot [his] part." Outside the intensely prescribed values of his self-fashioning display, he is forced into the uncomfortable position of improvising an identity in response to others' performances. His thinking is wishful, "*As if* a man were author of himself," but in this subjunctive moment he is intensely reminded—by the woman who is his most immediate and literal author—that within the parameters of social performance, each role is authored by many.

This scene is tragic anticlimax. Unlike the heroic victory over Antium in the first act, the battle for Rome is deferred, and an identity (authored by another) is grudgingly accepted. For this sole act of mercy in a long, violent career, Coriolanus is betrayed by his closest comrade, and publicly stabbed to death by a group of conspirators in the heart of the city that gave him his name-an assassination that offers tempting parallels to the scene of Caesar's death. Coriolanus is slain "In puny battle" after all; he is condemned, not for an act of mercy, but for an act of social interaction:

he stops to listen to a petitioner (his mother) and is persuaded by her. He abandons his habitual reticence, and accepts a change to the previously fixed self-image that would have led him to author a violent new representation of the city that he had banished.

Whereas the conspirators of *Caesar* meet with mortal punishments, the leader of this other group of conspirators escapes punishment, redeemed by recourse to public performance: Aufidius volunteers to mourn Coriolanus publicly and to help bear his body in procession through the streets of the city (V.vi.138-48).

Just as it is difficult for me to think about Coriolanus without thinking about James, it is difficult for me to think about Shakespeare's Rome without thinking about Shakespeare's London. For Shakespeare and others in this period (including James), Rome was as much an idea as a location, and this idea was suspended between a historical past and a material present. Shakespeare was not concerned by the fact that his Roman patricians spoke like English aristocrats, just as he was not concerned that the plebeians on stage might be indistinguishable from the commoners in the audience. These were not anachronous errors, but dramatic desiderata. Shakespeare set his Roman plays in a kind of Londinium, a Romanized representation of his own city. The social, political, and urban subject matter of *Coriolanus* may be located in ancient Roman source material, but the actual places of performance—the theatre itself and the city in which the theatre stood—were the real sources for this play's concerns, more than any history of ancient Rome.

James, from the outset of his rule, "placed a Roman stamp" on his public and political image (Goldberg 165), and *Coriolanus* reproduced Jacobean culture as James himself would have it. Both James and Coriolanus tried to achieve the fixed identity that de Certeau describes by making public spectacles of themselves. Such acts of civic representation can be used to structure and stabilize the identity of individuals and cities alike. Coriolanus, like James, wants the power to decide who and what is to be performed, but Coriolanus himself will not perform. In *Coriolanus*, as in *Caesar*, public performance is important to the representation of the city. Coriolanus' aggressive self-fashioning mirrors James's withdrawal from the public; the play reflects the dangers that a postmedieval author like Shakespeare saw in a reliance on private, visual representation and the rejection of public self-fashionings as a traditional form of identity formation. In *Coriolanus*, Shakespeare demonstrates the answer to his own question: "What *is* the city?" More than just a choice between citizens and structures, the city was a space to be produced in performance.

A CONCLUSION AND AN EMERGENCE

The hybrid spaces explored and developed in the 1599 performances of *Julius Caesar* contributed to the necessary cultural preconditions for the elaborately hybridized event of James's royal entry and the subsequent expression of Roman ideas in *Coriolanus*. Though Shakespeare's *Caesar* preceded James's entry by five years, both participated in the same "real-and-imagined" space—Jonson just gave it a name. The Londinium Arch straddled not only a narrow, ancient street in the City, it served as the threshold across which postmedieval London's traditional and emergent spaces briefly coexisted, suspended between representation and performance.

Caesar can be seen to be "in a way, the last play of its kind" because the text displays cultural traces, however atrophied, that link the representational forms of late sixteenth-century London to the spatiality of medieval performance culture. By contrast, a sense of *the first of its kind* pervades James's 1604 entry. While the performed event of the entry displayed a doubled spatiality under the name of Londinium, the king (in the role of Augustus, not Julius) attempted to retire into fixity: the *propre* was James's ruling representational force. Though the character of Caesar is "almost obsessively" concerned with fixing his political identity in his own name, nevertheless, in contrast with James, Caesar sees his authority as something to be publicly performed. Coriolanus achieved the fixed identity that de Certeau describes by eschewing performance altogether. Coriolanus, like James, refused to yield the *locus* of his own represented identity, choosing to remain on display in the stabilized site of his name-until, of course, his final, fatal capitulation. If the hybridized Rome of *Julius Caesar*-in which the city's ruler willingly performed in the space of the city-was the last of its kind, then what followed in James's entry, as in Coriolanus' self-nomination, was a Latin-derived, Romanized hybrid space in which the city's ruler absolutely refused to perform at all. But, Londinium was more than just a picture to be looked at.

The performance events considered here demonstrate the brief trajectory of this period of hybrid spatiality. Shakespeare's *Julius Caesar* and *Coriolanus* stand on either side of a cultural threshold, offering two views of this spatial transition: early and late, predecessor and successor, Julian and Augustan. While *Caesar* and other theatre texts of its ilk demonstrate "a strategic approximation to the uses of perspectival form" (Weimann, *Author's Pen* 182), James's entry strove (not quite successfully) to *approximate* nothing: with this event the visual paradigms that would come to dominate perspective-based theatre were imported to England, and its traditional performance paradigms demoted.[45] The force of visual representation at work in the entry superceded the role of embodied performance that had been a traditional aspect of urban pageantry (and an essential feature of the public theatre). Not long after James's entry, Inigo Jones would introduce Jacobean London to both the self-contained theatrical narratives of proscenium arch performance and the self-contained urban narratives of the piazza, precipitating the end of this period of spatial hybridity.

Londinium, a simultaneously real-and-imagined space, was the setting for the first and last Arches in James's entry. The Londinium Arch inaugurated the king's Roman vision of himself and of his capital city. Similarly, Shakespeare produced his own version of Londinium, an urban / theatrical paradigm that responded to his own experience of multivalent cultural, social, and urban practices. Shakespeare's *Caesar* and *Coriolanus* participated along with James's entry in the same "finite historical period" (Lefebvre 73); these hybrid spaces mark three points among the broad genealogy of space in Shakespeare's London.

The epigram from Lefebvre with which I began Chapter One insists on the materiality and historicity of cities as spaces that are "fashioned, shaped, and invested by social activities during a finite historical period" (73). But Lefebvre argued as well that social activity was in turn shaped by the city. Thus understood, theatrical performance in early modern London can be seen to have conditioned as it was conditioned by the social practices of the city and its inhabitants. Interactions between bodies and spaces remained crucial to the production of the city—on the stage, on the printed page, and in the streets themselves. Shakespeare's idea of the world was a theatrical one—the name of his theatre, The Globe, was not chosen by accident. If Shakespeare did indeed see all the world as a stage, then in his Roman plays he conceived the city as theatrical too: a space that was meant to be, not passively viewed, but actively performed.

Conclusion
"The Business of an Age"

Trafficke and travell hath woven the nature of all Nations into ours, and made this land like Arras, full of devise, which was Broade-cloth, full of workemanshippe. Time hath confounded our mindes, our mindes the matter; but all commeth to this passe, that what heretofore hath been served in several dishes for a feaste, is now minced in a charger for a Gallimaufrey.

John Lyly[1]

By 1616, "Trafficke and travell" had so worked on the imagination of post-medieval London that the audacious unconcern for spatial unity that produced a play like *Hickscorner* no longer governed theatrical practice, neither on the stage nor on the page. However confounding these cultural changes, the opportunity to express cultural anxieties, like those in Lyly's *Midas*, was also an opportunity to establish a new paradigm for the theatre. Shakespeare drew on anachronistic chronologies and idiosyncratic geographies as well as precisely mapped ideas of past time and distant location to craft quotational plays that introduced, for example, Roman events into the space of postmedieval London. *Caesar* and *Coriolanus* staged variations on Londinium; but more than just a "theme," these plays experimented with new cultural forms, producing innovations in social space with real-world consequences.

Art historian Richard Krautheimer has noted that the theatre served as one of the means by which the idea of the urban could be explored and an ideal metropolis posited in representational space, well before "Renaissance" ideas and ideals could actually be imposed on the physical terrain of the city. Such theories were predicated upon a fusion of rational philosophy and perspective art, the goal of which was to make "the shape of cities [. . .] conform to reason" (Paster 27). Krautheimer's study of painted theatrical backdrops situates these "experiments in stage design" in the context of early modern spatial and urban innovation (357). With reference to Serlio, Alberti, and others, Krautheimer observes that a representation of a new kind of city:

> could obviously be reconstructed on a stage set with the greatest ease, far easier, indeed, than it could be built. Antiquity, as interpreted by the Renaissance, was distinctly a never-never land-a higher reality which was fully consistent in itself. In a city such as Rome [. . .] an individual building, a church, a palace, perhaps a single house, could be set up to represent revived antiquity. It would stand out from the medieval surroundings, but it would stand out like a sore thumb. To remodel an entire town remained an ideal never achieved [. . .] and obviously difficult to achieve where hard reality was concerned. But it could be done on the canvas of a stage set. This, we should say, is the real link between Vitruvian studies and stage design. (355-6)

Unlike the lavish "prospective" events prepared for James's accession progress and his many private pageants, the stage of the Globe was not a space of visual spectacle where an audience would have *viewed* an abstract representation of idealized cityspace. Rather, the stage was a performance space where actors participating in a theatrical representation could perform an idealized reconception of space that relied on uses of text, *locus*, and spatial practice to communicate urban innovation. This was however not the case with the court masque.

While I may argue (along with Bergeron) that Harrison's Arches introduced London to scenographic and architectural innovations in advance of those contributed by Inigo Jones, Delano-Smith articulates the more widely held opinion: Jones was undoubtedly "the first to introduce [. . .] Renaissance town-planning ideas into England" (208). Regardless of the merits on either side of this historical debate, Krautheimer's suggestive study convincingly argues that the stage spaces of European coterie theatres (those of Jones's Jacobean masques included) may well have been the most innovative laboratories of spatial representation and urban reinvention of the 16th and 17th centuries.

Like the triumphal arch that introduced James to "Londinium," and a new idea of space to London, Jones's court masques invited the courtier / viewer into a conceptual space of geometric precision, architectural *ratio*, and a fixed cultural hierarchy with queen and king placed at its zenith. In England, Jones's work for James and Charles I—theatrical, architectural, urban— was clearly the execution in material space of some of the most sophisticated theories extant in Europe at the time. Orgel's assertion that the "most complete expression of the royal will in the age lay [. . .] in Inigo Jones's ability to do the impossible" suggests the political and social force that the new space of perspective theatre had in the early modern imaginary (*Illusion* 87). The space that Jones introduced in court "entertainments" was a force for conceptual reinventions that would have a transformational impact on the city. Subsequent projects that applied such concepts in built space were, in a sense, quotations of the theatrical: the interventions that Jones performed in Greenwich (1616) and Covent Garden (1630) were topographical application of concepts developed in performance.

The spaces presented in Shakespeare's plays and on Shakespeare's stages were visually unlike the spaces of Jonson and Jones's masques, but these seemingly divergent spaces were conceptually related. The latter reconceptions and new perceptions of theatrical space accelerated the pace of transformation in London's urban practices. The early modern world-picturing project that appeared in the court performances, particularly in those that framed the performance in the space of the proscenium arch, changed the way that space was performed and represented in Jacobean theatre in general, and changed as well the ways in which dramatic writing responded to and capitalized on these new spaces for theatrical discourse. While the popular theatre in Shakespeare's England did not rely on perspectival painted backdrops, it did come to rely on a kind of performance that created a sustained representation of place and time at a remove from the empirical place and time of the performance. Just as Weimann refers to the *locus* as a "strategic approximation to the uses of perspectival form," so perspective in court masques may be seen to provide a strategic approximation of the *locus*. When introducing his wedding masque, Prospero says, "No tongue! all eyes! Be silent" (IV.i.59). This is the appropriate mode of reception for royal spectacle of all sorts (see Chapter Three), but particularly so for the masque, in which visual representation worked to fix narrative location in an abstract image.[2] Subsequent construction in seventeenth-century London would make the visual reception of the city's sites and sights the most important feature of built space, rather than the physical, pedestrian experience of the city celebrated by Stow.

As by now has become obvious, the common theme in the preceding chapters is that the spaces and spatial practices in and of London was subject to major shifts and emergences in Shakespeare's lifetime. And, as discussed in Chapters Three and Four, one of the representational regimes that served as the basis for these conceptual developments was the Stuart myth of a Romanized London. Following the death of Shakespeare, fifty years would pass before Londoners were presented with an opportunity to construct in built space a wholesale reinvention of the City that was comparable to the conceptual reinvention imagined during James's reign. However, when that opportunity presented itself, London's architects and designers were ready with five decades of preparation. Notably, this physical reinvention would be conceived in Roman terms, and described as the apotheosis of those early seventeenth-century urban representations.[3]

Concerned as he is with "urban form" rather than with historicizing spatial practice, Spiro Kostof locates the origins of early modern London in a specific time and place (unlike the broad "postmedieval" transitional period that I have identified in this study). Kostof writes: "The transformation of London from a medieval half-timbered warren into a Renaissance city of paved streets and brick buildings began in a baker's house on Pudding Lane at around 1 a.m. Sunday, 2 September 1666" (245). Kostof argues that the first physical expression of what de Certeau calls "the concept city," an urban space defined by the organizational principles of the modern, could not have been achieved were it not for London's Great Fire which made away with the vast majority of the built structures that still stood from the medieval era.[4]

In 1667, Wenceslaus Hollar composed a map of London showing the damage done to the City in the Great Fire. This map represented an influential shift in the representational practices of urban cartography. At the margins of this map can be found the areas of the city that were not destroyed by the fire: in these portions of the map, the built features of the city are shown in dimensional, oblique view—in common with the conventions of many of the map images considered in Chapter Two. However, in what he refers to as the "blanke space" of the fire's devastation, Hollar elected to employ an abstract representation of space: instead of a dimensional view of the buildings that had been there, or of smoldering rubble, Hollar introduced a purely geometric system of lines that preserved an idea of space but did not represent that space as topographic. So influential was Hollar's new view, that the visual strategy was quickly copied: John Leake's 1669 map of the same terrain employs Hollar's approach [Fig. 13], with the added feature of an inset panorama of the city in flames, as if Leake felt an anxious need to represent the event that had rendered the most ancient spaces of London "blanke."

Restructurings of the physical city followed swiftly upon the destruction of the City of London, and representation would play a material role in this transformation. Ambitious plans for the reconstruction of the devastated areas were drawn up by a number of architects and engineers, including Christopher Wren, who submitted a full-scale plan for the rebuilding of

Figure 13: London, Map of Fire Damage. John Leake, 1669.
© The British Library. All Rights Reserved.

the City in less than two weeks—"while," Delano-Smith notes, "the burnt-out area of London was still smouldering" (209).[5] Delano-Smith goes on to observe that the best early modern English example of "the role of maps in the [urban] planning process occurred in association with the rebuilding of London after the Great Fire of 1666" (209). Gordon's observations reinforce this claim, citing the significant representational shift visible in Hollar's rendering:

> The extent to which geometric delineation in purely diagrammatic form challenged contemporary conceptions of the city is suggested by the fact that the area depicted in the ground plan is explicitly described as a 'blank space' signifying [. . .] precisely the absence of the city." (73)

This image, which is in part a truly abstract representation "from above," can be seen to re-imagine London's spaces in the geometrically precise abstraction that would become characteristic of the early modern world view. Not coincidentally, the way of looking at urban space associated with the concept-city is coterminous with the area destroyed by the fire.

In the geometrical fixity of Hollar's post-fire "groundplot," any trace of the pedestrian mappings of Matthew Paris, Norden, Stow, and others is erased. Presentational frames that might lead the viewer to a conceptual approximation of a physical relation to an image are absent. Instead, the tactile and topographical space of the surviving city frames the "blanke space" of Hollar's representation, a space where physical, human activity is not invited because there is no city left in which to act. While the passage on the map states that in this "blanke space" the territory of London is "exactly demonstrated," the practices by which the city had been represented as performed and performable are as fully erased from the map image as the buildings of medieval London were razed from the physical space of the city.

Hollar's representation of the damage done in the Fire is in many respects the genealogical predecessor of the abstract image of urban destruction that provides the frontispiece to this book. The quotation from *The New York Times* editorial that accompanies this image—published a year later on September 11, 2002—refers to this photograph, but has relevance to a consideration of the "blanke space" of Hollar's image too.

> We look at the satellite photograph of New York City taken on Sept. 12 [2001] and our eyes go to the plume of smoke blowing off [. . .] the tip of Manhattan. We barely notice the undisturbed grid of city streets reaching into the distance. They were, indeed, unnaturally quiet that day, but it was quietness, not extinction. (A32)

Upon considering this photo, the editors of *Times* were reassured by "the undisturbed grid of city streets" (A32). The source of that reassurance is the abstraction of this image: this photo is the realization of the concept city, a representation of cityspace. The satellite view has accomplished the evacuation of human meaning from a physical territory freighted with violence and grief. Instead of human-scale meaning, the image shows a grid and sets of buildings occupying their "proper" locations on that grid; it also shows a section of the grid with a gap in it where no buildings can be seen. This is a site (sight?) of disaster, but one rendered geometric, perhaps even "legible" in de Certeau's sense of the term.

A congruent theory of urban space and urban trauma obtains in Hollar's remarkable 1667 map, in which the illustrator not only documented the extent of the damage but responded to the social effects of the 1666 Fire. Abstraction serves to represent part of the city too charged with trauma to illustrate according to the conventions of the urban portrait, conventions that obtain in other parts of the same illustration. Kostof's description of post-fire London recalls the building project proclaimed by James in the year before Shakespeare's death: "Wee had found Our Citie and Suburbs of London of stickes, and left them of Bricke, being a Materiall farre more durable, safe from fire, beautifull and magnificent" (Stuart 346). Though not a project completed in James's lifetime, after the Fire, any evidence of medieval wooden construction was gone, to be rebuilt in the fashions and materials of early modern construction. After the Fire, the building of early modern London began in earnest. This beginning is marked, appropriately, by a Romanate monument: the massive, muralled obelisk designed by Christopher Wren, architect of many of London's new spaces. Wren's monument to the Great Fire (called simply, "The Monument") is a testament to the catastrophe that made possible the implementation in physical space of an idea of London that had been developing for decades.

The Monument is a single column 202 feet tall, a height (according to a plaque on the west side of the Monument) "being equal to the distance westward from the bakehouse in Pudding Lane where the fire broke out." The column is surmounted by a circle of brass flames. A Latin inscription on the south side of the Monument provides encomiums to the leadership of the king, the fortitude and industry of London's citizens, and to the remarkable accomplishments of the rebuilding project.

> Charles the Second, son of Charles the martyr, king of Great Britain [. . .] commiserating the deplorable state of things, whilst the ruins were yet smoking, provided for the comfort of his citizens, and the ornament of his city [. . .] immediately passed an act , that public works should be restored to greater beauty [. . .] the streets made straight and regular, such as were steep levelled, and those too narrow made wider, markets and shambles removed to separate places. They also enacted, that every house should be built with party walls, and all in front raised to equal height, and those walls all of square stone or brick [. . .]. Also anniversary prayers were enjoined; and to perpetuate the memory hereof to posterity, they caused this column to be erected.[6]

A bas relief sculpture at the base of the Monument, executed by Caius Gabriel Cibber, draws on Roman tradition. [Fig. 14] Cibber's sculpture depicts Charles II as a periwigged Caesar Augustus, directing the reconstruction efforts. On the left side of the sculpture:

> [A] female figure representing the city of London sits disconsolately on a pile of ruins. Time tries to raise her up; behind are goddesses of Plenty

Figure 14: Bas relief, C.G. Cibber; The Monument, C. Wren, 1677. Photo by author.

and Peace, and the citizens of London. [. . .] [B]elow, the dragon
from the city arms attempts to hold up the ruins.

(Schofield, *Building* 175)

On the right, Charles is surrounded by a throng of allegorical figures including Science, Architecture, Nature, Justice, and Fortitude; many of these
figures wield the emblematic tools of their trades, including surveying and
measuring implements (Schofield, *Building* 175). Lions are reined in, and
Ignorance is imprisoned. The Monument serves a dual function: eulogizing
London's medieval spaces from the epicenter of their demise while praising
the idea of early modern London, many of its spaces conceived and designed
"from above." Enshrining the theory behind this urban perspective, the
Monument is surmounted by an observation deck from which one may view
London, not quite as the "texturology" that de Certeau saw from the observation deck of the World Trade Center, but certainly from a vantage well
above the ruins of the fire—and from a point directly across the river from
St. Mary Overy, whose tower served the observations of so many of London's
portraitists.

The inscription on the Monument concludes with a final remark on
the cultural significance of the change that various forces—material and representational—had performed on the space of London: "[A]t three years' end,
the world saw that finished which was supposed to be *the business of an age*"
(emphasis added). Though the reconstruction of the City was performed in
just three years, the reinvention of London's spaces had been under construction for much longer than that, since well before Stow's *Survey*. Thus, the
initial assumption recorded on the Monument is not far wrong: the building
of early modern London, from conception to construction, was indeed the
business of an age.

Notes

NOTES TO THE INTRODUCTION

1. De Certeau 92.
2. See Meyerowitz.
3. For more on this satellite photo, see the conclusion. For a discussion of the relationship between performance and memorials, with special reference to the WTC memorial and the history of Lower Manhattan, see D.J. Hopkins and Shelley Orr, "Memory / Memorial / Performance," in the collection *Text and the City: Performing and Writing Urban Space*, Ed. Kim Solga, Hopkins, and Orr, forthcoming. Predictably, the WTC site, like any public memorial, has become a site of political and social contention. The plans for the site continue to evolve under private, civic, and financial pressures, and it is not clear that the retaining wall will be part of the final product. However the memorial designed by Michael Arad and Paul Walker would offer a similar "from below" perspective. See Paul Goldberger, *Up From Zero: Politics, Architecture, and the Rebuilding of New York* (New York: Random House, 2005) for a complete account (to 2005) of the WTC site controversy.
4. For a thorough study of contemporary cities, a review of influential urban theories, and a theorization of the "pedestrian" spatial values that can activate cities, see my article "Mapping the Placeless Place: Performing Community in the Urban Spaces of Los Angeles," *Modern Drama* 46.2 (Summer 2003): 261–84.
5. Another term from Foucault: "*emergence*, the moment of arising"; not "the final term in historical development," but an incident of historical "apparition" (1977 148, italics in original).
6. See Braider, Friedrichs, Mumford.
7. For a reliable discussion of the conventional uses of these terms, see Leah S. Marcus, "Renaissance/Early Modern Studies," *Redrawing the Boundaries: The Transformation of English and American Literary Studies*, Ed. Greenblatt, Stephen and Giles Gunn (New York: Modern Language Association of America, 1992), 41-63. For a debate over periodizing, see Margreta de

Grazia, "The Ideology of Superfluous Things: *King Lear* as Period Piece" *Subject and Object in Renaissance Culture,* Ed. Margreta de Grazia, Maureen Quilligan, and Peter Stallybrass (Cambridge: Cambridge University Press, 1996), 17-42. De Grazia has rejected the vast periodization of the term that she dismisses as the "early now," advocating instead materialist microhistories of the "renaissance."

8. I draw on another of Roach's studies for a concise definition of a term that will be used throughout this project: "[B]y the word *performance* [. . .] I mean the kinesthetic and vocal embodiment of social memory and self-invention" ("History, Memory, Necrophilia" 23).

9. See Schneider, Taylor, Worthen 1998.

10. See Hopkins 2003.

11. I say "seemingly 'ephemeral'" because conceptions of performance as inherently ephemeral have come under critique in recent years. See Taylor and Schneider. See also Hopkins and Blum, "Shakespeare: Early Modern / Postmodern (Performance, Pedagogy, Polemic)," in *Reconsidering Early Modern Ephemera* (forthcoming) for a discussion of Shakespearean production as a mode of performance that is particularly durable (i.e. not so ephemeral after all).

NOTES TO CHAPTER ONE

1. Calvino 136-139, italics in original.

2. Lefebvre 73.

3. For an overview of Saxton's output, and that of his growing number of colleagues in the practices of chorography and cartography in England, see Harvey, *Maps in Tudor England.*

4. *As You Like It* II.vii.139. All quotations from Shakespeare's works are from *The Riverside Shakespeare.*

5. Soja's phrase is indebted to Homi Bhaba. See Bhaba, where he articulates his theory of "sententious" history (56). Both Bhaba and Soja are influenced by Lefebvre, after whom I might describe this study as, not a consideration of "the history of space" (116), but of *the space of history.*

6. See also Carlson, *Places of Performance* 14.

7. See especially *Shakespeare and the Popular Tradition* 64-84, 196-207; "Textual Authority"; and *Author's Pen and Actor's Voice* 180-215. See also John Drakakis's study of Weimann's output, "Discourse and Authority: The Renaissance of Robert Weimann," *Shakespeare Studies* 26 (1 January 1998): 83–105; and the collection of essays *Rematerializing Shakespeare,* a volume dedicated to Weimann's work; most of the essays in this volume are engaged in some aspect of his output.

8. See in particular Phythian-Adams, Manley, and Geertz. Gillies calls this same phenomenon "the sacred drama of the bounded city" (6). The language of

performance studies provides much greater specificity for the description of meaningful, signifying human behaviors-both individual and cultural-that "sacred," "ritual," and "ceremonial" seem inadequate to describe events that may not have any direct religious connotation. Moreover, Gillies use of "drama" in this context attributes the textual obsessions of modernity to a culture in which reference to print is anachronistic.

9. For a critical history of the field of Performance Studies, along with its often contentious relationship with Theatre Studies, see Worthen.

10. Gillies draws the phrase "geographical imagination" from Frank Lestringant's work. See Lestringant, esp. 1-11.

11. All references to the "City of London" refer explicitly to the Corporation of the City of London, the so-called "Square Mile." This area constitutes the official territory historically bounded by the walls around medieval London, a territory established by the Romans in the first century, which had only slightly expanded by Elizabeth's accession to include suburbs immediately outside the walls to the northeast and to the west. My use of the term "London" follows that of Francis Sheppard. I use "London" or "the city" to refer to "the whole metropolitan urban area" (xvi), which includes not only the official suburbs of the City, but also the unofficial suburbs like Southwark and the slums which by the period of study were rapidly expanding outside the limits of the city walls. See Francis Sheppard, *London: A History* (New York: Oxford UP, 1998).

12. The term "synekism" is taken from Edward Soja, who himself appropriated the Greek-derived term "synoecism" from urban history and archeology. Synekism refers to "the stimulus to urban agglomeration," the impulse to form cities (Soja, "Putting" 27). Synekism refers not only to the origins of city-making, but to the forces which lead to continual change and wholesale reinvention of urban space and practice. It is in this latter sense that I use the term to describe postmedieval London.

13. Mulcaster 16.

14. The amount of critical material treating *The Quene's Majestie's passage* is considerable. See Bergeron, *English Civic Pageantry,* 11-64; Geertz, "Kings, Centers, Charisma"; McCoy; Frye; Logan; Goldberg; and Mullaney, *The Place of the Stage,* esp. 10-13. Montrose provides several analyses of the representational discourses surrounding Elizabeth: "'Eliza, Queen of the Shepheardes' and the Pastoral of Power," *The Purpose of Playing,* "Idols of the Queen," and *The Subject of Elizabeth: Authority, Gender, and Representation.*

15. See Anglo 344-359.

16. See Frye and Logan for astute, if divergent, readings of this scene. See also the contemporary accounts provided by Londoner Henry Machyn and Il Schifanoya, the Mantuan ambassador.

17. For details of the planning, see Bergeron, *English Civic Pageantry* 12–13; Anglo 346; Frye 30–33.

18. For an exploration and expansion of Weimann's theory of *locus* and *platea*, see Chapter 4.

19. For key studies in the issue of presence in performance, see Herbert Blau, *Take Up the Bodies: Theater at the Vanishing Point*; Peggy Phelan, *Unmarked: The Politics of Performance*; Philip Auslander, *Liveness: Performance in a Mediatized Culture*. See also Hopkins and Justin Blum, "Shakespeare: Early Modern / Postmodern (Performance, Pedagogy, and Polemic)," in *Re-Thinking Early Modern Ephemera* (forthcoming).

20. James's successor, Charles I, took the first fully early modern approach to these matters. He canceled his own entry altogether.

21. See F.J. Fisher, "Growth" and "Engine," and Agnew.

22. For these statistics, Shepherd's first appendix consolidates the most reliable material available. See also Sacks, Finlay, and Finlay and Shearer. Comparisons among cities generally exclude reference to Constantinople, a vast city which for centuries loomed large at the eastern edge of the European continent. Jardine as much as suggests that the early modern period may be set from 1453: the fall of Constantinople to Suleiman the Magnificent and its absorption into the Ottoman Empire. Subsequently, Constantinople can no longer be considered the Eastern outpost of Europe and the last remaining link to the uninterrupted cultural, religious, and intellectual heritage of imperial Rome. From this date, Jardine argues, European centers of culture, religion, and scholarship shifted to the west, where they became commodities circulating in western Europe along with other more clearly material forms of capital. Constantinople was a "global city" in advance of that term, in advance even of European and Asian global knowledge. See Jardine 37-45.

23. Diamond's parenthetical "(again)" invokes a critical history of the relationship between representation and theatre, the latter often disregarded by traditional philosophy as representationally redundant. See Worthen, "Drama, Performativity, and Performance," for a summary of this history. Paul Ricoeur seeks to redeem representation from philosophical denunciations as merely "a reduplication of presence" (15). Peggy Phelan seeks to reframe performance as a means of "representation without reproduction" (3).

24. This magnetically attractive chronological pole is noted in the title of a recent collection of essays on the subject of social change in early modern England. See Orlin *Material London, ca. 1600.*

25. For a review of the major figures in postmodern urbanism see Michael J. Dear.

26. See Munro, *Crowded Spaces: Population and Urban Meaning in Early Modern London.*

27. Lavedan, *Histoire d'urbanisme*, 2 vols. (Paris, 1959), 1:27.

28. For a discussion of the views of London, see Chapter 2.

29. See Peter Ackroyd's "biography" of London, which begins with a chapter, "The City as Body," in which London's figurations and personifications are considered.

30. Lefebvre makes the distinction between representational spaces, representations of space, and spatial practices. The distinction among the terms is subtle, and numerous authors have attempted summaries and definitions. See Arnade, Howell, and Simons; Dear, *Postmodern*; Hanawalt and Kobialka; and Lefebvre, 36–46.

31. Foucault's rather flexible distinction between the terms "space" and "place" is in contrast with Casey's studies of the two concepts. See Casey, *Getting Back Into Place* and *The Fate of Place*. For current work on the study of place, see Adams, Hoelscher, and Till.

32. This dedication, which appeared only in the first edition of Hakluyt's Ventures (1589), was addressed to Sir Francis Walsingham—the "Right Honourable" of the first line.

33. Destroyed in World War II, the Ebstorf now only exists in photographic reproductions.

34. See Chapter Two.

35. For a valuable discussion of the hegemonic ideas informing Ortelius's project and represented in the frontispiece to the *Theatrum*, see Cosgrove, *Apollo's* 130-132.

36. This is how maps work even today. No official, representational map ever suggests that it might be inaccurate. For more on the representational strategies of maps, see MacEachren, *How Maps Work: Representation, Visualization, and Design*; and Wood, *The Power of Maps*.

37. See the survey of 20th century ideas about urban space in Hopkins, "Mapping the Placeless Place."

38. Whatever the geographical origin of this play, the character of Hickscorner is a paradigmatically urban figure. The name is not, as one might surmise, a geographical referent (as in "Hick's Corner,"), but rather a description of the character: he is a "hick-scorner." Thanks to Michael Fox for this observation.

39. Quotes from Jonson are from *Volpone, or The Fox*, ed. Jonas Barish.

40. A critically important corollary to Jonson's map-like picturing of the world in *Volpone* is the picturing of the *word* "Volpone" at the beginning of the printed version of the play. Following the list of "The persons of the play," Jonson provides what he calls "The Argument":

    V olpone, childless, rich, feigns sick, despairs,

    O ffers his state to hopes of several heirs,

    L ies languishing. His parasite receives

    P resents of all, assures, deludes, then weaves

    O ther cross-plots, which ope themselves, are told.

    N ew tricks for safety are sought; they thrive; when, bold,

    E ach tempts th' other again, and all are sold. (1-7)

The passage which begins Jonson's play is exemplary of what Mitchell has called "the figure of the 'imagetext'" (9), a visual representation operating at the intersection of picture and word. While such a poeticized acrostic is not an innovation exclusive to Jonson, this textual trope participates in the historic publishing developments that Jonson helped pioneer. The title of the play and the lines of poetry appear in a way that would have been unavailable to the listening audience of a theatrical performance for Jonson's contemporaries. In fact, the imagetext of "The Argument" could have been material exclusive to the printhouse, rather than the playhouse, for an appreciation of this "picture" of the title of the play is clearly calculated for reception by a reader rather than an auditor. In *Volpone*, as in other printed versions of his plays, Jonson "succeeded in suppressing the theatrical production, and has replaced it with an independent, printed text" which signifies "not as a play but as a poem" (Orgel, "What?" 4). In "The Argument" to *Volpone*, Jonson uses picturing to erase the residue of performance and to establish "an authentic Ben Jonson text" free from the collaborative space of the theatre (Orgel, "Authentic" 6). Chapter Three will consider a single issue at the intersection of performance and print culture, but Jonson's role in the innovations of postmedieval London was not small. For consideration of such innovations at great length, see Hirschfeld and Loewenstein.

NOTES TO CHAPTER TWO

1. Though the name of the Temple area continued to refer to them, this property passed out of the control of the Knights Templar with the dissolution of the Order in 1312. See Inwood 126, Read 183.
2. The sparsely populated western suburb of Farringdon Ward Without, of which the Temple and the Inns were a part, was the first area to exceed the medieval walls of London, though industrial suburbs to the north and east would soon follow (Inwood 125–131).
3. Temple Bar was the site of the second of three pageants designed by Jonson for James's royal entry in 1604, the aptly named "Temple of Janus." This arch was the last of London's pageants for the king, set at the limit of the City's jurisdiction. The third pageant, paid for by the City of Westminster, was located in the Strand. See Chapter Three.
4. See also Cosgrove, *Apollo's Eye* 133-5.
5. A monk working in the library of Constantinople made the discovery in 1295, but a Latin translation was not made available until 1409 (Edson 165).
6. Paris's London-to-Rome itinerary exists in four versions. All are drawn by hand, presumably by Paris himself, and as a consequence there is considerable variation among the images. All of the versions of the itinerary are dated circa 1252. Despite differences, the route remains the same on each

itinerary. Each of the itineraries begins with an image of London, though some of the city images are more specific than others. See Delano-Smith and Kain 15–17, 150–151. I have seen three of the four thumbnail sketches of London that Paris drew; the one that I choose to discuss here is the most geographically specific.

7. For more on Paris's representation of Rome, see Delano-Smith 150.

8. See Glanville 18; Harvey, *Medieval* 8-9, 71-73; and Delano-Smith and Kain 15-17, 150-151.

9. For "*aide memoire*" and "*ars apodemica*," see Frangenberg. For travel in preindustrial England, see Harper.

10. For the bibliographical history of the Macro plays, see Bevington xvii-xxiii. For a book-length study of *The Castle of Perseverance* "and related matters," see Southern.

11. "The famous stage diagram serves as a kind of illustrated cover for the manuscript" (Bevington xviii).

12. For the history of this image, which exists only as an eighteenth-century copy, see Howgego 4-5.

13. See Manley, *Sites* 44 for a discussion of the significance of this urban corridor.

14. The overall size of the copperplate map would have been approximately three and a half feet high by seven and a half feet wide (Fisher v). The first two plates were found in 1955 and 1962, with sixteenth-century Flemish oil paintings on the reverse sides (Harvey 74); the third was found in 1996 in a similar condition, and an investigation of the reverse sides of Flemish paintings, particularly those illustrating the Tower of Babel, is under way (*Lost Map*).

15. See Barker and Jackson 12-13; Fisher v-vi; Glanville 72; Gordon 76; and Harvey, *Tudor* 74.

16. "[T]he congruence of Latin titles is an obvious indication of both works' generic companionship" (Klein 34).

17. "Bird's eye view" is a technical term of cartographic history, indicating an overhead "balloon" view that shows an oblique view of a city from a perspective that could not have been physically realized in the sixteenth century. By contrast, a "map view" is a largely ichnographic view to which is added the topographical detail of a very shallow oblique view. These terms are among those developed by British cartographic historian R.A. Skelton (Hyde 11). See also Alpers 72 and Delano-Smith 187-88.

18. This draftsman, Hoefnagel, was a close friend and professional associate of Ortelius (Cosgrove, Apollo 135).

19. "London, capital city of that most fertile kingdom, England." Author's trans.

20. For biographical information about Norden, see Kitchen 43-61.

21. For a brief history of this document itself, only two copies of which remain, see Hyde 42-43.

22. See the London Topographical Society's "A View of London in 1600 by John Norden," hereafter cited internally.

23. The Braun and Hogenberg image includes Bankside, though the location is rendered schematically, without the detail of the City. Moreover, the locations of what might be called the "entertainment district" on the Braun and Hogenberg are labeled "The Boull bay-ting" and "The Beare bay ting," and it is likely that the *Civitates* map image of London predates the presence of theatres as such in Bankside.

24. The City of London began acquiring control of Southwark in 1327, though the authority of the City in the Borough was sporadically enforced. See Sheppard 113-4 and Johnson.

25. The text of this legend is small and indistinct, and may read "Statio prospetiva" (without the "c"). The meaning nevertheless is clear. See Howgego 7, Hyde 43.

26. In November 2002, Southwark Cathedral offered visitors a historical exhibit of portraits of London. In addition to displaying a series of reproductions, including Hollar's "long view," the exhibit also offered visitors an opportunity to view contemporary London from approximately the same location as Hollar would have occupied when making his own image of the city. Using simple remote controls, the visitor could watch on a small monitor as a video camera mounted on the Cathedral tower pans across the north shore of the Thames. The camera even allows one to zoom in on distant structures, like Wren's St. Paul's Cathedral or the top of his Monument to the Great Fire—structures in stark contrast to the twentieth and twenty-first-century office towers that now bracket them.

27. For his discussion of Mercator, see Cosgrove (*Apollo's* 133).

NOTES TO CHAPTER THREE

1. Ackroyd, *London: The Biography*, 92–3.

2. Howes edited Stow's *Annales, or A generall chronicle of England*, extending its contents to include events of the seventeenth century.

3. See Dillon; see also Mullaney, *The Place of the Stage*.

4. Edward Soja draws the term "trialectics" from Homi Bhaba. Soja uses "trialectics" to open a consideration of the system of power(s) at work in the city, particularly the ways in which urban space, political authority, and social forces interact to jointly influence the urban subject. Soja's use of such trialectics is indebted to Foucault, for whom Soja insists: "The power-knowledge link [. . .] was embedded in a trialectic of power, knowledge, and space. The third term should never be forgotten." See Soja, *Thirdspace*, 148.

5. See Arthur Wilson's 1653 biography of James, *The History of Great Britain, Being the Life and Reign of King James the First*. Early in this text, Wilson celebrates James with this exact phrase (1).

6. See Andrew Gurr, *Playgoing in Shakespeare's London*, 31.

7. For classic examples see Barker, Belsey, Dollimore, Howard and Rackin, Stallybrass and White, Sinfield, Tennenhouse.

8. Bergeron has also provided a renewed evaluation of Dugdale's text, grounding an appreciation for Dugdale's contribution in an understanding of how the elements of the entry may have been perceived and interpreted by someone writing about the entry without the benefit of access to the texts of the entry's dramatists.

9. All references to these texts are from *Progresses of King James the First*, J.B. Nichols, ed. Nichols's work is antiquarian at best, but his volume consistently includes first printings of these texts that display their authors' anxieties more clearly than subsequent editions; and Nichols remains the only convenient source for Harrison and Dugdale. Fredson Bowers is considered the authoritative source for Dekker's work, but his text of *The Magnificent Entertainment*, ostensibly "based on a collation of the sixteen copies of Q1," draws on the organization of Q2, placing the "To the Reader" note at the end of the text. See Bowers. Jonson's *Royal and Magnificent Entertainment* can be found in Herford and Simpson and in Dutton. Dutton's text provides a conflation with Dekker (see note 33) which makes for easy classroom study of the entry but is not helpful for textual scholarship. The eleven volume work by Herford and Simpson is considered the authoritative source for Jonson, but the text of this *Entertainment* draws on Jonson's 1616 *Workes*, which excludes statements expressive of Jonson's performance anxieties. See *Ben Jonson*, C. H. Herford, Percy Simpson, and Evelyn Simpson, eds.

10. Most notable among the textual studies are Bergeron, Goldberg, and Parry.

11. Given the massive amounts of cloth required to fully drape a fifty foot tall triumphal arch, one must wonder if the proximity of the Clothworkers' Hall would indicate a collaboration between Harrison's artisans and the specialists of this guild. Schofield (*Building* ix) and Prockter and Taylor (1979) use the "Agas" map to indicate the likely location of property owned by the Clothworkers Guild.

12. Bergeron in particular has provided a thorough description of the entire entry. See Bergeron 1971. Goldberg provides a thorough description of Jonson's contributions.

13. In addition to holding his coronation during these months, James spent much of the time traveling and entertaining in the countryside. See Dekker 342-3, Jonson 385, Wilson 12.

14. Presumably, the arch contributed by the Dutch merchants living in the City would have been the one that James viewed before visiting the Exchange, located as it was so close to the site of the Exchange in Cornhill. See Dekker 349 and Manley 43-44.

15. This strategy of silent watching serves as a model of reception for court masques, as in Prospero's address to Miranda and Ferdinand before the

wedding masque he has prepared for them: "No tongue! all eyes! be silent" (4.1.59). See also James J.Yoch, "Subjecting the Landscape in Pageants and Shakespearean Pastorals" in Bergeron 1985.

16. Rouse is referring specifically to postmodern, post-dramatic performance, but his statement holds true in the early modern as well. See Rouse's valuable essay, "Textuality and Authority in Theater and Drama: Some Contemporary Possibilities."

17. See the valuable examination of this point in Worthen, *Shakespeare and the Force of Modern Performance*, esp. 1–27.

18. Logan's analysis of Elizabeth's entry convincingly argues that Mulcaster's text cannot be presumed to be any more stable than a text such as Dekker's, though the latter announces its divergence from the event that it "records."

19. For a discussion of the current debate over the relationship between text and performance, see Worthen, "Disciplines of the Text / Sites of Performance." This essay provides not only a summary of prevalent positions, it poses a challenge to the binary opposition between text and performance which is so often reinforced by disciplinary boundaries (literature / drama / theatre studies / performance studies). See also valuable "Responses" to Worthen's essay in the same issue, esp. that of Jill Dolan.

20. Bergeron's observation that the "dramatic dialogue" in James's entry is a "significant" deviation from traditional royal entry forms, particularly that of Elizabeth I (*English* 89), is a sound one, but given the noise of the crowd and James's censorship (both active and passive) the contribution of dialogue to the performance itself is unclear and should not be overestimated. Further, the claim that the entry texts are an example of "dramatic" performance takes for granted that the performance occurred exactly as it is documented in published form, an assumption that presumes a "performance *of*" relationship between text and entry, when it is clear that these particular texts were produced after, and because of, this performance.

21. See the following section, Londinium: Camera Regia.

22. For more on instability in performance and text, see Stephen Orgel, "The Authentic Shakespeare," 8-10.

23. For this typography, I refer directly to the quarto held by the British Library, since this same is available through Early English Books Online. The typography in Nichols is different in many respects.

24. Nichols notes that the title given for this event in Jonson's 1616 *Workes* includes an error that suggests as much: "King James's Entertainment in passing to the Coronation; the Author B.J." (Jonson 377 n1).

25. For the foundational discussion of the (often adversarial) working relationship of Jonson and Inigo Jones, see Gordon, 77–101; for a discussion of the Renaissance theory of "*ut pictura poesis*," see Orgel and Strong, esp. 1-11.

26. For a discussion of Jonson's "self-experience" via "editorial authorship" (103), see Loewenstein, *Ben Jonson and Possessive Authorship*, 133–210.

27. Dutton himself performs an interesting act of editorial inclusion. His text of the *Magnificent Entertainment* incorporates Jonson's and Dekker's contributions into a single text. His table of contents attributes "*The Magnificent Entertainment*" to "Thomas Dekker and Ben Jonson" (Dutton 5). This text presents the work of these two dramatists as a single continuous piece, and though Dutton occasionally marks where one author's work begins, the editorial division between the two is inconsistent and at times would be unclear to the unfamiliar reader. In this, Dutton's textual approach resembles, however unintentionally, that of Dekker.

    Dutton's text raises interesting questions about the uses of editing for pedagogical purposes. The goal of his book is to assemble noteworthy examples of Stuart civic pageantry for use "in the classroom" (Dutton 7). But a student reading Dutton's conflated text "by" Dekker and Jonson might not appreciate or even notice the division between the two texts, missing more than just opportunities for productive intertextual readings. The texts of Shakespeare are often received by students who are unaware of comparable editorial practices. Ann Thompson's editorial work-in-progress for the Arden *Hamlet* may break new ground in this area, providing all three extant texts of the play separately, rather than the conventional conflation of the second quarto and folio (and corresponding neglect of the first quarto).

28. The illustrations of the arches in *The Arches of Triumph* were engraved for Harrison by William Kip. See Bergeron, *Practicing* 168.

29. However remarkable the accomplishment that Harrison himself "performed," I choose to emphasize the collaborative process that led to the creation of the Londinium Arch, and indeed, all the arches in the entry. What architect and theorist Rem Koolhaas calls "hybrid authorship" (Koolhaas and OMA xxix) offers an appropriately way of describing the composition of the Londinium Arch, certainly a more nuanced approach than the conventional literary histories that refer to the Arch as exclusively "Jonson's design" (Paster, "Idea" 54).

30. For "emergence," see also Foucault, "Nietzsche, Genealogy, History" 148-52.

31. For further discussion of Jonson and language, see Martin Elsky, esp. 101-109.

32. The term "mega-event" is introduced by Harry H. Hiller. Hiller defines mega-events as "Special events" occasioned by "celebration, commemoration, or declaration" that "altered the daily routines of urban dwellers" and "altered the nature of urban living" (181). Even "short-term, one-time, high profile" events "hosted by a city" (182) can have "a significant and / or permanent urban effect" (183).

33. Bergeron's challenge to Nichols's conclusion is insubstantial (*Practicing* 156-7).

34. My thanks to Louis Montrose for suggesting this rich speculation.

35. See also Hopkins and Blum.
36. See Cosgrove, *Apollo's* 130-1.
37. See Corbett and Lightbown, *The Comely Frontispiece*.
38. See Baker.
39. Londinium was founded in CE 43 by the Roman invasion force under the Emperor Claudius. Though the location of the current City of London was at the time part of the territory of the Catuvellauni tribe, there is no record of a permanent settlement in this area before Roman occupation. For the most authoritative history of Londinium, see Francis Sheppard, *London: A History*. For a non-linear, associative study of London's history, see Ackroyd's "biography." See also Mary Cathcart Borer, *The City of London: A History*; Stephen Inwood, *A History of London*; Jenny Hall and Ralph Merrifield, *Roman London*; John Morris, *Londinium: London in the Roman Empire*; David J. Johnson, *Southwark and the City*; and Bruce Watson, Trevor Brigham, and Tony Dyson, *London Bridge: 2000 Years of a River Crossing*.
40. See Frye's chapter title "Who Represents Elizabeth?"
41. I find this aspect of the Londinium arch to be an evocative genealogical predecessor of the Velàzquez painting that Foucault discusses in his famous essay, "Las Meninas." See *The Order of Things*, 3-16. The painting locates its viewer in relation to "the necessary disappearance of that which is its foundation": the absent presence of royal perspective (*Order* 16).

NOTES TO CHAPTER FOUR

1. Stoppard 107. Thanks to Andre W. Case for suggesting this quotation.
2. See esp. Stow 33–39.
3. For the text *on* this monument, see Nichols 395.
4. The abbreviation is still used throughout Rome to designate municipal buildings, projects, and property.
5. Again, as per formatting in British Library copy. See also Jonson in Nichols (395), and Early English Books Online.
6. James had already arranged for his coronation to be held on 25 July (1603), the Anglican feast day of St. James; one is lead to conclude that scheduling events to coincide with significant dates on the calendar was part of the new king's *modus operandi*, and indeed it was a popular practice in early modern England.
7. See also Paul A. Cantor, who notes that "something is happening to Rome" in Shakespeare's plays that will produce a change in the subjectivity of its inhabitants (28).
8. Serlio's work, *The Five Books of Architecture*, appeared in print in London in 1611: an English translation of a Dutch translation of the Italian original. This first English language edition, published by Robert Peake, was dedicated to James I's son. Even prior to this translation, all five books of the

Architettura had been available in a single volume throughout Europe since 1584 (Serlio i).

9. The field of study "the Roman plays of Shakespeare" was established by Mungo MacCallum in *Shakespeare's Roman Plays and Their Background* (1910). Other "classic" studies in this field include: Maurice Charney, *Shakespeare's Roman Plays: The Function of Imagery in the Drama* (1961); Norman Rabkin, *Shakespeare and the Common Understanding* (1967); Paul A. Cantor, *Shakespeare's Rome: Republic and Empire* (1976); Platt; Robert S. Miola, *Shakespeare's Rome* (1983); and Vivian Thomas, *Shakespeare's Roman Worlds* (1989).

10. In the most remarkable use of quotation in recent critical history, Gayatri Chakravorty Spivak concludes her "Translator's Preface" to *Of Grammatology* with a short paragraph that begins in quotation marks. This short passage is actually the beginning of Derrida's own preface to *Of Grammatology*, but Spivak quotes his preface at the end of her own. Moreover, Spivak interpenetrates this quotation with italicized text, addressing herself and her translation to the reader: "*Now I insert my text within his and move you on, situating here*" (lxxxvii, italics in original). Significantly, at the end of this eight-line paragraph, there is no second set of quotation marks, no closure to the open quotation. Instead, there is only an ellipsis, intentionally blurring the boundary between "Spivak" and "Derrida." By opening but not closing the quotation at the end of her "Preface," Spivak situates all of Derrida's *Of Grammatology* as merely the supplement to her own introduction to it.

11. Vernacular construction is, as the term suggests, the popular "language" of building materials and habitation; a practice that "reproduces cultural given [sic] spatial and formal patterns" (Hillier 4).

12. The imagery of Rome in James's reign is extensively explored in Goldberg.

13. As before, all quotations from *The Riverside Shakespeare*.

14. See Michael Platt, who argues: "By seldom or never speaking of himself as 'I,'" Caesar "is already a monument, a colossus" (187). See also Geoffrey Miles, *Shakespeare and the Constant Romans*, 123-148.

15. Troynovant, the legendary precursor to Rome and London, was invoked by Dekker in James I's royal entry, though with less success than Jonson's use of the name for the Roman settlement. See Dekker 359.

16. I cannot follow the approach to these plays taken by Paul A. Cantor, who argues that "any attempt at understanding Shakespeare's Rome must begin with *Coriolanus*" (52). His suggestion that the order of the plays based on Roman history must be followed and that the order in which the plays were written is unimportant overlooks the fact that, unlike the history plays, Shakespeare's four Roman plays were written over a period of roughly two decades and do not present a single, organized approach to Rome, or, more important, to theatrical representation itself. Given my argument that the

influence of London's culture was as much a factor in the development of these plays as was Shakespeare's understanding of Rome, locating these plays in their written chronology is significant.

Bearing in mind as well that this project addresses issues at the intersection of spatial representation, the city, and theatre and performance history, I have chosen to exclude from the discussion *Titus Andronicus* and *Antony and Cleopatra*. These plays engage issues of violence, desire, trans-national power, and the early modern "other" that, however interesting in their own rights, extend well beyond the "city limits" that I have chosen as boundaries for this study.

17. Garber, "Dream" 43.

18. Sohmer 18

19. Wilson, "Holiday" 66.

20. Examples include Barton, Danson, Drakakis, Garber "Dream," Paster *Idea*. An endorsement of multiple meanings such as that of William and Barbara Rosen is rare: "*Julius Caesar* is above all a play of ambiguities and alternatives" (114).

21. For the primary source for Platter's visit to Southwark, I draw on Gurr, *Playgoing* 213-4. See also Gurr, *Shakespearean* 197-8.

22. For a succinct summary of this information, see Kermode, "Julius Caesar" 1146-7; for a longer study, see Wilson, "'Is this a holiday?'"; for a book-length study, not only of the dating of *Caesar* but of dates and dating in the play, see Sohmers, esp. 3-16.

23. For a discussion of other major developments in the postmedieval city, topographical and practical, see Schofield, "Topography."

24. Note that Gillies is not referring to any particular map, though his formulation "the ancient map" would seem to suggest so (6). For this assertion, he draws on Vico who refers to "mapping" practices, but not to map-making per se.

25. On violence and ritual in *Caesar*, see Girard and Liebler.

26.

27. Garber astutely observes that: "The presence of a modern clock in Caesar's Rome abruptly reminds the audience of the double time period in which the play is set. Not only a history of the classical past, it is also a story of the present day" (*Shakespeare After All* 411). Other studies of anachronism in Shakespeare's Roman plays include: Terence Spencer, "Shakespeare and the Elizabethan Romans"; Northrop Frye, "The Tragedy of Order: *Julius Caesar*"; Cantor 21-52; A.D. Nuttall 99-161; Gary B. Miles, "How Roman Are Shakespeare's 'Romans'?"; Charles and Michelle Martindale, *Shakespeare and the Uses of Antiquity*; and Clifford Ronan, *"Antike Roman."*

28. For further consideration of relations between text and performance in Shakespeare, see Hopkins and Reynolds, "The Making of Authorships."

29. "*Spass*" is the German word for "fun," associated in the field of Theatre Studies with the work of Bertolt Brecht, who called for more space for Spass in the theatre. See John Willett's translation of Brecht's "Emphasis on Sport."

30. This section title is an appropriation of the chapter title "*Locus* and *Platea* Revisited" in Weimann, *Author's Pen*, 187. For the introduction of the terms *locus* and *platea*, see Weimann, *Shakespeare and the Popular Tradition*, 73–85.

31. My thanks to Weimann for bringing this artful pun to my attention. See also Paster, *The Idea of the City* 61.

32. Not to mention underestimating the contributions of Weimann to studies of the Elizabethan stage. See Jean Howard's favorable review of Weimann's *Author's Pen and Actor's Voice* for a recent, though well meaning, example of this error (311). In his rather more acerbic estimation of Weimann's work, Brian Vickers limits the relevance of his remarks by relying on a number of oversimplifications, of *locus* and *platea* as well as other key Weimanian concepts (214-271). Lorraine Helms also misconstrues *locus* and *platea* as specific "venues" or stage locations (555), but her idea of a "tragic *platea*" is suggestive. Erika Lin provides a productive study of the wide-ranging influence of Weimann's concepts; the article includes a thoroughgoing study of the upstage-downstage controversy and the sensorium of Weimanian spectatorship. See Lin, "Performance Practice and Theatrical Privilege: Rethinking Weimann's Concepts of *Locus* and *Platea*."

33. Lin comes to a conclusion that offers an interesting contrast with my own: "the more characters are aware of the playhouse conventions through which visual, aural, and verbal cues onstage come to signify within the represented fiction, the more they are in the *platea*" (292). Lin's position privileges the narrative as a force that acts upon the character, and regards characters as textual effects with greater or lesser degrees of awareness; by contrast, my view conceives of the actor as a performing agent operating in conjunction with the dramatic narrative, but without surrendering awarness of the social occasion and material conditions of theatrical performance.

34. I use the term "topography" here, not only in its geographical sense, but in that developed by contemporary US director Anne Bogart, whose approach to stage space and actor training, the "Viewpoints," has had a remarkable influence on contemporary American theatre. Topography in this sense refers to the physical and conceptual organization of stage space. For a review of Bogart's "method," see Landau.

35. For a full consideration of Lupercal and its uses in *Julius Caesar*, see Naomi Conn Liebler, "'Thou Bleeding Piece of Earth': The Ritual Ground of *Julius Caesar*"; see also Brents Sterling, "'Or Else This Were a Savage Spectacle." Of course, in the "double vision" of the opening scene, there is no

holiday *per se*: the tribunes address the audience of the play as much as the Commoners in the scene, teasing the former for coming to the Globe on a "laboring day" (I.i.4).

36. Note that my performance reading of this and other scenes in *Caesar* is at odds with Goldberg, who finds in the Roman plays of Shakespeare and Jonson a uniform reflection of representational strategies: Caesar, like James, "stood aloof; for him to see was enough" (Goldberg 32). This reading strikes me as a consequence of Goldberg's approach, whereby he finds in "the Roman plays [. . .] a convenient place to examine closely the politics of *literature*" (166 emphasis added), rather than the properties (political or otherwise) of *performance*.

37. While I rely on Drakakis's astute reading of theatrical representation in this play, I cannot let pass without criticism his use of "theatre" as the opposite of "truth." While his essay often suggests a subtle comprehension of historical theatre practices, his use of "theatre" as synonymous with "deceit" betrays Drakakis's own antitheatrical bias. For a useful analysis of contemporary academic discourse surrounding (and often misrepresenting) theatre studies, see W.B. Worthen, "Drama, Performativity, and Performance."

38. Charney expresses suspicion for the conflation of civic ceremony and public theatre, noting that *Julius Caesar* repeatedly offers the "ominous image of the people as audience" (75). Ian Donaldson is rather more comfortable with the ways in which the audience is often implicated in the meaning-making practices of the play. Charney, "The Images of Caesar"; Donaldson, "'Misconstruing Everything': *Julius Caesar* and *Sejanus*."

39. For history as representation, see Nora.

40. For historically situated readings of Elizabeth's conflicts with Leicester over *The Entertainment at Elvetham*, and the connection between the Essex rebellion and *Richard II*, see Frye and Logan. For studies of paintings and other visual art representations of Elizabeth, see Strong, *The Cult of Elizabeth*; and Montrose, "Idols of the Queen" and *The Subject of Elizabeth*.

41. In an intertextual (and, ultimately, chilling) reading, Reynolds compares Shakespeare's *Coriolanus* and Brecht's *Coriolan*. Reynolds notes an "ideological compatibility between *Coriolanus* and *The Communist Manifesto*" (113), a conclusion that recalls Christopher Hill's anachronistic assertion regarding *Coriolanus*: "Shakespeare had clearly heard communist propaganda" (92).

42. For examples, see Aubrey, Calderwood, Cantor, Garber (*Coming of Age*, esp. 52-116), Londré, Thomas.

43. Garber notes that *Coriolanus* is "a play much concerned with the losing and finding of names" (*Coming of Age* 59).

44. Cynthia Marshall sees Coriolanus' character as defined by a resistance to "verbal signification," rather than a refusal to participate in political and social performance (109).

45. Wilson locates one such emergence in *Caesar*, which shows "the process of separation as the new theatre distanced itself from [. . .] an older participatory
form" ("*Julius Caesar*" 43).

NOTES TO THE CONCLUSION

1. *Midas*, 3: 115.
2. Vitruvius, the only architect whose work survives from antiquity, "defined
'*scenographia*' as the set of rules for representing three-dimensional space on
a plane" ("Geometry"). Consequently, for the early modern theatre artist,
the Vitruvian terms for "perspective" and for "stage design" were the same.
3. For a discussion of a different representational apotheosis, see Goldberg on
Rubens's painting *The Apotheosis of James I*, commissioned by Charles I for
the ceiling of Jones's Banquet Hall (250).
4. The idea of the "concept city" is taken from de Certeau, but has become
widely used throughout urban studies to describe the city as conceived
"from above." See de Certeau 94-95.
5. See Delano-Smith (208-9) for Wren's contribution to London's urban features in brief; see Jardine, *On A Grander Scale*, for a book-length study of
his contribution to London's architecture and topography.
6. Translated in Schofield, *Building* 174-175.

Bibliography

Ackroyd, Peter. *London, The Biography*. New York: Anchor Books, 2000.

Adams, Paul C., Steven Hoelscher, Karen E. Till, eds. *Textures of Place: Exploring Humanist Geographies*. Minneapolis: U of Minnesota P, 2001.

Agnew, Jean-Christophe. *Worlds Apart: The Market and the Theater in Anglo-American Thought*. New York: Cambridge UP, 1986.

Alpers, Svetlana. "The Mapping Impulse in Dutch Art." Woodward 1987. 51-96.

Anglo, Sydney. *Spectacle, Pageantry, and Early Tudor Policy*. Oxford: Clarendon P, 1969.

Archer, Ian. *The Pursuit of Stability: Social Relations in Elizabethan London*. New York: Cambridge UP, 1991.

———. "The Nostalgia of John Stow." *The Theatrical City: Culture, Theatre and Politics in London, 1576–1649*. Smith, Strier, and Bevington 1995, 17-34.

Arnade, Peter, Martha C. Howell, and Walter Simons. "Fertile Spaces: The Productivity of Urban Space in Northern Europe." *Journal of Interdisciplinary History* 32:4 (Spring 2002): 515-548.

Arnold, Dana. *Re-Presenting the Metropolis: Architecture, Urban Experience, and Social Life in London, 1800–1840*. Burlington, VT: Ashgate, 2000.

Aubrey, Karen. "Shifting Masks, Roles, and Satiric Personae: Suggestions for Exploring the Edge of Genre in *Coriolanus*." Wheeler 1995, 299-338.

Auslander, Philip. *Liveness: Performance in a Mediatized Culture*. New York: Routledge, 1999.

Baker, David Weil. "'Master of the Monuments': Memory and Erasure in Jonson's *Bartholomew Fair*." *English Literary Renaissance* 31.2 (Spring 2001): 266-287.

Bakhtin, Mikhail. *The Dialogic Imagination*. Trans. Michael Holquist and Caryl Emerson. Austin: U of Texas P, 1981.

Balshaw, Maria and Liam Kennedy. "Introduction: Urban Space and Representation." Balshaw and Kennedy 2000, 1-21.

Balshaw, Maria and Liam Kennedy, eds. *Urban Space and Representation*. London: Pluto Press, 2000.

Banham, Reyner. *Los Angeles: The Architecture of the Four Ecologies*. New York: Harper & Row, 1971.

Barker, Felix and Peter Jackson. *The History of London in Maps*. London: Barrie & Jenkins, 1990.

Barker, Francis. *The Tremulous Private Body: Essays in Subjection*. London: Methuen, 1984.

Barton, Anne. "Rhetoric in Ancient Rome." Bloom 1988, 79-89.

Belsey, Catherine. *The Subject of Tragedy: Identity and Difference in Renaissance Drama*. New York: Metheun, 1985.

———. "Shakespeare and Film: A Question of Perspective." *Shakespeare On Film*. Ed. Robert Shaughnessy. Basingstoke, UK: Macmillan, 1998: 61–70.

Benjamin, Walter. *Charles Baudelaire: a lyric poet in the era of high capitalism*. Trans. Harry Zohn. London: Verso, 1983.

Berger, Harry, Jr. "Bodies and Texts." *Representations* 17 (Winter 1987): 144-166.

Bergeron, David M. *English Civic Pageantry, 1558–1672*. London: Edward Arnold, 1971.

———. "Introduction." Bergeron 1985, 1–16.

———. *Practicing Renaissance Scholarship: Plays and Pageants, Patrons and Politics*. Pittsburgh, Pennsylvania: Duquesne UP, 2000.

Bergeron, David M., ed. *Pageantry in the Shakespearean Theater*. Athens: U of Georgia P, 1985.

Bevington, David, ed. *The Macro Plays*. New York: Johnson; Washington, DC: Folger, 1972.

Bhaba, Homi. "Postcolonial Authority and Postmodern Guilt." *Cultural Studies*. Ed. Lawrence Grossberg, Cary Nelson, Paula Treichler. New York: Routledge, 1992.

Biddick, Kathleen. "Universal Histories as Genre." *Medieval Practices of Space*. Ed. Barbara A. Hanawalt and Michal Kobialka. Minneapolis: U of Minnesota P, 2000. 224-241.

———. *The Typological Imaginary: Circumcision, Technology, History*. Philadelphia: U of Penn P, 2003.

Bloom, Harold, ed. *William Shakespeare's* Julius Caesar. New York: Chelsea, 1988.

Borer, Mary Cathcart. *The City of London: A History*. London: Constable, 1977.

Bowers, Fredson. *Thomas Dekker: Dramatic Works*. Vol. II. New York: Cambridge UP, 1955.

Bradley, David. *From Text to Performance in the Elizabethan Theatre: Preparing the Play for the Stage*. New York: Cambridge UP, 1992.

Braider, Christopher. *Refiguring the Real: Picture and Modernity in Word and Image*. Princeton: Princeton UP, 1993.

Brecht, Bertolt. "Emphasis on Sport." *Brecht on Theatre: The Development of an Aesthetic.* Trans. John Willett. New York: Hill and Wang, 1964. 6-9.

Bristol, Michael D. "Lenten Butchery: Legitimation Crisis in *Coriolanus.*" *Shakespeare Reproduced: The Text in History and Ideology.* New York: Methuen, 1987.

Brophy, Brian. "Perspectives on Urban Community-Based Theater: Peter Sellars in East Los Angles: The Postcolonial Dilemma of Artistic Occupation." MA Thesis, UCLA, 1999.

Bulman, James C., ed. *Shakespeare, Theory, and Performance.* New York: Routledge, 1996.

Burke, Peter. *Popular Culture in Early Modern Europe.* Rev. ed. Aldershot, UK: Scolar-Ashgate: 1994.

———. *Eyewitnessing: The Uses of Images as Historical Evidence.* Ithaca, NY: Cornell UP, 2001

Calderwood, James L. "*Coriolanus*: Wordless Meanings and Meaningless Words." Wheeler 1995, 77-91.

Calvino, Italo. *Invisible Cities.* Trans. William Weaver. New York: Harcourt Brace, 1974.

Cantor, Paul A. *Shakespeare's Rome: Republic and Empire.* Ithaca, NY: Cornell UP, 1976.

Carlson, Marvin. *Places of Performance: The Semiotics of Theatre Architecture.* Ithaca: Cornell UP, 1989.

———. *Performance: A Critical Introduction.* New York: Routledge, 1996.

———. *The Haunted Stage: The Theatre as Memory Machine.* Ann Arbor: University of Michigan Press, 2001.

Casey, Edward S. *Getting Back Into Place: Toward a Renewed Understanding of the Place-World.* Bloomington: Indiana UP, 1993.

———. *The Fate of Place: A Philosophical History.* Berkeley: U of California P, 1997.

Cavell, Stanley. "'Who does the wolf love?': Coriolanus and the Interpretations of Politics." *Shakespeare and the Question of Theory.* Ed. Patricia Parker and Geoffrey Hartman. New York: Methuen, 1985. 245-272.

Certeau, Michel de. *The Practice of Everyday Life.* Trans. Steven Rendall. Los Angeles: U of California P, 1984.

Charney, Maurice. *Shakespeare's Roman Plays: The Function of Imagery in the Drama.* Cambridge, MA: Harvard UP, 1961.

———. "The Images of Caesar." *Twentieth Century Interpretations of Julius Caesar.* Ed. Leonard F. Dean. Englewood Cliffs, N.J.: Prentice-Hall, 1968. 73-75

Chaudhuri, Una. *Staging Place: The Geography of Modern Drama.* Ann Arbor: U of Michigan P, 1995.

Cohen, Walter. *Drama of a Nation: Public Theater in Renaissance England and Spain.* Ithaca, NY: Cornell UP, 1988.

Corner, James. "The Agency of Mapping: Speculation, Critique and Intervention." *Mappings*. Cosgrove 1999, 213-252.

Cosgrove, Denis. *Social Formation and Symbolic Landscape*. London: Croom Helm, 1984.

———. "Introduction: Mapping Meaning." Cosgrove 1999, 1-23.

———. *Apollo's Eye: A Cartographic Genealogy of the Earth in the Western Imagination*. Baltimore: Johns Hopkins UP, 2001.

Cosgrove, Denis, ed. *Mappings*. London: Reaktion, 1999.

Counsell, Colin. *Signs of Performance*. London: Routledge, 1996.

Danson, Lawrence. "Ritual and *Julius Caesar*." Bloom 1988, 29-41.

Davis, Mike. *City of Quartz: Excavating the Future in Los Angeles*. New York: Vintage, 1990.

———. *Ecologies of Fear: Los Angeles and the Imagination of Disaster*. New York: Vintage, 1998.

Dawson, Anthony B. "Correct Impressions: Editing and Evidence in the Wake of Post-Modernism." *In Arden: Editing Shakespeare*. Ed. Ann Thompson and Gordon McMullan. London: Arden Shakespeare / Thomson, 2003.

Dear, Michael J. *The Postmodern Urban Condition*. Malden, MA: Blackwell, 2000.

Dear, Michael J., H. Eric Schockman, and Greg Hise, eds. *Rethinking Los Angeles*. Thousand Oaks, CA: Sage, 1996.

Dekker, Thomas. *The Magnificent Entertainment*. Nichols 1828, 337-376.

Delano-Smith, Catherine and Roger J.P. Kain. *English Maps: A History*. Buffalo, NY: U of Toronto P, 1999.

Deleuze, Gilles and Félix Guattari. *A Thousand Plateaus*. Trans. Brian Massumi. Minneapolis: Minnesota UP, 1987.

Derrida, Jacques. *Of Grammatology*. Trans., Intro. Gayatri Chakravorty Spivak. Baltimore: Johns Hopkins, 1974.

Diamond, Elin. *Unmaking Mimesis: Essays on Feminism and Theater*. New York: Routledge, 1997.

Dolan, Jill; Roach, Joseph; Schechner, Richard; Zarrilli, Phillip B.; Worthen, W.B. "Responses to W.B. Worthen's 'Disciplines of the Text/Sites of Performance.'" *TDR* 39.1 (Spring 1995): 28–45.

Dillon, Janette. *Theatre, Court and City, 1595-1610: Drama and Social Space in London*. New York: Cambridge UP, 2000.

Dollimore, Jonathan. *Radical Tragedy: Religion, Ideology, and Power in the Drama of Shakespeare and His Contemporaries*. Brighton, UK: Harvester, 1984.

Donaldson, Ian. "'Misconstruing Everything': *Julius Caesar* and *Sejanus*." *Shakespeare Performed: Essays in Honor of R.A. Foakes*. Ed. Grace Ioppolo. Newark: U of Delaware P; London: Associated UP, 2000. 88-107.

Drakakis, John. "'Fashion It Thus': *Julius Caesar* and the Politics of Theatrical Representation." Wilson 2002, 77-91.

———. "Discourse and Authority: The Renaissance of Robert Weimann." *Shakespeare Studies* 26 (1 January 1998): 83–105.

Dugdale, Gilbert. *The Time Triumphant.* Nichols 1828, 408-419.

Dutton, Richard, ed. *Jacobean Civic Pageants.* Staffordshire, UK: Ryburn-Keele UP, 1995.

Edgerton, Samuel Y., Jr. "From Mental Matrix to Mappaemundi to Christian Empire: The Heritage of Ptolemaic Cartography in the Renaissance." Woodward 1987. 10-50.

Edson, Evelyn. *Mapping Time and Space: How Medieval Mapmakers Viewed Their World.* London: British Library, 1997.

Eisenstein, Elizabeth L. *The Printing Press as an Agent of Change.* London: Cambridge UP, 1979.

Egginton, William. *How the World Became a Stage: Presence, Theatricality, and the Question of Modernity.* Albany, NY: State University of New York P, 2003.

Ellenbogen, Josh. "Representational Theory and the Staging of Social Performance." *The Theatrical Baroque.* Ed. Larry F. Norman. Chicago: Smart Museum of Art, University of Chicago, 2001. 21–31.

Elsky, Martin. *Authorizing Words: Speech, Writing, and Print in the English Renaissance.* Ithaca: Cornell UP, 1989.

Enders, Jody. *Death by Drama and Other Medieval Urban Legends.* Chicago: U of Chicago P, 2002.

Etchells, Tim. "Nights In This City: Sheffield 1995 / Rotterdam 1997." *Site-Specific Art: Performance, Place and Documentation.* Kaye 2000, 13-24.

Finlay, Roger. *Population and Metropolis: The Demography of London, 1580–1650.* New York: Cambridge UP, 1981. 51.

Finlay, Roger and Beatrice Shearer. "Population Growth and Suburban Expansion." *London 1500–1700: The Making of the Metropolis.* Ed. A.L. Beier and Roger Finlay. London: Longman, 1986. 11, 42, 49.

Fisher, F.J. "London as an 'Engine of Economic Growth." *London and the English Economy, 1500-1700.* Ed. P.J. Corfield and N.B. Harte. London: Hambledon, 1990. 185-198.

———. "The Growth of London." *London and the English Economy, 1500-1700.* Ed. P.J. Corfield and N.B. Harte. London: Hambledon, 1990. 173-184.

Fisher, John. "Introductory Notes." *The A to Z of Elizabethan London.* Compiled by Adrian Prockter and Robert Taylor. London: Harry Margary-London Topographical Society; Guildhall Library, 1979.

Foucault, Michel. *The Order of Things: An Archeology of the Human Sciences.* New York: Vintage, 1973.

———. "Nietzsche, Genealogy, History." *Language, Counter-Memory, Practice.* Ed. Donald Bouchard. Ithaca, NY: Cornell UP, 1977. 139-164.

———. *Discipline and Punish.* Trans. Alan Sheridan. New York: Vintage, 1979.

———. "Of Other Spaces." *Diacritics* 16.1 (Spring 1986).

Frangenberg, Thomas. "Chorographies of Florence: The Use of City Views and City Plans in the Sixteenth Century." *Imago Mundi* 46 (1994): 41-64.

Friedrichs, Christopher R. *The Early Modern City: 1450-1750.* New York: Longman, 1995.

Frye, Northrop. "The Tragedy of Order: Julius Caesar." *Twentieth Century Interpretations of Julius Caesar.* Ed. Leonard F. Dean (Englewood Cliffs, N.J.: Prentice-Hall, 1968), 95-102.

Frye, Susan. *Elizabeth I: The Competition for Representation.* New York: Oxford UP, 1993.

Fuller, Mary C. *Voyages in Print: English Travel to America, 1576-1624.* New York: Cambridge UP, 1995.

Garber, Marjorie. *Shakespeare's Ghost Writers: Literature as Uncanny Causality.* New York: Methuen, 1987.

———. "Dream and Interpretation: *Julius Caesar.*" Bloom 1988, 43-52.

———. *Coming of Age in Shakespeare.* New York: Routledge, 1997.

———. *Shakespeare After All.* New York: Pantheon, 2004.

Garreau, Joel. *Edge City: Life on the New Frontier.* New York: Doubleday, 1991.

Geddes, Patrick. *Cities in Evolution.* London: Williams & Norgate, 1949.

Geertz, Clifford. "Blurred Genres: The Refiguration of Social Thought." *American Scholar* 49.

———. *The Interpretation of Cultures.* New York: Basic Books, 1973.

———. *Local Knowledge: Further Essays in Interpretive Anthropology.* New York: Basic Books, 1983.

Geometry of Seeing. Getty Center. Los Angeles. May-June, 2002.

Gillies, John. *Shakespeare and the Geography of Difference.* New York: Cambridge UP, 1994.

Girard, René. "Collective Violence and Sacrifice in *Julius Caesar.*" *Salmagundi* 88 (1991): 399-419.

Glanville, Philippa. *London In Maps.* London: Connoisseur, 1972.

Goldberg, Jonathan. *James I and the Politics of Literature.* Baltimore: Johns Hopkins UP, 1983.

Goldberger, Paul. *Up From Zero: Politics, Architecture, and the Rebuilding of New York.* New York: Random House, 2005.

Gordon, Andrew. "Performing London: The Map and the City in Ceremony." *Literature, Mapping, and the Politics of Space in Early Modern Britain.* Ed. Andrew Gordon and Bernard Klein. New York: Cambridge UP, 2001. 69-88.

Gordon, D.J. "Poet and Architect: The Intellectual Setting of the Quarrel Between Ben Jonson and Inigo Jones." *The Renaissance Imagination: Essays and Lectures by D.J. Gordon.* Ed. Stephen Orgel. Berkeley: U of California P, 1975. 77–101.

Grazia, Margreta de. "The Ideology of Superfluous Things: *King Lear* as Period Piece." *Subject and Object in Renaissance Culture.* Ed. Margreta de Grazia,

Maureen Quilligan, and Peter Stallybrass. Cambridge: Cambridge University Press, 1996. 17-42.

Greenblatt, Stephen. *Renaissance Self-Fashioning: From More to Shakespeare*. Chicago: U of Chicago P, 1980.

Greenblatt, Stephen, ed. *Representing the English Renaissance*. Berkeley: U of California P, 1988.

Gurr, Andrew. *The Shakespearean Stage, 1574–1642*. New York: Cambridge UP, 1980.

———. *Playgoing in Shakespeare's London*. New York: Cambridge UP, 1987.

———. "The Bare Island." *Shakespeare Survey* 47 (1994): 29-43.

Hakluyt, Richard. *The Tudor Ventures*, selected from *The Principal Navigations, Voyages, Traffics and Discoveries of the English Nation, made by Sea or Over Land*. Ed. John Hampden. London: Folio Society, 1970.

Hall, Jenny and Ralph Merrifield. *Roman London*. London: Museum of London-HMSO, 1986.

Hall, Peter. *The World Cities*. London: Weidenfeld and Nicolson, 1966.

Hampton, Timothy. *Writing from History: The Rhetoric of Exemplarity in Renaissance Literature*. Ithaca, NY: Cornell UP, 1995.

Hanawalt, Barbara A. and Michal Kobialka, eds. *Medieval Practices of Space*. Minneapolis, MN: U of Minnesota P, 2000.

Hayden, Dolores. *The Power of Place*. Cambridge, MA: MIT Press, 1995.

Harley, J.B. "Maps, Knowledge, and Power." *The Iconography of Landscape*. Ed. Denis Cosgrove and Stephen Daniels. New York: Cambridge UP, 1988. 277-312.

———. "Meaning and Ambiguity in Tudor Cartography." *English Map-Making, 1500-1650*. Ed. Sarah Tyacke. London: Moxon, 1983. 22-45.

Harley, J.B. and David Woodward, eds. "Preface." *The History of Cartography*. Chicago: U of Chicago P, 1987. xv-xxi.

Harper, Charles George. *The Old Inns of Old England*. 2 vols. London: Chapman & Hall, 1906.

Harrison, Stephen. *The Arches of Triumph*. Nichols 1828, 329-330, *330-*334.

Harvey, P.D.A. *Medieval Maps*. U of Toronto P, 1991.

———. *Maps In Tudor England*. Chicago: U of Chicago P, 1993.

Heidegger, Martin. "The Age of the World Picture." *The Question Concerning Technology and Other Essays*. Trans. William Lovitt. New York: Harper and Row, 1977: 115–54.

Helgerson, Richard. "The Land Speaks: Cartography, Chorography, and Subversion in Renaissance England." *Representing the English Renaissance*. Ed. Stephen Greenblatt. Berkeley: U of California P, 1988. 327-361.

Herford, C.H., Percy Simpson, and Evelyn Simpson, eds. *Ben Jonson*. Oxford: Clarendon Press, 1954-65.

Heywood, Thomas. *The Fair Maid of the West*. London: Methuen, 1986.

Hickscorner. *Everyman and Other Miracle and Morality Plays*. New York: Dover, 1995.

Hill, Christopher. *Change and Continuity in Seventeenth-Century England*. New Haven: Yale UP, 1991.

Hiller, Harry H. "Toward an Urban Sociology of Mega-Events." *Constructions of Urban Space*. Ed. Ray Hutchison. Stanford, CT: JAI Press, 2000. 181-205.

Hillier, Bill. *Space Is the Machine: A Configurational Theory of Architecture*. New York: Cambridge UP, 1996.

Hirschfeld, Heather Anne. *Joint Enterprises: Collaborative Drama and the Institutionalization of the English Renaissance Theater*. Amherst, MA: U of Massachusetts P: 2004.

Hodgdon, Barbara. "Re-Incarnations," *Remaking Shakespeare: Performances Across Media, Genres, and Cultures*. New York: Palgrave, 2003.

Hodnett, Edward. *English Woodcuts, 1480-1535*. 2nd ed., with additions and corrections. London: Bibliographical Society, 1973.

Hopkins, D.J. "The Londinium Arch: Representing the Urban Subject in Performance and Print (London, 1604)." *Symbolism Yearbook*, Ed. Douglass Bruster and Robert Weimann (2006).

———. "Mapping the Placeless Place: Performing Community in the Urban Spaces of Los Angeles." *Modern Drama* 46.2 (Summer 2003): 261–84.

———. Rev. of *A Brief History of Western Theatre Space* by David Wiles. *Theatre Journal* 57.2 (May 2005): 319–320.

Hopkins, D.J. and Shelley Orr. "Memory / Memorial / Performance: New York City, 1776 / 2004." *Text and the City: Performing and Writing Urban Space*. Ed. D.J. Hopkins, Shelley Orr, and Kim Solga. Forthcoming.

Hopkins, D.J. and Bryan Reynolds. "The Making of Authorships." *Performing Transversally*. New York: Palgrave, 2003. 29-51.

Hopkins, D.J. and Justin Blum. "Shakespeare: Early Modern / Postmodern (Performance, Pedagogy, Polemic)." *Reconsidering Early Modern Ephemera*. Ed. Joshua B. Fisher. Forthcoming.

Howard, Jean. Rev. of *Author's Pen and Actor's Voice: Playing and Writing in Shakespeare's Theatre* by Robert Weimann. *Shakespeare Quarterly* 53.3 (Fall 2002): 390-393.

Howard, Jean and Phyllis Rackin. *Engendering a Nation: A Feminist Account of Shakespeare's English Histories*. New York: Routledge, 1997.

Howes, Edmund. *John Stow's Annales, or A Generall Chronicle of England*. London, 1631.

Howgego, James. *Printed Maps of London circa 1553-1850*. Folkestone, UK: Dawson, 1978.

Hyde, Ralph. *Gilded Scenes and Shining Prospects: Panoramic Views of British Towns, 1575-1900*. New Haven, CT: Yale Center for British Art, 1985.

Inwood, Stephen. *A History of London*. New York: Carroll and Graf, 1998.

Jacob, Christian. "Mapping in the Mind: The Earth from Ancient Alexandria." Cosgrove 1999, 24-49.

Jacobs, Jane. *The Death and Life of Great American Cities*. New York: Vintage, 1992.

James, Mervyn. "Ritual, drama and the social body in the late medieval English town." *Society, Politics and Culture: Studies in Early Modern England.* New York: Cambridge UP, 1986. 16–47.

Jardine, Lisa. *Worldly Goods: A New History of the Renaissance.* New York: Doubleday, 1996.

———. *On A Grander Scale: The Outstanding Career of Sir Christopher Wren.* New York: HarperCollins, 2002.

Johnson, David J. *Southwark and the City.* London: Corporation of London-Oxford UP, 1969.

Jonson, Ben. *Volpone, or The Fox.* Ed. Jonas Barish. Arlington Heights, IL: Crofts Classics, 1958.

———. The Royal and Magnificent Entertainment. Nichols 1828, 377-399.

———. *B. Jon: His Part of King James his Royall and Magnificent Entertainment.* British Library, Name / Number: STC (2nd ed.) / 14756. London: By V[alentine] S[immes and George Eld] for Edward Blount, 1604.

Kahn, Coppelia. "Roman Virtue on English Stages." *Roman Shakespeare: Warriors, Wounds, and Women.* London: Routledge, 1997.

Kastan, David Scott. "The Mechanics of Culture: Editing Shakespeare Today." *Shakespeare Studies* 24 (1996): 30-37.

———. *Shakespeare After Theory.* New York: Routledge, 1999.

———. *Shakespeare and the Book.* New York: Cambridge UP, 2001.

Kaye, Nick. *Site-Specific Art: Performance, Place and Documentation.* New York: Routledge, 2000.

Kennedy, Dennis. *Looking at Shakespeare: A Visual History of Twentieth-Century Performance.* New York: Cambridge UP, 1993.

Kermode, Frank. "Coriolanus." Introduction. *Riverside* 1997, 1440-1443.

———. "Julius Caesar." Introduction. *Riverside* 1997, 1146-1150.

Kershaw, Baz. *The Politics of Performance: Radical Theatre as Cultural Intervention.* New York: Routledge, 1992.

Kirby, Kathleen. *Indifferent Boundaries: Spatial Concepts of Human Subjectivity.* New York: Guilford, 1996.

Kitchen, Frank. "John Norden (c. 1547-1625): Estate Surveyor, Topographer, County Mapmaker and Devotional Writer." *Imago Mundi* 49 (1997): 43-61.

Klein, Bernhard. *Maps and the Writing of Space in Early Modern England and Ireland.* New York: Palgrave, 2001.

Klein, Norman M. *The History of Forgetting: Los Angeles and the Erasure of Memory.* New York: Verso, 1997.

Kline, Naomi Reed. *Maps of Medieval Thought: The Hereford Paradigm.* Woodbridge, UK: Boydell Press, 2001.

Kobialka, Michal. Seminar presentation. ASTR Conference, Philadelphia, November 2002.

Koolhaas, Rem and Harvard Project on the City, et al. *Mutations.* Barcelona: Actar; Bordeaux: arc en rêve centre d'architecture [sic], 2001.

Koolhaas, Rem, OMA, and Bruce Mau. *S, M, L, XL*. New York: Monacelli Press, 1995.

Kostof, Spiro. *The City Assembled: The Elements of Urban Form Through History*. New York: Bulfinch-Little Brown, 1992.

Krautheimer, Richard. "The Tragic and Comic Scene of the Renaissance: The Baltimore and Urbino Panels." *Studies in Early Christian, Medieval, and Renaissance Art*. New York: New York UP; London: U of London P, 1969.

Landau, Tina. "Source Work, The Viewpoints and Composition: What Are They?" *Anne Bogart: Viewpoints*. Lyme, New Hampshire: Smith and Kraus, 1995.

Lefebvre, Henri. *The Production of Space*. Trans. Donald Nicholson-Smith. Oxford: Blackwell, 1991.

Lestringant, Frank. *Mapping the Renaissance World: The Geographical Imagination in the Age of Discovery*. Trans. David Faucett. Berkeley: U of California P, 1994.

Letts, Rosa Maria. *The Renaissance (Cambridge Introduction to the History of Art)*. New York: Cambridge UP, 1981.

Liebler, Naomi Conn. "'Thou Bleeding Piece of Earth': The Ritual Ground of *Julius Caesar*." *Shakespeare's Festive Tragedy: The Ritual Foundations of Genre*. New York: Routledge, 1995. 88-111.

Lin, Erika T. "Performance Practice and Theatrical Privilege: Rethinking Weimann's Concepts of Locus and Platea." *New Theatre Quarterly* 22.3 (August 2006): 283–98.

Loewenstein, Joseph. *Ben Jonson and Possessive Authorship*. London: Cambridge UP: 2002.

———. "The Script in the Marketplace." *Representing the English Renaissance*. Ed. Stephen Greenblatt. Berkeley: U of California P, 1988. 265–78.

Logan, Sandra. *Willing Subjects: Historical Events and Rhetorical Occasions in Early Modern England*. Unpublished dissertation, University of California, San Diego. 2000.

———. "Making History: The Rhetorical and Historical Occasion of Elizabeth Tudor's Coronation Entry." *Journal of Medieval and Early Modern Studies* 31.2 (Spring 2001): 251–282.

London Encyclopedia. Ed. Ben Weinreb and Christopher Hibbert. Bethesda, MD: Adler & Adler, 1986.

London in the Age of Shakespeare: An Anthology. Ed. Lawrence Manley. London: Croom Helm, 1986.

Londré, Felicia. "*Coriolanus* and Stavinsky: The Interpenetration of Art and Politics." *Theatre Research International* 11 (Summer 1986): 119-32.

Lost Map. Museum of London. 5 March 2003 <http://www.museum-london.org.uk/MOLsite/exhibits/lostmap/lostmap.htm>.

Lyly, John. *The Complete Works of John Lyly*. 3 vols. Ed. R. Warwick Bond. Oxford: Clarendon Press, 1902.

Lynch, Kevin. *The Image of the City*. Cambridge, MA: MIT Press, 2000.

McCoy, Richard C. "'Thou Idol Ceremony': Elizabeth I, *The Henriad*, and the Rites of the English Monarchy." *Urban Life in the Renaissance*. Ed. Susan Zimmerman and Ronald F.E. Weissman. Newark: U of Delaware P, London: Associated UP, 1989. 240-266.

MacEachren, Alan M. *How Maps Work: Representation, Visualization, and Design*. New York: Guilford Press, 1995.

MacCallum, Mungo. *Shakespeare's Roman Plays and Their Background*. London: Macmillan, 1910.

Machyn, Henry. *The diary of Henry Machyn, citizen and merchant-taylor of London from A.D. 1550 to A.D. 1563*. Ed. John Gough Nichols. New York: AMS Press, 1968.

McKenzie, Jon. *Perform or Else: From Discipline to Performance*. New York: Routledge, 2001.

Maguire, Laurie E. *Shakespearean Suspect Texts: The "Bad" Quartos and Their Contexts*. New York: Cambridge UP, 1996.

Manley, Lawrence. *Literature and Culture in Early Modern London*. New York: Cambridge UP, 1995.

———. "Of Sites and Rites." Smith, Strier, and Bevington 1995, 35-54.

Marcus, Leah S. *Unediting the Renaissance : Shakespeare, Marlowe, Milton*. New York: Routledge, 1996.

———. "Renaissance/Early Modern Studies." *Redrawing the Boundaries: The Transformation of English and American Literary Studies*. Ed. Greenblatt, Stephen and Giles Gunn. New York: Modern Language Association of America, 1992. 41-63.

Marshall, Cynthia. "Wound-man: *Coriolanus*, gender, and the theatrical construction of identity." *Emerging Subjects: Feminist Readings of Early Modern Culture*. Ed. Valerie Traub, M. Lindsay Kaplan, and Dympna Callaghan. New York: Cambridge UP, 1996.

Martindale, Charles and Michelle. *Shakespeare and the Uses of Antiquity: An Introductory Essay*. London: Routledge, 1990.

Massey, Doreen. *Space, Place, and Gender*. Minneapolis: U of Minnesota P, 1994.

Metropolis and its Image: Constructing Identities for London, c. 1750-1950. Ed. Dana Arnold. Malden, MA: Blackwell, 1999.

Meyerowitz, Joel. "Saving the Wall That Saved New York." *The New York Times* 27 February 2003: A31.

Miles, Gary B. "How Roman Are Shakespeare's 'Romans'?" *Shakespeare Quarterly* 40.3 (Autumn 1989): 257-283.

Miles, Geoffrey. *Shakespeare and the Constant Romans*. Oxford: Oxford UP, 1996.

Miola, Robert S. *Shakespeare's Rome*. Cambridge, UK: Cambridge UP, 1983.

Mitchell, W.J.T. *Picture Theory: Essays on Verbal and Visual Representation*. Chicago: U of Chicago P, 1994.

Montrose, Louis. "'Shaping Fantasies': Figurations of Gender and Power in Elizabethan Culture." *Representing the English Renaissance*, Ed. Stephen Greenblatt. Berkeley: U of California P, 1988. 31-64 .

———. "The Work of Gender in the Discourse of Discovery." *Representations* 33 (Winter 1991): 1-41.

———. *The Purpose of Playing: Shakespeare and the Cultural Politics of the Elizabethan Theatre.* Chicago: U of Chicago P, 1996.

———. "Spencer's domestic domain: poetry, property, and the Early Modern subject." *Subject and Object in Renaissance Culture.* Ed. Margreta de Grazia, Maureen Quilligan, and Peter Stallybrass. New York: Cambridge UP, 1996. 83-130.

———. "Idols of the Queen: Policy, Gender, and the Picturing of Elizabeth I." *Representations* 68 (Fall 1999): 108-161.

———. *The Subject of Elizabeth : Authority, Gender, and Representation.* Chicago: U of Chicago P, 2006.

Mooney, Michael E. *Shakespeare's Dramatic Transactions.* Durham: Duke UP, 1990.

Morris, John. *Londinium: London in the Roman Empire.* Rev. Sarah Macready. London: Weidenfeld and Nicolson, 1982.

Mukerji, Chandra. *From Graven Images: Patterns of Modern Materialism.* New York: Columbia UP, 1983.

———. *Territorial Ambitions and the Gardens of Versailles.* New York: Cambridge UP, 1997.

Mulcaster, Richard. *The Quene's Majestie's Passage. Elizabethan Backgrounds.* Ed. Arthur Kinney. Hamden, CT: Archon Books, 1975. 7-39.

Mullaney, Steven. *The Place of the Stage.* Chicago: U of Chicago P, 1988.

———. "Strange Things, Gross Terms, Curious Customs: The Rehearsal of Cultures in the Late Renaissance." *Representing the English Renaissance.* Ed. Stephen Greenblatt. Berkeley: U of California P, 1988. 65-92.

Mumford, Lewis. *The City in History: Its Origins, Its Transformations, and Its Prospects.* New York: Harcourt Brace & World, 1961.

Munro, Ian. *Crowded Spaces: Population and Urban Meaning in Early Modern London.* Unpublished dissertation. Harvard University: 1998.

The New York Times. "9/11/02; America Enduring." Editorial. 11 Sept. 2002: A32.

Nichols, J.B., ed. *Progresses of King James the First.* Vol. 1. London: Society of Antiquaries, 1828.

Nora, Pierre. "Between Memory and History: *Les Lieux de Mémoire.*" Trans. Marc Roudebush. *Representations* 26 (Spring 1989): 7-25.

Nuti, Lucia. "Mapping Places: Chorography and Vision in the Renaissance." Cosgrove 1999, 90-108.

Nuttall, A.D. "Shakespeare's Imitation of the World." *A New Mimesis: Shakespeare and the Representation of Reality.* London: Methuen, 1983.

Orgel, Stephen. "What is a Text?" *Research Opportunities in Renaissance Drama* 24 (1981): 3-6.

———. "The Authentic Shakespeare." *Representations* 21 (1988): 1-25.

———. *The Illusion of Power: Political Theater in the English Renaissance.* Berkeley: U of California P, 1991.

————. "What is an Editor?" *Shakespeare Studies* 24 (1996): 23–29.

Orgel, Stephen and Roy Strong. *Inigo Jones: The Theatre of the Stuart Court*. Berkeley: U of California P, 1973.

Orlin, Lena Cowen. *Material London, ca. 1600*. Philadelphia: U of Pennsylvania P, 2000.

Parry, Graham. *Hollar's England: a mid-seventeenth-century view*. Salisbury, UK: Michael Russel, 1980.

————. *The Golden Age Restor'd: The Culture of the Stuart Court, 1603-42*. London: Manchester UP, 1981.

Paster, Gail Kern. *The Idea of the City in the Age of Shakespeare*. Athens, GA: U of Georgia P, 1985.

————. "The Idea of London in Masque and Pageant." Bergeron 1985, 46-58.

Pavis, Patrice. *Languages of the Stage*. New York: PAJ, 1982.

Perry, Curtis. "The Citizen Politics of Nostalgia: Queen Elizabeth in Early Jacobean London." *Journal of Medieval and Renaissance Studies* 23 (1993): 89-111.

Peters, Julie Stone. *Theatre of the Book, 1480–1880: Print, Text, and Performance in Europe*. New York: Oxford UP, 2000.

Phelan, Peggy. "Numbering Prospero's Books." *Performing Arts Journal* 41 (May 1992): 43-49.

————. *Unmarked: The Politics of Performance*. New York: Routledge, 1993.

Platt, Michael. *Rome and Romans According to Shakespeare*, Rev. Ed. New York: UP of America, 1983.

Postlewait, Thomas. "Historiography and the Theatrical Event: A Primer with Twelve Cruxes." *Theatre Journal* 43 (1991): 157-178.

Phythian-Adams, Charles. Societies, Cultures, and Kinship, 1580–1850. Leicester: Leicester UP, 1993.

Rabkin, Norman. *Shakespeare and the Common Understanding*. New York: Free Press, 1967.

Read, Piers Paul. *The Templars*. Cambridge, MA: Da Capo, 1999.

Rebhorn, Wayne. "The Crisis of the Aristocracy in *Julius Caesar*." *Julius Caesar*. Wilson 2002, 29-54.

Reynolds, Bryan and Joseph Fitzpatrick. "The Transversality of Michel de Certeau: Foucault's Panoptic Discourse and the Cartographic Impulse." *diacritics* 29.3 (Fall 1999): 63–80.

Reynolds, Bryan. "'What is the city but the people?': Transversal Performance and Radical Politics in Shakespeare's *Coriolanus* and Brecht's *Coriolan*." *Shakespeare Without Class: Misappropriations of Cultural Capital*. Ed. Donald Hedrick and Bryan Reynolds. New York: Palgrave, 2000. 107-132.

Ricoeur, Paul. "Mimesis and Representation." *Annals of Scholarship* 3 (1981): 15-32.

Riverside Shakespeare, The. Ed. G. Blakemore Evans and J.J.M. Tobin. New York: Houghton Mifflin, 1997.

Roach, Joseph R. *Cities of the Dead: Circum-Atlantic Performance*. New York: Columbia UP, 1996.

———. "History, Memory, Necrophilia." *The Ends of Performance*. Ed. Peggy Phelan and Jill Lane. New York: New York UP, 1998.

———. "Reconstructing Theatre / History." *Theatre Topics* 9:1 (1999): 3–10.

———. "Covent Garden: Situating Theatre History." Conference Presentation. "Redefining British Theatre History: Practice and Theory, A Conference at The Huntington." The Huntington Library, San Marino, CA. 15 March 2002.

Ronan, Clifford. *"Antike Roman": Power Symbology and The Roman Play in Early Modern England, 1585-1635*. Athens, GA: U of Georgia P, 1995.

Rorty, Richard. *Philosophy and the Mirror of Nature*. Princeton, NJ: Princeton UP, 1979.

Rosen, William and Barbara. *"Julius Caesar*: The Specialty of Rule." *Twentieth Century Interpretations of Julius Caesar*. Ed. Leonard F. Dean. Englewood Cliffs, N.J.: Prentice-Hall, 1968. 109-115.

Rouse, John. "Textuality and Authority in Theater and Drama: Some Contemporary Possibilities." *Critical Theory and Performance*. Ed. Janelle G. Reinelt and Joseph R. Roach. Ann Arbor: U of Michigan Press, 1992. 146–157.

Rubin, Miri. *Corpus Christi: The Eucharist in Late Medieval Culture*. New York: Cambridge UP, 1991.

Rykwert, Joseph. *The Idea of a Town*. London: Faber and Faber, 1976.

Sacks, David Harris. "London's Dominion." *Material London, ca. 1600*. Ed. Lena Cowen Orlin. Philadelphia: U of Pennsylvania P, 2000. 20-54

Sassen, Saskia. *Cities in a World Economy*. New York: Pine Forge Press, 1994.

———. "How Downtown Can Stand Tall and Step Lively Again." *The New York Times* 26 Jan 2003: AR 35.

Sauter, Willmar. *The Theatrical Event: Dynamics of Performance and Perception*. Iowa City: U of Iowa P, 2000.

Schechner, Richard. *Between Theater and Anthropology*. Philadelphia: U of Pennsylvania P, 1985.

Il Schifanoya. *Venetian Calendar of State Papers*. Vol. 7. Ed. Rawdon Brown and G. Bentinck. London, 1890.

Schneider, Rebecca. "Performance Remains." *Performance Research* 6.2 (2001): 100–108.

Schofield, John. *The Building of London: From the Conquest to the Great Fire*. London: Colonnade-British Museum, 1984.

———. "The Topography and Buildings of London, ca. 1600." Orlin 2000, 296-321.

Scott, Walter, ed. "A Report of her Majestie's most gratious Answere, delivered by her selfe verbally, to the first Petitions of the Lords and Commons . . . the xii Day of November 1586." *A Collection of Scarce and Valuable Tracts*. Vol. 1. London: T. Cordell and W. Davies, 1809. 220.

Serlio, Sebastiano. *The Five Books of Architecture: An Unabridged Reprint of the English Edition of 1611*. New York: Dover, 1982.

Serpieri, Allesandro. "Reading the signs: Towards a Semiotics of Shakespearean Drama." *Alternative Shakespeares*. Ed. John Drakakis. London: Routledge, 1985. 119-143.

Shapiro, I.A. "The Bankside Theatres: Early Engravings." *Shakespeare Survey* 1 (1948): 25-37.

Sheppard, Francis. *London: A History*. New York: Oxford UP, 1998.

Simmons, J.L. "*Antony and Cleopatra* and *Coriolanus*, Shakespeare's Heroic Tragedies: A Jacobean Adjustment." Wheeler 1995, 111-122.

Sinfield, Alan. *Faultlines: Cultural Materialism and the Politics of Dissident Reading*. Berkeley: University of California Press, 1992

Smith, Bruce R. "Pageants into Play: Shakespeare's Three Perspectives on Idea and Image." Bergeron 1985, 220-246.

Smith, David L., Richard Strier, and David Bevington, eds. *The Theatrical City: Culture, Theatre and Politics in London, 1576-1649*. New York: Cambridge UP, 1995.

Sohmer, Steve. *Shakespeare's Mystery Play: The Opening of the Globe Theatre, 1599*. New York: Manchester UP, 1999.

Soja, Edward W. *Postmodern Geographies: The Reassertion of Space in Critical Social Theory*. New York: Verso, 1989.

———. "Putting Cities First: Remapping the Origins of Urbanism." *A Companion to the City*. Ed. Gary Bridge and Sophie Watson. London: Blackwell, 2000. 26-34.

———. *Thirdspace: Journeys to Los Angeles and Other Real-and-Imagined Places*. Malden, MA: Blackwell, 1996.

Southern, Richard. *The Medieval Theatre in the Round: A Study of the Staging of* The Castle of Perseverance *and Related Matters*. New York: Theatre Arts, 1956.

Spencer, Terence. "Shakespeare and the Elizabethan Romans," *Shakespeare Survey* 10 (1957): 27-38.

Stallybrass, Peter and Allon White. *The Politics and Poetics of Transgression*. Ithaca, NY: Cornell University Press, 1986.

Stow, John. *A Survey of London written in the year 1598*. Phoenix Mill, UK: Sutton, 1994.

Strong, Roy. *The Cult of Elizabeth: Elizabethan Portraiture and Pageantry*. New York: Thames and Hudson, 1977.

Stoppard, Tom. *Rosencrantz & Guildenstern Are Dead*. New York: Grove, 1967.

Stuart Royal Proclamations. Ed. James Larkin and Paul Hughes. Vol. I. Oxford: Oxford UP, 1973.

Taylor, Diana. *The Archive and the Repertoire: Performing Cultural Memory in the Americas*. Durham, NC: Duke UP, 2003.

Tennenhouse, Leonard. *Power on Display: The Politics of Shakespeare's Genres*. New York: Methuen, 1986.

Thomas, Vivian. *Shakespeare's Roman Worlds.* New York: Routledge, 1989.

Tschumi, Bernard. *Event Cities.* Cambridge, Mass.: MIT Press, 1994.

Turner, Victor. "Variations on a Theme of Liminality." *Secular Ritual.* Ed. Sally F. Moore and Barbara E. Myerhoff. Amsterdam: Van Goreum, 1977. 36-52.

Vaughn, Richard. *Matthew Paris.* London: Cambridge UP, 1958.

Vickers, Brian. *Appropriating Shakespeare: Contemporary Critical Quarrels.* New Haven: Yale UP, 1993.

"A View of London in 1600 by John Norden." Publication No. 94. Reprod. de la Gardie Collection, Royal Library, Stockholm. London: London Topographical Society, 1961.

Walker, Julia M. *Medusa's Mirrors: Spenser, Shakespeare, Milton, and the Metamorphosis of the Female Self.* Newark: U of Delaware P, London: Associated UP, 1998.

——. "Bones of Contention: Posthumous Images of Elizabeth and Stuart Politics." *Dissing Elizabeth: Negative Representations of Gloriana.* Ed. Julia M. Walker. Durham, NC: Duke UP, 1998. 252-76

Watson, Bruce, Trevor Brigham, and Tony Dyson. *London Bridge: 2000 Years of a River Crossing.* London: Museum of London Archaeology Service-English Heritage, 2001.

Weimann, Robert. *Shakespeare and the Popular Tradition in the Theater: Studies in the Social Dimension of Dramatic Form and Function.* Johns Hopkins UP: 1978.

——. "'Appropriation' and Modern History in Renaissance Prose Narrative." *New Literary History* 14 (Spring 1983): 459-96.

——. "Towards a Literary Theory of Ideology: Mimesis, Representation, Authority." *Shakespeare Reproduced: The Text in History and Ideology.* Ed. Jean E Howard and Marion F. O'Connor. New York: Methuen, 1987.

——. "Textual Authority and Performative Agency: The Uses of Disguise in Shakespeare's Theater." *New Literary History* 25 (Autumn 1994): 789–808.

——. *Authority and Representation in Early Modern Discourse.* Ed. David Hillman. Baltimore: Johns Hopkins UP, 1996.

——. *Author's Pen and Actor's Voice: Playing and Writing in Shakespeare's Theatre.* New York: Cambridge UP, 2000.

——. "From 'Hodge-Podge' to 'Scene Individable.'" *European Journal of English Studies* 7.1 (April 2003).

Wells, Charles. *The Wide Arch: Roman Values in Shakespeare.* New York: St. Martin's Press, 1992.

Westrem, Scott D. *The Hereford Map: A Transcription and Translation of the Legends with Commentary.* Turnhout, Belgium: Brepols, 2001.

Wheeler, David, ed. Coriolanus*: Critical Essays.* New York: Garland, 1995.

Wilson, Arthur. *The History of Great Britain, Being The Life and Reign of King James The First, Relating To what passed from his first Access to the Crown, till his Death.* [UC Riverside Special Collections.] London: Richard Lownds, 1653.

Wilson, Richard. "Introduction." Wilson 2002, 1-28.

——. "'Is this a holiday?' Shakespeare's Roman Carnival." Wilson 2002, 55-74.

Wilson, Richard, ed. *Julius Caesar: Contemporary Critical Essays*. New York: Palgrave, 2002.

Wood, Denis, with John Fels. *The Power of Maps*. New York: Guilford, 1992.

Woodward, David. *Maps as Prints in the Italian Renaissance: Makers, Distributors & Consumers*. London: The British Library, 1996.

———. "Introduction: Art and Cartography." Woodward 1987, 1-9.

———. "The Medieval *Mappamundi*." *The History of Cartography*. Ed. J.B. Harley and David Woodward. Chicago: U of Chicago P, 1998. 286-300.

Woodward, David, ed. *Art and Cartography: Six Historical Essays*. Chicago: U of Chicago P, 1987.

Woolf, D.R. "Two Elizabeths? James I and the Late Queen's Famous Memory." *Canadian Journal of History* 20 (1985): 167-191.

Worthen, W.B. *Shakespeare and the Force of Modern Performance*. New York: Cambridge UP, 2003.

———. "Drama, Performativity, and Performance." *PMLA* 113 (October 1998): 1093–1107.

———. "Disciplines of the Text / Sites of Performance." *TDR* 39.1 (Spring, 1995): 13-29.

Yoch, James J. "Subjecting the Landscape in Pageants and Shakespearean Pastorals." Bergeron 1985, 194-215.

Index